The Visitor's
to
PERU

THE VISITOR'S GUIDE TO
PERU

MPC

Published by:
Moorland Publishing Co Ltd,
Moor Farm Road,
Airfield Estate,
Ashbourne,
Derbyshire DE6 1HD
England

© Goldstadtverlag Karl A. Schäfer,
Pforzheim
© Moorland Publishing Co Ltd
1989 (English Edition)

Authors: Gerd and Elfriede Möller
Translated by: A. J. Shackleton

British Library Cataloguing in
Publication Data:
Möller, Gerd
  The visitor's guide to Peru
  1. Peru - Visitor's guides
  I. Title II. Möller, Elfriede
  918.5'0463

ISBN 0 86190 303 X (paperback)
ISBN 0 86190 302 1 (hardback)

Colour and black & white
origination by:
Scantrans, Singapore

Printed in the UK by:
Richard Clay Ltd, Bungay, Suffolk

Cover photograph: *The Urubamba Valley* (Walt Unsworth).

All photographs have been supplied by Elfriede Möller.

Maps and diagrams by Gerd Möller.

CONTENTS

Key to Symbols Used in Text Margin

 Parkland

 Church/Ecclesiastical site

 Archaeological site

 Building of interest

 Nature reserve/Animal interest

 Museum/Art gallery

 Gardens/Plant life

 Beautiful view/Scenery/Natural phenomenon

 Castle/Fortification

 Other place of interest

Note on the maps
The maps drawn for each chapter, while comprehensive, are not designed to be used as precise route maps, but rather to locate the general route, main towns, villages and places of interest.

INTRODUCTION

Landscape and Scenery

The Peruvians divide their country into three main zones on the basis of their scenery: the *costa*, *sierra* and *selva*, or coast, mountains and forest. The differences between these zones are so clearly defined that they will be obvious even to the most unobservant visitor. The contrasts are enormous, from the arid deserts that run the whole length of the Pacific coast, to the impassable mountain chains (*cordilleras*) of the Andes that run parallel to the coast, and finally to the impenetrable Amazonian jungles in the east of the country.

THE COAST

Costa is the name given by geographers to the Pacific coastal strip (from the Spanish word meaning 'coast'). It rises to about 500m (1,640ft), and its width varies from about 30km (18½ miles) in the south to 150km (93 miles) in the north.

This coastal zone is quite remarkable in a number of ways. Although situated in a geographical zone that is normally characterised by lush vegetation, it is actually covered by desert, which in places is even less inviting than some of the more godforsaken parts of the Sahara. And although the area almost straddles the equator, it is not in fact a hot desert. The sky is not the unremitting blue of other deserts (bar the odd sandstorm), but is almost always obscured by low, grey clouds. The air, moreover, is not dry, but is usually full of nasty cold drizzle. What is even more remarkable is that almost half the population of Peru lives in this relatively narrow coastal region, and that it is the country's most important agricultural region. The unusually cool and dry climate is due to a cold sea current that runs along the coast, known as the Humboldt or Peruvian Current.

The coastal scenery is much the same for hundreds of kilometres, both north and south of Lima. The traveller along the Panamerican Highway will see nothing for the most part but kilometres of bare stones, rocky gorges and rippling sand dunes. The dismal grey landscape is occasionally interrupted by a green valley full of flowering cotton fields, lush orchards and forests of sugar cane. Around the edges of the valley are a few mud cottages, followed by yet more desert, with barren mountains and desolate plains.

Agriculture was highly developed in many of these coastal valleys long before the Spanish conquest. All that was required for this was sufficient water flow in the rivers during the period from December to March, when there is heavy rainfall in the mountains of the hinterland.

Nowadays the natural water flow in the rivers is no longer sufficient to satisfy modern agricultural needs. More and more aqueducts are being tunnelled through the mighty barrier of the Andes to bring valuable water supplies from the rainsoaked Amazon regions and transform the western deserts into fertile land.

Just occasionally the desert blooms without the help of technical means, but there are only a few places where this happens. These are the so-called *lomas* — hills where the coastal fog almost always lingers. In damp years between June and October, there is enough grass and other vegetation here to support grazing cattle and sheep, which are then brought in from other regions.

THE MOUNTAINS

Travellers who venture into the Andes will soon realise why Amerindians and Europeans alike preferred to settle in the barren wilderness along the coast. The mountains, or *sierra*, are an inhospitable region criss-crossed by steep, narrow gorges that are continually subject to landslides and flooding.

There are passes through the mountains, but these are so high that they cause mountain sickness (only in the north are they lower than 4,500m, 14,760ft). No wonder, therefore, that there are so few usable transport links, and vast regions that have yet to be explored.

One of the main transport links is the so-called Carretera Central, a road which runs east from Lima. This may be less awe-inspiring than some other routes, but it is undoubtedly the most comfortable way of getting to know the beauty of the Andes. The scenery is extremely varied, thanks to the great height differences and the enormous variation in rainfall between east and west.

Yunga is the name given by Peruvian geographers to the transitional zone between the barren coast and the warm valleys of the interior. These areas are particularly impressive between the months of May and December. The temperature rises by as much as 10˚C (50˚F), and the sky over the *yunga* is typically blue and cloudless.

The mountain slopes are still mostly bare and rocky. In a few places there is just enough groundwater or rainfall for a little vegetation, and hosts of prickly cactus have found a foothold in the stony ground. Where the valley floor can be irrigated and is safe from flooding, it has been transformed into orchards full of oranges, avocados, custard apples, papayas and bananas.

The next zone is called the *quechua* (pronounced 'ketchwa'); it begins at about 2,300m (7,544ft) and goes up to about 3,500m (11,480ft). In contrast to the *yunga* zone, there is some rainfall here, especially between December and March. In some places there is enough rain to grow wheat and maize without irrigation. The larger valleys at this height are the main areas of Indian settlement. Most of the Andean cities are in this zone, which is pleasantly warm during the day and relatively free from night frosts.

Above 3,500m (11,480ft) is the *puna* zone — a damp, infertile grassland that is subject to severe night frosts. A few favourably situated areas support barley and potatoes, but for the most part the land is good for nothing but grazing sheep and llamas.

In the wetter northern and eastern Andean regions, the *puna* gives way to another kind of landscape called *jalca* or *páramo*. The climate here is continually foggy, and the vegetation includes shrubs between 1 and 6ft tall and woolly rosette plants.

The highest of the Andean zones is the *janca* — a region of scree and rocky precipices, topped with snow-covered peaks and subject to frequent landslides. The most impressive range is that of the Cordillera Blanca or White Mountains, which includes Peru's highest peak, Huascarán (6,768m, 22,199ft).

The eastern side of the mountains presents a stark contrast to the western side and the central valleys. Many of the slopes above 3,000m (9,840ft) are full of moisture rising from the Amazonian basin below; they are covered in thick cloud and forests of trees covered with mosses and ferns. The lower slopes lie mostly in the rain shadow of the mountains, and the forests there are sparser or even non-existent. For this reason the Peruvians call the higher forests the *ceja de la montaña* or 'eyebrow of the mountains'.

Below 1,000m (3,280ft), however, the forests become an uninterrupted sea of green. The climate becomes hot and steamy in the impenetrable upland jungles of the *selva alta* or *montaña*.

THE JUNGLE

The eastern region of Peru covers an area more than twice the size of Great Britain, but it is completely covered by the vast green carpet of the Amazonian jungle or *selva*.

The region is virtually uninhabited. For although there are large quantities of bananas and fish available, the climate is extremely inhospitable. The heat and humidity are highly ennervating, and the numerous body parasites are deleterious to health. The tropical rainstorms and the associated floods are a threat to any cultivation.

The main transport links are the River Amazon and its tributaries

Indians and livestock at the roadside

— the Ucayali (1,900km, 1,178 miles), the Huallaga (1,100km, 682 miles), the Marañón and countless others — which meander endlessly through the jungle.

The people of the *selva* build their palm-roofed huts on the higher river banks that are safe from flooding, or else on floating rafts along the shore, which they reach by means of motor boats or traditional log canoes (dug-outs). Just a few venture out into the forest in search of valuable timber, while others collect fruit or latex for rubber. But most of them live quite simply from what nature provides, namely fish and bananas.

The Climate

Few countries in the world can boast such contrasts as Peru, where permanent ice lies in close proximity to tropical jungle and arid desert. This fact in itself points to enormous climatic differences. However, there are several features that are common to all regions of Peru.

Peru stretches south from the equator to the 18th parallel, and thus lies entirely within the tropics. This means that there are two points in the year when the sun reaches its highest point in the sky (zenith), and similarly its lowest point (nadir). This does not mean that there are two winters and two summers in the year. Indeed, often the

Mist over the coastal desert

only seasons one can really speak of are those based on variations in rainfall.

Peru is also typical of tropical countries in having a relatively large difference between day and night temperatures, especially in the mountains; whereas the differences between the hottest and coldest months are only very small. On the other hand, there are marked seasonal differences in rainfall, both in the mountains and in the east of the country. The stark climatic contrasts between different regions are due mainly to the enormous differences in altitude; the prevailing south-easterly trade winds, which produce high rainfall and the cold Humboldt Current along the Pacific coast.

High Altitude

The mountain climate is unusual in other ways that may be of great significance to tourists. Because the air is relatively thin, there is a high level of ultraviolet radiation from the sun, and visitors from lower altitudes can easily become sunburnt in a very short time.

There are great temperature differences between sun and shadow, so that if you take your jacket off you may have to put it back on again immediately you enter the shade of a house. The differences are even greater between day and night. In Cuzco or around Lake Titicaca, for example, it is not infrequent for the thermometer to

*Crossing a mountain
ravine*

rise to over 20˚C (68˚F) at midday during the winter (May to August),
only to drop well below freezing at night so that all water surfaces are
frozen by next morning.

Flora and Fauna

THE VEGETATION

The climatic variation is also responsible for an extraordinary variety
of plant species in Peru. This may not be apparent to anyone arriving
in Lima for the first time, since the surrounding deserts reveal little of
this richness of flora. But even the desert, though mostly bare of vegetation, has a few interesting surprises for the more observant visitor.

The traveller along the Panamerican Highway may be struck by
what appears to be giant writing or decorative designs covering the
hills all around. These may seem at first glance to be made up of
stones. But in fact they are large numbers of weird rosette-like plants
called tillandsia, which are closely related to the pineapple. They
have no roots and lie loosely on top of the barren ground. They
survive by absorbing nutrients from the moisture and dust in the air.
In places where the fog lingers, they can cover whole slopes with a

Cotton picking

display of lovely flowers.

A large number of plants flourish in hollows which are flooded from time to time. They include the 'wild cane' (*Gynerium saggitatum*), which closely resembles sugar cane, and the giant reed (*Arundo donax*). Both plants are important for coast-dwellers, as they provide roofing material instead of wood. In the shanty towns around Lima, whole dwellings are sometimes made out of reed matting.

In the northern deserts of Peru, a few trees manage to gain a foothold in the dust where the water table is not too far down. The predominant species is the algarrobo (*Prosopsis juliflora*), a plant covered in thorns and feathery leaves that is closely related to the acacia. The young plants are remarkable in being able to survive for years without water. Their pod-like fruits are edible, but are normally rendered down into an extract that is used in a popular Peruvian cocktail called algarrobina.

Improved irrigation has enabled the Peruvians to grow a variety of different crops along many parts of the coast. The most important of these are sugar cane, cotton, maize and rice. Many of the valley oases support a variety of fruit crops, including vines, peaches, oranges and bananas.

Chillies drying in the sun

The vegetation in the valleys of the Andes depends very much on local rainfall. On the western side especially, cacti often form the only plant cover up to a height of 2,300m (7,544ft). There are columnar cacti, especially *Cactus pitajaya* and *Cereus macrostibas*, and other leafless succulents that store water in their thick, fleshy stems.

The upper valleys between 2,300m (7,544ft) and 3,500m (11,480ft) are an area of intense cultivation, where since time immemorial the Amerindians have grown maize, quinoa and calabash gourds. Quinoa (*Chenopodium quinoa*) is a plant with lilac-coloured flowers that is closely related to spinach. But only its seeds are used for human consumption; they are made into products similar to flour and porridge. The calabash or bottle gourd (*Cucurbita moschata*) is a large sausage-shaped, spherical or bottle-shaped gourd, from which the Indians make decorative containers that are popular as souvenirs.

Any trees growing in the upper valleys are nowadays mostly eucalyptus. Eucalyptus trees are easy to recognise from their slender habit and long, aromatic leaves. The only native trees still found here are a few surviving examples of the queñoa (*Polylepis racemosa*). They are low and stunted, with brightly-coloured gnarled trunks, and can even occur as high as 4,500m (14,760ft).

Areas above 3,500m (11,480ft) are covered with wide expanses

Indian reed boats on Lake Titicaca

of yellow-brown grassland known as *puna*. Here and there are a few small-leaved shrubs and giant daisy-like flowers, whose leaves are covered with a thick layer of down to protect them against the cold. One speciality of this region is sadly dying out: the remarkable *Puya raimondii* is a relative of the pineapple that shoots up inflorescences more than 5m (16ft) high.

On the eastern side of the Andes, the slopes below 3,000m (9,840ft) are permanently covered in hill fog, and are a region of thick forests known as cloud forest. There are numerous ferns and thick bamboo-like undergrowth, while the trees grow into strange, stunted shapes and are covered with mosses, lichens and epiphytes. Lower down, where there is enough moisture, the trees grow taller, and include many good hard timber species. But where the natural vegetation has been cleared, there is only grass interspersed with fast-growing trees that provide virtually no timber.

The Amazonian Basin is almost completely covered with ever-green rain forests, which are characterised by a remarkably rich variety of species. Often there are no two trees alike over a considerable area, and the search for valuable timbers such as mahogany, rosewood or caoba can be a long and painstaking one. But transporting the timber can be even more difficult and dangerous.

A lot of special apparatus is needed to fell these colossal trees, which are supported in the soft ground by vast root systems several metres thick. Even after they have been cut up, the only way of transporting them is by water, and then only in the rainy season. Often long canals must be dug in order to float the logs — and if the tree fellers miscalculate the lie of the land, or there is not enough rain, then their trouble will have all been in vain. It is no surprise, therefore, that these valuable trees have mostly disappeared from areas adjoining the main waterways.

The traveller today is unlikely to see the original primaeval jungle. Most of the areas near the transport routes are covered with secondary forest that has grown up since the original forest was burned down or cleared. This forest is much poorer in species, and consists mostly of fast-growing soft-timbered trees. The undergrowth forms an impenetrable mass of ferns, creepers and prickly palms.

Even a boat trip along one of the meandering waterways will reveal only a part of the original Amazonian jungle. The flood plains of the rivers can be as much as 20-30km (12-18 miles) wide, and remain considerably waterlogged for much of the dry season. The resulting swamp forests are similarly poor in species. They consist mostly of palms, bamboos and trees with a complex network of mangrove-like roots. This area is the original home of the rubber tree (*Hevea brasiliensis*), a member of the spurge family that was responsible for the sudden increase in the development of Amazonia at the beginning of this century.

BIRD AND ANIMAL LIFE

The cold Humboldt Current, with its hosts of micro-organisms, provides an inexhaustible food supply for all kinds of sea creatures — especially the shoals of tiny anchovettas (*Engraulis ringens*) that form the staple diet of all the larger fish and the hosts of sea birds along the coast. Unfortunately the balance of nature has been disturbed by the overfishing of anchovettas to supply the demands of the fishmeal industry. The resulting lack of available food has caused a noticeable drop in the population of large fish and sea birds.

The commonest birds along the Peruvian coast are pelicans, boobies and cormorants. They all nest on inaccessible cliffs or offshore islands, which are often covered with a thick white layer of guano excreted by the birds. This guano is such a good fertiliser that at one time it was Peru's chief export.

The Andean condor is also seen occasionally on the coast. These giant vultures have a wingspan of 3m (10ft). They come down from the mountains in the morning, and use the heat thermals in the afternoon to glide back up to their nests, which they build at altitudes of 4,000m (13,120ft) or more.

The animal that most typifies the Andean plateaux is the llama, which was domesticated by the Indians as long as 4,000 years ago. Llamas provided them with everything they needed to survive in that inhospitable terrain, including meat for food, wool for clothing and leather for footwear. The bones were used to make ornaments and spearheads, and the dung was invaluable as a burning material in a region so bereft of trees.

As early as the Inca period, there were two distinct species of domestic llama: the llama proper (*Lama glama*) and the alpaca (*Lama pacos*). The llama was bred for its size and strength, and used as a beast of burden, while the smaller alpaca's thick, shaggy coat provided wool that was usually soft and warm. Sadly the great llama and alpaca herds are being supplanted by the faster-breeding sheep, so that today they are confined to the southern steppes of Peru above 4,000m (13,120ft). The two wild llama species, the guanaco (*Lama guanicöe*) and the vicuña (*Lama vicugna*), are very nearly extinct.

Apart from llamas and sheep, the Indians also keep guinea pigs (*Cavia cobaya*) as domestic animals. These pretty little rodents are very much prized for their meat, and the Indians may keep several dozen of them at home inside their mud-roofed cottages.

The best-known of the wild rodents is the chinchilla (*Chinchilla laniger*), which was almost hunted to extinction on account of its valuable fur. These grey rabbit-sized creatures can sometimes be seen at heights of 4,500m (14,750ft) or so, hopping along the road on their long hindlegs.

Insects are particularly abundant in these hot, sultry climes, and they include more than just unwanted pests. There are brilliantly coloured but harmless flies, giant beetles the size of your fist and magnificent butterflies that flutter gently through the forest shade. Among the most beautiful of these are the brilliant blue morphos, many of them as large as teaplates. Ants are particularly abundant here, often living in the hollow recesses in umbrella trees and other plants. Also common are the wood-eating termites, whose nests cling to tree trunks like large bee swarms.

Of the numerous colourful bird species in the jungle, the parrots are the most likely to be seen. The dazzling green or red macaws often perch on rooftops or in nearby trees, and will regularly come down to be fed. Toucans can occasionally be seen near to human dwellings. These are known as the clowns of the jungle on account of their enormous brightly coloured beaks and their hilarious behaviour. The many club-shaped formations that hang down from branches are the nests of the South American weaver bird. This starling-sized bird creates these remarkable structures about a metre in length out of woven plant material.

Flowering herbs and pretty plants thrive around Lake Llanganuco

The jungle rivers are similarly full of fish. These include not only the many colourful little creatures that brighten up many an aquarium, but also much larger fish that are delicious to eat. The arapaima (*Arapaima gigas*), for example, is a primitive bony fish that grows to 3m (10ft) in length with a weight of up to 200kg (440lb).

Many grisly stories are told of the bloodthirsty habits of shoals of piranhas, which can use their razor-sharp teeth to remove all the flesh from larger animals and even humans within seconds. These stories are difficult to believe when you see native Indians bathing happily in the river while one of these 20cm (8in) long carnivores is caught by an angler nearby.

It is much more dangerous to bathe where the banks are covered in undergrowth hiding poisonous snakes, or in muddy places where freshwater stingrays burrow around. Their 12cm (4½in) long spines are heavily barbed, and leave deep wounds that almost always become dangerously inflamed. The most lovable of the water creatures are undoubtedly the playful river dolphins, which never tire of rolling among the waves.

Most visitors to Amazonia are disappointed not to see some of the larger wild animals that live there. This is because many of them only leave their shelters at night, and others such as the giant anteater are very shy and avoid human company, while others such as the great

Llama caravan

cats have been almost totally exterminated for their fur.

The many snakes, though relatively common, are fortunately seen only rarely, because native guides bang the trees with bush knives to scare off these lethal reptiles before they come too close.

Economic Life

Considering the enormous wealth of natural resources that Peru possesses, with enormous reserves of land and an ample supply of manpower, it would appear that Peru has a bright economic future ahead of it. But in order to achieve this it must first try to solve the enormous social problems created by the present population explosion, and must somehow manage to raise the necessary capital.

Even today the Peruvian economy seems healthier in the long term than that of neighbouring countries. It does not depend on the success or failure of one particular product, but has a relatively broad spectrum of activities based on the resources provided by fisheries, agriculture and mining. It is true that the recent absence of fish shoals continues to be a major problem, but this has been in no way as disastrous as the drop in the price of tin has been for Bolivia.

Although nearly half the population works in agriculture, only 1.6

per cent of the land surface is actually under cultivation. In the Andes especially, where by far the majority of people are employed in agriculture, the stone-age methods used mean that they can barely produce enough to subsist on, and often even less than that. Thus Peru is still largely dependent on imports of meat, wheat, rice, fats and milk products.

But the agriculture is by no means backward everywhere. On the contrary, the numerous farm complexes in the coastal region use the latest farming methods. Since the agrarian reforms they have been under the co-operative ownership of their workers. They maintain complicated irrigation plants, grow only the most productive crops, and use their scientific knowledge in the application of fertilisers.

The *selva* also produces a small surplus of coffee and tea for export. But the vast agricultural resources of this enormous region will no doubt remain untapped for some time to come. The only intensive agriculture so far takes place in the so-called development areas between Tingo María and Pucallpa, and around Tarapoto. But the soils there are already being exhausted due to inappropriate methods of cultivation.

Great efforts are being made along the coast to turn yet more of the desert into fertile land by means of skilful irrigation. It was for this reason that the great Tinajona Reservoir was created to the east of Chiclayo. It is supplied by water diverted from the Amazon Basin via a tunnel through the Andes, and will be able to provide enough water to irrigate whole areas of the vast desert to the north of Chiclayo.

The importance of mining can be seen from the statistics. The figures below show Peru's production of four important metals as a percentage of total world production (figures given for 1969): silver: 12.8 per cent; zinc: 6.0 per cent; lead: 4.8 per cent; copper: 3.3 per cent.

The older mines are mainly concentrated in a region to the east of Lima (Cerro de Pasco, Casalpaca, Morococha). The ores mined there are smelted in the isolated mountain settlement of La Oroya. Peru also possesses some valuable iron ores along the coast to the west of Nazca. Some of these are turned into steel at the smelting works at Chimbote.

South America's first oil wells were opened as early as 1863 in the north Peruvian town of Talara. The oilfields there are now sadly nearing exhaustion, and production is no longer anywhere near sufficient to supply Peru's needs. Hopes of new oil finds in Amazonia have only been partially fulfilled. A new pipeline was laid across the Andes at enormous expense to the north Peruvian port of Bayóvar, but this has proved to be no more than an expensive white elephant.

Fisheries form the third plank of the Peruvian economy after agriculture and mining. The vast majority of the Peruvian fishing

Weaving in Chinchero, near Cuzco

catch is made up of those tiny anchovettas that swim in vast shoals off the coast. They form the basis of the fishmeal industry in Callao, Chimbote, Pisco, Supe and other towns along the coast.

Industry accounts for as much as a quarter of Peru's national product, and in recent years has become amazingly varied. The food industry employs by far the largest number of workers. But the textile and metalworking industries have also achieved considerable importance. One speciality is the manufacture of paper and cardboard from the squeezed-out cane that is left over from sugar production.

In the seventies an increasingly large number of foreign companies set up manufacturing bases in Peru, producing items such as machinery, electronic goods, cars and pharmaceuticals. But the enormous foreign debts incurred since then have produced a serious shortage of currency, which has created more and more problems for these industries that depend so much on imports from abroad.

Separating the chaff from the wheat

The Peruvian People

THE POPULATION

With an area of 1,285,215sq km, (496,220sq miles) Peru covers at least five times the area of Great Britain. The population in 1988 was estimated to be 23.5 millions — well under half that of Britain. The population density can thus be calculated as 18.3/sq km, which when compared with 250/sq km in Britain makes Peru a very thinly populated country. This is especially true of the Amazonian region, which accounts for 60 per cent of the area but only 9 per cent of the population, giving a population density of only 1.8/sq km.

The coastal desert by contrast is almost overpopulated, especially in view of the inhospitable nature of the terrain. What is more, one in three Peruvians lives in the urban area around Lima. The statistics show a significant movement of population towards the coast that is if anything accelerating. As many as a third of Peruvians have left from their home area to seek their fortune elsewhere. The depopulation of the mountain regions is further encouraged by the economic backwardness and undeveloped resources of these areas, while there are few who venture into the unexplored jungle areas to the east.

The vast majority of migrants have settled in the slum areas

Mine at Yanashalla Pass

around the coastal cities, and especially around Lima. Integrating them into the community is more than just an economic problem. Most of them are coming into contact with modern industrial society for the very first time; they have no education, and many of them do not even speak Spanish.

Peru is one of the countries in which the American Indians still make up a large proportion of the population. The figure is estimated to be around 50 per cent, although a large mixed-race population means that an accurate figure is impossible. The Indians of South America can scarcely be described as redskins. They are of Mongoloid origin, and similar to Tibetans both in skin colour and in physical build. They normally only come up to the shoulder of an average European. They have shiny black hair and rather pronounced cheek bones, and often have oriental-style eye folds. The yellowish-brown skin of mountain-dwellers becomes wrinkled and leathery in the raw mountain air.

The majority of Indians come from the mountain regions. Most of these are Quechuas, descendants of the Incas that once ruled Peru. The area around Lake Titicaca is inhabited by another race called the Aymarás. Both groups have their own language, and their understanding of Spanish (the official language) is often poor if not totally non-existent.

The number of Indians living in the *selva* is estimated to be around 100,000. They belong to many different races, each of which has a completely different set of customs. American linguists in Pucallpa print school books for them in over thirty different languages. Their way of life varies, from primitive hunters that still wander through the jungle, to half-assimilated city-dwellers who are perfectly capable of doing simple repairs to the outboard motors on their dug-outs.

Creole was originally the term applied to descendants of European settlers who were born in South America, most of them in Peru being of Spanish descent. Considerable racial mixing has obscured the distinction between whites and *mestizos* (those of mixed descent). However, a figure of 10 per cent whites is commonly given. Two other groups account for about 1 per cent of the population. These are the blacks, who arrived as slaves for the sugar and cotton plantations, and the Chinese, most of whom were originally hired for building the railway to La Oroya. Both these groups live almost exclusively around Lima.

Government and Administration

Compared to its revolution-ridden neighbour Bolivia, Peru has enjoyed relatively stable government. That is not to say that its history has been free of coups. For it too has seen the frequent alternation between civilian governments and military dictatorships that is so characteristic of Latin America.

The military regime that ruled from 1968 to 1980 brought about total economic chaos through a series of social experiments. The present democracy has inherited an enormous legacy of almost insuperable problems: a poor infrastructure, a stagnating agricultural economy, unprofitable industries, a catastrophic depopulation of the countryside, mounting national debts, and increasing misery and oppression among large sections of the population.

Peru is divided into 25 *departamentos* or administrative districts, each of which has a prefect appointed over it.

Education

In spite of enormous efforts on the part of the government, Peru has yet to fulfil its ultimate aim of achieving six years' basic primary education for every child in Peru. The lack of teachers is an insuperable problem, especially in the isolated mountain and jungle regions, where the illiteracy level is correspondingly very high.

Five years' secondary education lead in some cases to university. Private schools are particularly prestigious, some of which are run by the Catholic Church and others by various education associations. The latter include the Swiss-run Pestalozzi School and the German-run Alexander von Humboldt School, which caters for all levels from kindergarten up to the German *Abitur*.

The country's twenty universities vary enormously in the standard of education provided. All of them are oversubscribed, and this has resulted in drastic cut-backs in admissions.

Religion

There is complete freedom of religion in Peru. The majority of the population belong to the Roman Catholic Church, which in Peru is divided into seven archbishoprics with fourteen bishoprics. There is a lot of missionary activity in the jungle regions, mostly under the auspices of various American denominations and sects.

ATTITUDES AND CUSTOMS

Listening to the people of Lima, one is given the impression that there are four different kinds of people living there: *criollos*, *cholos*, *macacos* and *gringos*. None of these terms are meant seriously, and none are exactly flattering. They should certainly not be repeated by foreign visitors, as the line between teasing and insult is a very narrow one in Peru. All four terms allude to some weakness in the person to whom they are applied.

Cholo refers specifically to a person of mixed descent who is more Indian than European. The American term hillbilly has some of the same connotations, though its context is entirely different. *Cholo* implies an Indian from some outlying area who has little grasp or understanding of the modern world.

The word *macaco* is not really any nicer. The word is Spanish for macaque, a kind of monkey that is also known in English as the barbary ape. The term is used in Lima to refer to the Chinese, who according to the proud *criollos* are not quite human on account of their strange faces and 'terrifying' industriousness.

Criollo is probably the nicest of these four epithets, though even this term is not without a certain irony. The *criollo* is to be admired for his artfulness and cunning, but his cunning often goes beyond what is allowed. What is more, the *criollo* has little concern for punctuality or observing regulations, whatever the circumstances may be.

The last term is *gringo*, which basically refers to a foreigner, the implication being that he has acquired undeserved wealth by underhand means, but is no match for the *criollo* who attempts to do him out of that wealth. On the other hand, when a mountain Indian says *gringo*, it may be no more than a harmless expression of surprise at the arrival of a stranger in his isolated abode.

So the tourist must come to terms with always being called a *gringo*, though this is easier to accept if he realises that *cholos*, *criollos* and *macacos* are not without their faults too. More than that, he will be treated with great kindness if he tells the Peruvians how much he likes their country, which they are proud to show him, and disappointed if it is not appreciated as it should be.

Life in Lima is hardly any different from that of any large city in southern Europe. But the mountains are another world entirely. The mountain Indians live in little thatched cottages made of stone and mud. The whole household sleeps on the straw-covered floor of a single windowless room, which they share with the chickens and guinea pigs that serve to enrich their diet. The steep slopes around the houses are covered with stony fields that they cultivate with a primitive plough, and where the maize plants stand in distant array. Sometimes there is not even that — just a few sheep or llamas grazing on the coarse grass, while the people sit silently working the wool in front of their miserable dwellings. And one is led to wonder how they can possibly scrape a living in such a paltry environment.

The Indian costumes are so many and varied that one could fill a book just describing them. There are nearly twenty different costumes in Cuzco alone. Alas, these beautiful hand-woven costumes are becoming increasingly rare, especially in urban areas, where both Indians and *mestizos* now prefer manufactured clothes, albeit at second-hand. But if the men sometimes look like tramps, one should not immediately assume that is what they are.

Some traditional items of clothing are still in general use, even among those who now wear manufactured clothes. The poncho, for example, is worn throughout Latin America from Mexico down to Chile. It consists of a large square-shaped piece of cloth with a slit for the head, and is a very practical way of keeping out the rain and the cold. Apart from the poncho, the *chullo* is also very popular — a tasselled cap that comes in hundreds of different varieties.

The Indian women still love their brightly coloured dresses. They wear the most they can afford to on the basis that 'the broader the waist, the greater the beauty'. And no woman would ever be without the cloth that she wears over her back, which fulfils the dual role of shopping bag and baby carrier.

The mountain Indians are usually quiet, introverted and sparing with words. Many of them chew coca leaves; the juice turns their teeth a black colour, but also makes them less sensitive to pain, cold or hunger. They often drink *chicha,* an alcoholic drink produced from chewed maize. *Chicha* can make the harmless, peaceable Indian both hostile and aggressive.

Indian festivals are a colourful occasion that one would hardly think possible in the dreary grey-brown mountain environment. Their faces disappear behind strange masks, and their imagination knows no bounds in the costumes they dress up in. Festivals usually take place on the occasion of the local patron saint's day, though they often contain themes borrowed from ancient Indian mythology.

Christian missionaries swept through the country like a whirlwind, destroying much in their path but leaving many elements untouched.

Indian market at Chinchero, near Cuzco

The Indians have been converted to Christianity — they pray devoutly in their little churches and make reverential pilgrimages — but they still seek the protection of the gods, and pray to Mama Pacha the earth mother for a good harvest.

PERUVIAN FESTIVALS
The least interesting are the national festivals, such as the Day of National Honour on 9 October, and the Independence Days on 28 and 29 July. Just as in many other countries, they are mostly an occasion for military parades and official speeches. The church festivals, on the other hand, are often well worth seeing. The Holy Week processions in Ayacucho, for example, are such a marvellous experience that they are worth a trip for their own sake.

The patron saints' days in the mountain villages are magnificent occasions. The Spanish missionaries, who were keen to stamp out heathen practices, chose saints' days to coincide with the most important pagan festival in each village. This enabled them to transform the original festival into something with at least some Christian significance. The result is that many of the saint's-day festivals are combined with great fairs, firework displays and strange pagan dances.

Probably the most richly colourful of all these festivals is that of the

Purification of the Blessed Virgin Mary in Puno at the beginning of February, in which many groups of costumed dancers stage a unique and unforgettable pageant. There are hundreds of different strangely masked figures, of which the most exciting are without doubt the devil's dancers for which the Bolivian city of Oruro is so famous.

The capital Lima has several festivals too. They may not be as colourful or exotic as those in the mountains, but they involve great masses of people. One such occasion is the festival of the patron saint of South America, Santa Rosa of Lima, on 30 August. Other festivals centre around the veneration of a painting of Christ crucified called the *Señor de los Milagros* (Lord of Miracles), which is supposed to have miraculous properties. On the 18, 19 and 20 October, thousands of women in purple penitential robes form a long procession behind the painting as it is carried through the town on a silver litter. Many of them wear these robes for the whole of the month.

There is a third category of festival, namely those events that are laid on specially for tourists. Most of them are intended to bring the glory of the Inca empire back to life. The biggest of these is Inti Raymi, the great sun festival of the Incas, which takes place annually in the last week of June outside the gates of Cuzco.

History

BEFORE THE INCAS

The first Incas, so the legend goes, came down from the sun god to bring civilisation to mankind, who before that had wandered around like wild animals, without the blessings of agriculture, handicrafts, art and science. This myth was systematically propagated by the Incas in order to bolster up the rulers' claim to god-given supremacy, and thus succeeded in extinguishing all memories of previous civilisations. So given that there was no writing system for recording events, it is not surprising that the history of the pre-Inca period is very much a mystery.

However, much evidence has been discovered in the sand of the Peruvian desert, which has preserved thousand-year-old treasures as though they had been buried only yesterday. The dry climate has made coastal Peru into an archaeological treasure-trove that is unparalleled elsewhere except possibly Egypt.

These discoveries indicate quite clearly that there were important civilisations on the Peruvian coast long before the Inca period. However, they reveal very little about the religious, social and political structure of those coastal communities. Even less is known about the peoples of the mountains and the Amazonian jungle, because the climate there left only a few remains of buildings, many of which still lie undiscovered beneath the jungle.

It is now known for certain that there were people living along the coast of Peru before 10,000BC. The first settlers appear to have been hunters living on fish and sea-lions. But it is quite possible that the world's first farmers lived here, because beans and pumpkins were being grown here as early as 6500BC. By 1500BC the rivers were already being diverted to irrigate the fields, which were planted with cotton, maize and peanuts. This development marked the beginnings of weaving and pottery.

These communities lived in small and isolated valley oases that were separated by desert and mountains, and so each led a very independent existence. But it was nonetheless possible for three cultures to spread their influence over the whole of the central Andean region: the Chavín, the Tiahuanaco and finally the Incas. However, all three cultures were centred not on the coast but in the high mountains of the hinterland.

The Chavín culture grew from the ninth century BC onwards, and was centred around the worship of a deity represented by a cat-like creature that is nowadays known as a *felino*. There are still doubts as to whether the associated cult was influenced from outside, say from Central America. Nor is it known for certain whether the ancient city of Chavín on the eastern flank of the Cordillera Blanca was the centre of this cat-god cult, or whether its spread was associated with politics.

One of the great unresolved mysteries of Peru's past is the nature of the community that lived on the Paracas Peninsula from the seventh century BC onwards. The burial site of Paracas is just over 200km (124 miles) south of Lima, and there is no visible evidence that very many people actually lived there. However, the remarkable fact remains that the mummies found in these underground chambers were wrapped in some of the most beautiful cloth in the whole of ancient Peru. The mummification process itself, the skull deformities and signs of successful brain operations are equally remarkable. The mummification of the dead was a complicated process. First the entrails were extracted and the skin and flesh removed. The skin was then dried out in the sand and possibly treated with chemicals before being replaced over the skeleton. The mummy was then placed in a crouched position and wrapped up in a series of valuable cloths.

The skull deformities were created by binding planks of wood around the heads of children. This custom was by no means confined to Paracas. However, it is not known for certain whether it was associated with some religious cult or some ideal of beauty. Trepanation was a dangerous operation whereby a hole was made in the skull. That many people survived this procedure is evident from the bone growth in adult skulls where the operation had been carried out (about 2 per cent of the bodies found show signs of trepanation).

Cuzco — colourful costume at the Inti Raymi Festival

The period following the Chavín culture was again characterised by several geographically separate developments, which eventually culminated in the Nazca culture along the coast to the south and the Mochica culture to the north. Both cultures reached their peak in the fifth and sixth centuries AD. The magnificent colours of Nazca pottery, and the many representational figures of Mochica pottery, were never again to be matched. The Mochicas in particular seem to have been a warlike people, and their tight organisation enabled them to build enormous buildings such as the Huaca del Sol near Trujillo.

The origins of the Tiahuanaco or Huari culture (also spelled Tiwanacu or Wari) are still hotly debated. The cult of the weeping god appeared in the ninth century AD in the central Andean plateau; but it is not known whether it came from Tiahuanaco (now in Bolivia) to the south of Lake Titicaca, where massive ruins show clear evidence of a major cult, or whether it was spread by a warlike people called the Huari who lived in the area around present-day Ayacucho.

The classical period of Tiahuanaco-style art was followed in the eleventh century AD by further geographically separate develop-

Costumes from Chivay

ments. In the Chancay region 80km (50 miles) north of Lima, thieves still come to plunder the many tombs from this period and steal the apparently inexhaustible supply of precious cloth that was wrapped around the mummies.

The Chimú Empire flourished along the coast to the north from the early thirteenth to the mid-fifteenth century, and was the cultural heir to the Mochicas. The Incas conquered this area only shortly before the arrival of the Spanish, and were not able to extinguish the earlier folk memories. Thus much more is known about Chimú mythology.

According to legend, King Naimlap arrived with his fleet from across the sea to found the Chimú Empire and its capital Chan Chan. This city soon numbered some 100,000 inhabitants, and at the time was probably one of the world's largest cities. Naimlap was made into a god after his death, and was represented by a winged figure. The other major deities were those of the moon, fox, sea and storm.

The Chimús resisted the Incas fiercely, but in 1450 the vital water supply to Chan Chan was cut off, and they were forced to surrender. The Incas carried the king off to Cuzco, together with the best of the

Dress from the Sacsayhuamán festival, Cuzco

Chimú craftsmen, some of whom were the most skilful metalsmiths of the time.

THE INCA PERIOD

When Francisco Pizarro the Spanish conquistador landed near the present-day Ecuadorean border in April 1532, he had no idea that he was entering a large and highly organised empire, in which every inhabitant was subject to a strict code of laws.

It was a land full of well-ordered cities, impressive temples, magnificent palaces and large storage chambers full of food and precious metals. It was a land of sophisticated irrigation plants and well-kept roads although wheels and horses were unknown. There were beautiful textiles made of cotton and alpaca wool, colourfully decorated china and marvellous ornaments made of gold, silver and bronze, but there was no iron for making ploughs or other tools.

The administrative system was quite remarkable, considering the absence of writing. Exact statistics were recorded by means of knotted strings or *quipus*. But without writing there was no means of recording important events.

The Incas called their empire Tahuantinsuyo, which effectively means 'Four Regions'. And it was indeed subdivided into four administrative regions: Chinchaysuyo to the north, Collaysuyo to the south, Cuntisuyo to the west and Antisuyo to the east.

The capital Cuzco (which means 'navel') was appropriately situated at the point where these four regions met. According to legend it was founded in about AD1200 by the first Inca, Manco Cápac. Little is known for certain about this ruler or about his successors. Indeed, the whole of the early history of the Incas is lost in the mists of time. The first events that are known for certain occurred around the time of the military expansion under Pachacutec Inca Yupanqui (1438-71), who is presumed to have been the ninth ruler of the Inca dynasty.

The Inca rulers' greatest achievement was to unite a variety of different peoples into a single empire. It was to this end that conquered rulers were allowed to continue to participate in administrative duties. Quechua was the official language, and its influence was spread by forcing people in conquered regions to exchange homes with Quechua-speakers.

A massive road-building programme was undertaken in order to expedite troop movements in the event of a rebellion. Rest stations known as *tambos* were set up at regular intervals along these roads (about a day's march apart). These provided rest and refreshment for llama caravans, military troops, running messengers and passing noblemen. The communications system was particularly effective. Relay stations were set up along the roads at regular intervals of a few kilometres. Each station was manned by two fast runners or *chasquis*, one of whom carried the next message received as fast as possible to the next station. This relay system enabled messages to be carried as far as 400km (248 miles) in one day.

The Inca's second great achievement was the creation of a comprehensive social system, in which no one went hungry but personal freedom was non-existent. Every subject had to pay a tribute to the state by working in the fields, in the mines, on public building sites or in military service. Idleness was often punished by death.

Fertile land was farmed communally by each village community or *ayllu*. This ensured that no gaps occurred when part of the population was called away to military service or other duties. The agricultural land was divided into three categories: the people's land, which usually provided just enough food to satisfy the needs of the peasant population; the Inca's land, which served the needs of the local nobility, the military and most officers of state; the land of the sun, which belonged to the priesthood; surplus food was distributed to the old and infirm, or else stored away for emergencies.

The main duties of both the nobility and officers of state were organisation and supervision. They were not required to work in the fields or do military service. But the ruling classes were different in

Souvenir masks from Arequipa

other ways from simple peasant folk. The nobility, most of whom were blood relatives of the Incas, wore expensive clothing and ornaments made of silver and gold. They also attached heavy metal plates to their earlobes, which gradually stretched them so that they dangled against the neck. In contrast to the simple folk, the nobility were allowed to have several wives.

Inca was the name given to the supreme ruler, who held all the strings of power together and was granted the status of a god. Apart from his main wife, who was always a sister or half-sister, he possessed a large number of concubines. Before his death the Inca appointed one of his sons as his successor. The last-but-one Inca, Huayna Cápac, decided to divide his empire between two sons. This resulted in serious quarrels between the two heirs, leading eventually to civil war. Atahuallpa had only just managed to gain the upper hand when the Spaniards arrived.

The Inca religion was characterised by a plethora of different gods and spirits. The most important of these deities in the Inca state was the sun god, whose earthly representative was the Inca himself. The Inti Raymi or sun-god festival was the main event of the year — so much so that it is still staged in Cuzco for the benefit of tourists. This took the form of a kind of harvest festival. Homage was also paid to other gods, such as the moon, Venus, lightning, thunder and the

A golden ceremonial Chimú knife

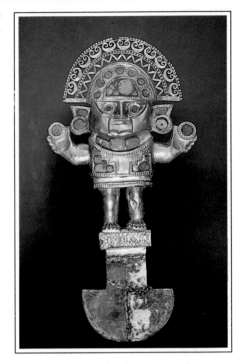

rainbow. Among the peasant folk Mama Pacha, the earth mother, has been continually revered right down to the present day. But apart from these mainly benevolent gods, there was a host of various evil spirits, who lived on mountain peaks and in gorges and lakes. The Indians still fear these spirits today.

THE COLONIAL PERIOD (1533-1821)

In April 1532 Francisco Pizarro landed near Tumbes in the far north of Peru with a small band of some 130-250 adventurers. They met no great difficulties as they marched inland, and in the November they were warmly received by the Inca Atahuallpa in the small mountain city of Cajamarca. But the Spaniards took the Inca prisoner and massacred his followers in the most gruesome way. The state organisation was effectively beheaded. The people were unaccustomed to thinking for themselves, and had no means of organising any resistance. The Spaniards were further helped by the fact that the Incas knew nothing about horses or explosive weapons, and that some of the nobility who had lost in the recent civil war sided with the

Spaniards in order to regain some of the power they had lost.

Thus Pizarro met little resistance as he advanced through the mountains, and on 15 November 1533 he captured the Inca capital of Cuzco. In order to keep the Indians happy, he appointed Atahuallpa's brother Manco Inca as successor to the Inca throne. Pizarro himself returned to the coast, where in 1535 he founded the city of Lima, which from then on was the capital of the Spanish colony in America.

Many adventurers followed to South America, drawn by stories of the vast wealth of the Incas. Thus a large number of Spanish settlements were founded within the space of a few years. But it was a long time before peace was secured. In 1536 Manco Inca led a rebellion in Cuzco, and very nearly overthrew the Spanish rulers. Meanwhile the conquistadors could never stop fighting among themselves. Pizarro had sent his companion at arms Diegro de Almagro to Chile. But Almagro was disillusioned by the poverty of this region, and returned to try and carve off a piece of Peru for himself. Thus began the year-long struggle between the Pizarristos and the Almagristos. Almagro was executed in 1538, but in 1541 Pizarro himself was murdered.

In an attempt to restore peace to the region by bringing it more under the control of the Crown, the king of Spain made the new colony into the viceroyalty of Nueva Castilla (New Castile). But Pizarro's younger brother Gonzalo thought he had been robbed of his rightful inheritance. He rebelled against the new viceroy, who was murdered shortly afterwards. But the second viceroy eventually managed to regain control, and Gonzalo Pizarro was executed.

The farmlands which had previously belonged to the Inca were taken over by the Spanish Crown and the Church. But the so-called *encomienderos* who were charged with administrating these lands tended to run them like their own private estates. They claimed the same rights over their Indian subjects as their Inca predecessors had done, but showed none of the same moderation. On the contrary, they often ignored the people's needs entirely. The Indians died in their tens of thousands, both in the mines and on the plantations. Other Indians succumbed to infectious diseases introduced by the Europeans and to which they had no natural resistance. The Indian population is estimated to have been some 10-15 million under the Incas, but by the late eighteenth century it had been reduced to only 600,000. Manpower shortages eventually became so severe that black slaves and Chinese had to be brought into the country.

Soon there were more creoles (Spaniards born in South America) and upwardly mobile people of mixed-race than there were Spaniards who had been born in Spain. But all the top administrative posts were reserved for immigrants from Spain, so the creoles became increasingly unhappy with their lot. Crises in the local administration, combined with difficulties in the Spanish homeland and the example of North America, eventually led to wars of independence throughout South America.

THE PERIOD OF INDEPENDENCE

Although there were several earlier abortive attempts, the wars of independence did not begin in earnest until 1817 in Venezuela under the leadership of Simón Bolívar. In Argentina the struggle was begun by José de San Martín, who in 1820 landed with his troops in Peru. Independence was declared the following year, but the king's troops had not yet given up. On 6 August 1824, Simón Bolívar's liberation army swept down from the north and began a bloody battle near Junín, which he only won at the last possible moment. But full independence was not achieved until 9 December 1824, when the king's army was finally routed near Ayacucho.

Though independent, Peru had further conflicts to contend with. In 1879 she joined with Bolivia in a war against Chile, who wanted the rich saltpetre deposits of the Atacama Desert in the south. The conflict lasted until 1884. Chile won, and Peru was forced to hand over the two southernmost provinces of Arica and Tarapacá. The result was more favourable in 1941, when differences over territory led to war with Ecuador, after which Ecuador was compelled to hand over most of the Amazonian territory that Peru had laid claim to.

Peruvian Art

ANCIENT AMERINDIAN ART

Art before the Spanish conquest concentrated almost entirely upon the production and ornamentation of pottery and textiles. Such was their beauty and variety that any architecture and stonework seems almost uninspired by comparison. Amerindian pottery and textile designs were characterised by a large number of different styles, which developed in geographical isolation from one other. However, some parallel developments appear to have occurred in each separate area, albeit at different times. Thus Amerindian art can be divided into three main periods, commonly known as the preclassical, classical and postclassical periods.

Towards the end of each of these periods, certain styles appeared which seem to have become universal throughout the whole of Peru. These were no doubt spread in conjunction with military power or certain religious practices.

The Preclassical Period

The formative period began around 900BC, at a time when pottery and textiles were becoming less confined to religious cults and increasingly general in their use. But since everyone produced their own pottery and materials for everyday use, art as such remained confined to the religious sector.

The universal style of this period is associated with the cat-god cult of the Chavíns. The cat-like motif (*felino*) crops up all over the place in finds from this period. The design was highly stylised in form, but also acquired certain bird-like, sometimes even snake-like or human traits. Horrific demons from this period are also depicted on the buildings and columns of Chavín. The most famous of these is the Raimondi Column, now housed in the Archaeological Museum in Lima.

The Classical Period

From the year 0 onwards, textile and pottery design became more and more the exclusive domain of specially trained experts. This brought both an improvement in quality and a refinement of design, and resulted in a flowering of art during this period.

The Paracas culture is named after a peninsula about 250km (155 miles) south of Lima, which became famous on account of the beautiful grave clothes found there. These represent the zenith of textile design. Motifs used included fishes, reptiles, birds, mammals and half-human creatures. Later pieces from Paracas contain such a variety of motifs that some experts think that they may eventually turn out to be some kind of writing.

The Nazca culture developed from the early fourth century AD on the coast to the south, and is famous for its magnificent pottery designs. The shapes of the actual vessels seem primitive by comparison, especially where people and animals are depicted. Most of them are near-spherical in shape, with two thin spouts linked by a handle.

Painting on pottery reached its zenith in the seventh and eighth centuries. Eleven different colours were used, but for some strange reason greens and blues were mostly absent. The painters seem to have been almost afraid of leaving any space blank, for every spare centimetre was covered with human or animal monsters, evil demons or weird beings with arms like snakes and tongues like millipedes.

The Mochica culture grew up almost simultaneously with the Nazcas on the coast to the north, and was similarly expert in the area of pottery design. However, in stark contrast to the Nazcas, the Mochicas used very little colour and concentrated on producing elaborate-shaped vessels. They turned pottery into a form of plastic art, in which everyday objects were represented with astonishing realism. There was scarcely any area of life that was not represented: human portraits, sexual activity, people with toothache or hare-lips, and every imaginable animal or plant. And yet all these items had one

Nazca pottery

aspect in common: a round handle with a spout at the top.

The Mochicas also painted on pottery, but their designs were markedly different from the usual Nazca style in that they were realistic down to the smallest detail. They show innumerable battles and episodes from everyday life, and provide invaluable information about ancient Amerindian cults along the coast of northern Peru.

The Tiahuanaco style was the second to become universal throughout Peru, in this case in the ninth and tenth centuries. The Tiahuanaco style is characterised by highly geometrical designs. The motifs used are stylised representations of humanoid creatures with some of the appendages of cats, snakes and condors. The round spots under the eyes of these deities are thought to represent tears, although there is considerable uncertainty about this. In contrast to the coastal peoples, who made flimsy buildings out of mud bricks, these mountain-dwellers built their temples out of great blocks of stone hewn from the mountainside. Thus many remnants of Tiahuanaco architecture have been preserved to this day. The most important examples are in Tiahuanaco itself, which is just across the

Bolivian border. Perhaps the 'weeping-god' figure that is engraved there on the famous monolithic Gate of the Sun formed the basis for similar designs on pottery and texiles.

The Post-Classical Period

The final period began in the eleventh century, and is dominated by the military expansion of the Chimú and Inca empires. Such military expansions naturally encouraged the spread of the artistic styles too. Textiles and pottery became increasingly mass-produced, and show distinct signs of decadence. However, metalworking and architecture reached their peak during this period.

Chimú pottery reached its peak in the fourteenth and fifteenth centuries, and was mostly mass-produced by means of moulds. Earlier Chimú pottery shows Mochica and Tiahuanaco-like influences, but decorative work gradually disappeared, and later examples are uniformly black with lead glazing.

Chimú metalsmiths worked mostly in silver, gold and copper. It is not yet known where they obtained these metals from, since they were certainly not available within the northern coastal territories ruled by the Chimús. Among the most remarkable finds are some fine death masks, beautiful beakers inlaid with precious stones, which were used in religious ceremonies, and enormous earrings that were worn by the nobility as a sign of their rank.

Chimú metalsmiths also produced numerous sacrificial knives called *tumis*, copies of which are available in every souvenir shop in Lima. Carved above the short semi-circular blade is a male figure with almond-shaped eyes and a broad helmet. This is thought to be a representation of Naimlap, the legendary founder of the Chimú empire.

The Chimú buildings were flimsy structures made of mud. However, some impressive remains of the Chimú capital of Chan Chan have been preserved down to this day, thanks to the unusually dry climate of the Trujillo area. On some of the walls it is still possible to make out long rows of fishes, pelicans and geometrical designs.

The artistry of the Inca culture is mostly shown in their buildings, though these admittedly reveal more technical expertise than true artistic sense. Stonecraft had already been developed in Chavín and Tiahuanaco, but it reached its zenith under the Incas. Massive blocks of stone were sculpted out with stone or bronze tools, then smoothed off with sand and dragged up and down the mountainsides by human strength alone. Blocks weighing many tons were placed on top of each other with such accuracy that no earthquake could budge them. Walls were never built quite vertical, though more for aesthetic than for technical reasons. All doors and alcoves were characteristically trapezoid in form. It is often very difficult to imagine how these buildings must have looked originally, for although they now look very bare and austere, they were once covered in costly gold decorations. The alcoves no doubt contained statues of gods and other objects of worship. Alas, all these rich treasures fell victim to the greed of the Spanish conquistadors.

AFTER THE SPANISH CONQUEST

Architecture

As soon as the Spaniards arrived, new buildings began to spring up everywhere. Whole cities were laid out in the chequerboard pattern that is typical of the whole of South America. Numerous churches appeared, together with public buildings and residences for well-to-do Spaniards.

The Spanish must have relied largely on local materials and the help of Indian craftsmen, painters and architects, especially in areas a long way from Lima. Given this fact, it is quite incredible that colonial architecture differed so little from that of the Spanish homeland — apart, that is, from certain modifications that were necessary to counteract earthquakes. Spanish architecture crossed to the American continent after only a short delay, and was usually changed very little to suit local circumstances.

The mansions of Lima were exact replicas of Andalusian residences, with their central courtyards and colonnaded galleries. The buildings of Lima were if anything even more magnificent than the originals in Spain, as befitted the richness of the American colonies. This was reflected not only in their dimensions but in the rich carvings and the lovely porcelain tiles imported from Andalusia.

The Spanish conquest was associated with vigorous missionary activity, so that churches and monasteries formed an important part of the building programme. Every town had to have monasteries for the Jesuits (La Compañía), the Franciscans (San Francisco), the Mercedarians (La Merced), the Augustinians (San Agustín) and other religious orders. One of the best examples of the artistry employed in such buildings is the church of La Compañía in Cuzco.

Church architecture was chiefly modelled on the Spanish renaissance and the rather ponderous Spanish early baroque, which lasted on the Iberian peninsula up until the eighteenth century. However, these European styles began increasingly to show signs of native Indian influence, leading to a style known as *mestizo*. This was particularly noticeable in the highly decorated façades, which were often covered with scrolled leaf and plant designs. Precolumbian motifs such as suns and puma heads sometimes appear amongst the foliage, while the figures of saints often seem naive and childlike. The best examples of *mestizo* architecture are the churches around Puno, in Cajamarca and in Arequipa, where special circumstances

Colonial palace, Cuzco

led to the development of a completely individual style.

It seems hardly surprising that the Spaniards also brought the mudejar style to Latin America, with its strong Moorish influences. Its Arabic origins are revealed in the horseshoe-shaped arches, the inlaid work on the furniture and the star-shaped designs in the ceiling vaults, while the famous wooden balconies of Lima hark back to the trellis-work that divides off the women's chamber in a mosque. But the '*cedarwood*' that is used is not from the coniferous cedar of Morocco, but from a group of tropical trees (*Cedrela*) belonging to the mahogany family, imported from Columbia and Central America.

There are two main types of altar design. In the so-called retablo style the altarpiece, which originally consisted of hinged panels, is decorated all the way up to the ceiling with columns, paintings and carved statues of saints. The other style is the plateresque, which flourished in Spain in the sixteenth century and also shows signs of Moorish influence. The altarpiece was mostly unsculpted, but was decorated with paintings of saints surrounded by a kind of carpet of fine gold or silver plate.

Finally in the eighteenth century the churrigueresque arrived in Peru. This late baroque style was named after the Spanish architect José de Churriguera, and is characterised by an extreme richness of decoration. The best Peruvian examples are in Lima, namely the façade of San Agustín and the altar at the church of Jesús y María.

Paintings

The many rich churches and monasteries required suitable interior decoration, and this led to a great demand for paintings. These were imported at first, but were soon copied by Indian and *mestizo* artists according to European methods. However, the lack of canvas and of paint dyes made in Europe from traditional secret recipes meant that Peruvian paintings soon took on a distinctive character of their own.

The first paintings were in the mannerist style of the Italian late renaissance. This was due to the influence of the Italian painter Bernardo Bitti, who emigrated to Peru in 1548. Later paintings show the increasing influence of Flemish painters, whose works came to Peru in the form of engravings. The most important Flemish-style painter was Diego Quispe Tito (probably 1611-81), an outstandingly versatile artist of Indian descent who brought landscape into Peruvian painting. His works depict weird tropical landscapes in strangely distorted perspectives. Because he was a *mestizo*, the Inquisition forbade him from signing his paintings. So he came upon the idea of leaving his own distinctive mark in the form of tropical birds or randomly placed huts.

As painters became more self-confident, so their style became less and less European-dominated. This led to the development of a distinctive Cuzco style, in which artists turned their attention away from the visible world and concentrated instead on fairy-tale and fable. The landscapes seem to stem from a child's imagination. Angels are armed with guns, while saints are clothed in royal robes. A love of decoration is expressed in the fine gold-leaf haloes and the jewels, brooches and necklaces that are incorporated into the paintings. The best examples of this style are to be found in the Museum of Art in Lima, the Archbishop's Palace in Cuzco and the monastery at Ocopa.

1
THE CITY OF LIMA

Lima was founded on 18 January 1535 by the Spanish conquistador Francisco Pizarro, who made it the capital of his newly conquered empire. His choice was a good one, for the city gates looked out onto the fertile fields of the largest oasis on the coast, while the Río Rimac brought down ample supplies of water from the mountains the whole year round. He could also keep in contact with his homeland via the port of Callao, which was only 10 miles away, and where in the sixteenth century there were usually between thirty and forty ships at anchor.

The city grew apace thanks to its favourable position, and in 1544 it became the capital of the whole Spanish colony in South America. The viceroy with his court and his considerable bureaucracy brought luxury and riches to the city, which proudly called itself the *Ciudad de los Reyes* or 'City of the Kings'.

The oasis has long since been obscured by asphalt and concrete, and the bare hills of the surrounding desert are covered with a vast sea of houses. The waters of the Rimac have long been insufficient to supply the city's needs, and water has to be brought via tunnels through the mountains from the other side of the watershed.

Lima and the neighbouring port of Callao have grown together to form a vast metropolis with a resident population of some 7 million. But this figure ignores the large numbers of so-called *pueblos jóvenes* or 'new residents' who occupy the shanty towns — a broad swathe of mud and straw huts that surrounds the city's main business and residential quarters. No one can say for certain how many people are forced to live here in abject poverty. But it is a known fact that Lima's population grows by at least 200,000 a year.

The repeated earthquakes no longer strike fear into those living in modern houses, thanks to today's stringent building regulations. But they have sadly destroyed the majority of the beautiful older buildings. What is more, the rising tide of traffic has meant sacrificing whole blocks of streets. But in spite of all this there are still some beautiful squares and a large number of fine churches and mansions

44

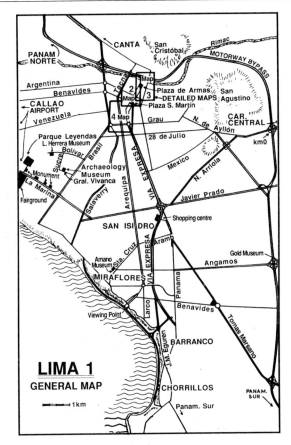

LIMA 1
GENERAL MAP
1km

PLACES OF INTEREST ON LIMA MAP 1
• **San Cristóbal:** A hill crowned with a cross just to the north of the city centre. There is a fine view from the top, but visitors should not go up there, either on foot or in a car, unless accompanied by a police guard!
• **Centro:** The old city is given in more detail on subsequent maps.
• **Museo Rafael Larco Herrera**, Avenida Bolívar 1515, Pueblo Libre. A museum of precolonial Amerindian culture.
• **Museo Nacionale de Antropología y Arqueología:** National Museum of Anthropology and Archaeology, Plaza Bolívar, Pueblo Libre. The best museum of precolonial Amerindian culture.
• **Avenida La Marina:** A broad avenue linking the southern suburbs with Callao and the airport. Many souvenir shops, fairground, zoo, **Parque las Leyendas.**
• **San Isidro:** The nicest quarter of the city, with villas mostly occupied by diplomats, and a large shopping centre next to an eight-lane highway called the Via Expresa.
• **Museo Amano**, Calle Retiro 160, Miraflores. An excellent museum with ancient Amerindian textiles.
• **Miraflores:** An important suburb with its own town centre, the main shopping street being the Avenida Larco.
• **Viewing point:** A marvellous view along the coast. Five minutes' walk from the centre of Miraflores along the Avenida Mariscal Oscar de Benavides (known under its old name of Diagonal).
• **Barranco** and **Chorrillos:** Older suburbs with nice beaches.

from the colonial period.

Anyone on a brief visit to Lima should at least visit the Plaza de Armas and the Gold Museum . The churches of San Francisco and San Agustín are the most interesting buildings from the colonial period. A half-day trip to Pachacámac provides a general view of the city, together with some desert scenery and a visit to an Inca site. The Gold Museum and the newly built Museum of Anthropology and Archaeology give a good overview of the ancient Amerindian cultures, while the Museum of the Inquisition provides interesting insights into medieval methods of torture.

Transport

Lima is not yet served by a proper rail or underground network. Buses and taxis are therefore the only public means of transport, and these unfortunately have all the traffic to cope with.

Taxis can be hailed anywhere. The officially prescribed taxi-meters do not usually work properly, so the fare must be negotiated before setting off. It is best to inquire in the hotel beforehand as to the standard fare for the journey.

Minibuses (*colectivos*) can be hailed at any corner in the city. To get off you must call '*bajar*' (pronounced 'bahar'). Minibuses are cheap but are usually full to bursting. It is also extremely difficult for a visitor to make head or tail of the extremely complicated network of routes.

Buses will only stop at an official bus stop (*paradero*). Timetables are available at street stalls in the city centre, giving details of all bus and minibus routes.

Tour 1

Lima Map 3
Best time: 3-6pm; also Sat and Sun am
Length: 1.5km (nearly a mile)

This suggested tour through the old city passes some of Lima's old churches and includes one of the finest of the colonial palaces. Those wishing to avoid the worst of the traffic can shorten the tour by going straight from San Francisco Church to San Pedro along the Jirón Azángaro and visiting the Museum of the Inquisition by taxi on a separate occasion.

✳ The **Plaza de Armas** *(Bus no 1)* is one of the most historic locations in the whole of South America. It was here that in 1535 Francisco Pizarro drew up the plan for his city using a sword on the ground. True to his Spanish tradition, he had all the main state and religious buildings built in close proximity to this central square, which was to witness all the ups and downs of the colonial period.

This was where the viceroys held their audiences with the people. This was where the crowds thronged to festivals, and cheered on the bullfights and processions. But this too was where the victims of the Inquisition were burned, and where rebel leaders were beheaded.

The earthquake of 1746 destroyed all the buildings around, and most of the visible structures are of modern origin. But the square nonetheless retains some of its old colonial glory. The lovely old fountain goes back to 1651, and the houses have been built in the old style, with fine wooden balconies and a sense of grandeur and space.

The present structure of the **Cathedral** (La Catedral) in the Plaza de Armas goes back to the seventeenth century, when the people decided to build a new cathedral on the site where Pizarro laid the foundation stone of Lima's first church. The building was consecrated in 1624, but was severely damaged in the earthquakes of 1687 and 1746. Changing tastes meant the introduction of many Gothic, baroque and classical features, but these have not changed the overall effect of the original structure.

The first chapel on the right-hand side houses the mortal remains of Francisco Pizarro, the conqueror of the Inca empire. In the second chapel on the right is an altar that was made in 1649 for another church, with beautiful carvings depicting the life and death of John the Baptist. The carved choirstalls are thought by experts to be the finest in the whole of America. These were made around 1623 by Pedro Noguera from Spain. To the left of the high altar is the entrance to the **Museum of Religious Art** (Museo de Arte Religioso), which contains some lovely paintings in the Cuzco style, together with other interesting works of art.

Iglesia del Sagrario is a small church sandwiched between the Cathedral and the Archbishop's Palace and is remarkable for its lovely Sevillian tilework and two beautiful gilded balconies, one for the bishop and one for the viceroy. The **Archbishop's Palace** (Palacio Arzobispal) includes some superb examples of the carved balconies that were so typical of colonial Lima. On important religious festivals the apostolic nuncio gives a blessing from the balcony above the entrance.

Francisco Pizarro built the **Government Palace** (Palacio del Gobierno) on this site between the Plaza de Armas and the Río Rimac. After his death this became the home of the viceroys and later of the presidents of the independent republic. The present building dates from 1938, and is guarded by soldiers in uniform. The changing of the guards takes place at 12.50pm every day except Sunday, and is part of a long ceremonial tradition. The building is due to be converted into a museum.

The street to the east of the Government Palace leads straight to Lima's **main railway station** (Estación del Ferrocarril), which seems ridiculously small to European eyes. The one train of the day departs

Lima Cathedral

very early in the morning to begin its difficult climb up into the mountains. The terrace to the right of the station provides a fine view of the back of the Government Palace and across the Rimac (usually no more than a trickle) to the cross on top of San Cristóbal. This hill is the haunt of armed robbers, and tourists should not go up there unless accompanied by a police guard.

The square in front of the **Monastery of St Francis** (Convento San Francisco) is one of Lima's finest architectural compositions, though the church looks rather unusual with its horizontal bands. To the left of the church is the entrance to the monastery, which is one of Lima's favourite tourist haunts.

The entrance hall is impressive with its colourfully decorated balconies. Above the stairs in the next room is a marvellous wooden dome, one of the finest examples in Lima of the mudejar style. The lovely vaulting was unfortunately badly damaged in the 1940 earthquake, and has not yet been fully restored. There is a small hall with a collection of works by the Spanish painter Francisco de Zurbarán (1598-1664) showing the twelve apostles. The chapter house is decorated with paintings and a gilded baroque altar. The cloister is famous for its Sevillian tilework, which was made specially for this

Santa Rosa procession in front of the Archbishop's Palace

monastery, as is shown by pictures on the columns of St Francis of Assisi. The pictures above the tilework also show scenes from the life of St Francis.

The museum room gives a taste of the former wealth of this monastery, which once spanned four blocks of houses and was one of the largest in Lima. The exhibits include silver lanterns and thuribles, monstrances and costly gold-threaded chasubles. At the back of the room is a reconstruction of the carved balcony of the former viceroy.

The **catacombs** form an underground passage to the Government Palace, where until 1808 the mortal remains of worthy citizens of Lima were laid to rest. The vaults are estimated to contain the bones of as many as 70,000 people. But some tidy-minded person has pulled the skeletons apart and sorted the bones according to type. Thus there are, for example, some vaults with only thigh bones and others filled with skulls. However, in the last renovation in 1975, grisly piles of human ribs, vertebrae and heads were removed once and for all.

The upper gallery leads into the **choir** of the church, where there are some of the most richly decorated choirstalls in the whole of Lima.

These were carved in 1673 from Nicaraguan 'cedarwood'. Where the ceiling is damaged, the roof structure becomes visible; as in other churches in Lima, the danger of earthquakes means that the usual stone arches are replaced by wattle and daub covered with plaster.

The route continues alongside the monastery and across a busy wide street called the Avenida Abancay to the **Plaza Bolívar**, *Bus nos 48, 59a* (*Miraflores*), *59b* (*Monterrico*). Here there is a statue of Simón Bolívar, the Venezuelan freedom-fighter who fought for the independence of Venezuela, Colombia, Ecuador, Peru and Bolivia.

A gateway through the classical façade of the **Museum of the Inquisition** (Museo del Inquisición) along the south side of the Plaza Bolívar leads to the former Courtroom of the Inquisition, which is remarkable for its carved wooden ceiling. The library leads through to the partially restored prison cells and torture chambers, where the Spanish Inquisition carried out their grisly handiwork. This group of specially appointed Dominican monks tortured their victims here from 1570 until 1813, when the people rebelled by storming the building and burning it down. The restored rooms contain exhibits of instruments of torture, in which dummies are shown being hanged, drawn and quartered, and martyred in many other horrific ways, just like all the thousands of condemned heretics who suffered during this reign of terror.

In spite of the rather bare exterior, the richly decorated interior of **St Peter's Church** (Iglesia de San Pedro) makes it one of the most beautiful of Lima's colonial buildings. Thanks to its solid construction it has withstood all the earthquakes, and is the only church in Lima to have remained substantially unchanged since its consecration in 1638, preserving its original decor right down to the present day.

The side aisles are particularly interesting, with Sevillian tilework below and elaborate gilded carvings above, surrounding painted panels, most of which have become somewhat faded. Each of the side altars is a masterpiece of medieval wood carving. The balconies either side of the high altar are also worth seeing. Again, one was for the viceroy and the other for the religious leader. To the right of the high altar is a door leading into the vestry, which is similarly remarkable, with its carved furniture, gilded wall decorations, old paintings and brightly painted window openings.

The early eighteenth-century mansion of the **Torre Tagle Palace** (Palacio Torre Tagle) belongs nowadays to the Foreign Ministry, but it is one of the finest examples in Lima of secular colonial architecture. The asymmetrical façade is particularly impressive, with its richly decorated entrance and two carved balconies. The inner courtyard shows similar evidence of Andalusian mudejar influence, especially in the shape of the window arches, the gate ornamentation and the carved wooden ceilings. A small chapel with a churrigueresque altar

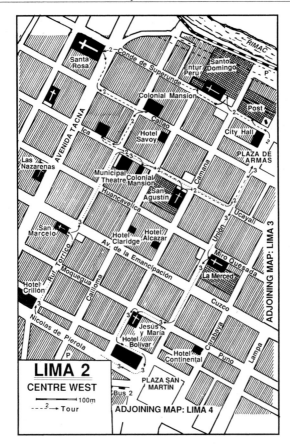

LIMA 2
CENTRE WEST
■—— 100m
---²—→ Tour
ADJOINING MAP: LIMA 4

PLACES OF INTEREST ON LIMA MAP 2
- **Santuaria de Santa Rosa**, Avenida Tacna. An interesting chapel.
- **Convento Santo Domingo**, Jirón Camaná. An interesting monastery.
- **Teatro Municipal**: Municipal Theatre, Jirón Ica.
- **Iglesia de San Agustín**, Jirón Camaná, Esquina Ica. A church with a beautiful façade.
- **Iglesia de las Nazarenas**, Avenida Tacna. Home of the *Señor de los Milagros* (Lord of Miracles) that is processed through the streets in October.
- **Iglesia de la Merced**, Jirón de la Unión. A church with a beautiful façade.
- **Jirón de la Unión**: The most important shopping street in the old city.
- **Iglesia de San Marcelo**, Avenida de la Emancipación. A church with a beautiful façade.
- **Iglesia de Jesús y María**, Jirón Camaná. A very interesting church.
- **Avenida Nicolas de Pierola/La Colmena**: Important tourist thoroughfare, with numerous souvenir shops, booking offices for most international airlines and two of the city's best hotels (Crillón, Bolívar).
- **Plaza San Martín**: Busy square with the Liberator's Monument.

is also open to the public, together with a few rooms furnished in the original style. The palace is open on weekdays from 2pm until 4pm and at weekends, 9am until 6pm.

Tour 2

Lima Map 2
Best time: 9.30-12noon; 3.30-5.30pm
Length: 1.3km (nearly a mile)

This tour also passes a number of fine colonial buildings and old churches. They may not quite match up to San Pedro or Torre Tagle, but they are nonetheless worth a visit. The tour again begins in the Plaza de Armas, but this time goes north-west along the Jirón Conde de Superunda/Jirón Lima, which comes out of the square between the city hall and the Pizarro Monument.

To the right of the courtyard of the **Main Post Office** (Correo Central) is a small **Stamp Museum** (*Museo Filatelisco*), where special stamps are also available. The long passage beyond the first courtyard is the domain of the travelling postcard sellers. There are picture cards of places all over Peru, including some that are not available at the places they show. The stamp collectors gather here on Sunday mornings, and it is possible to obtain some lovely old sets for a ridiculously small sum.

The church belonging to **St Dominic's Monastery** (Convento Santo Domingo) has lost most of its original sixteenth-century mudejar decorations to the classical fashions of the late eighteenth century. So apart from a few statues of saints, there is little of great interest to be found there.

However, the monastery itself is more interesting. The entrance is to the right of the church. A door to the left of the entrance passage leads into the reception room, which is graced by a particularly fine mudejar ceiling. The inner court is decorated with Sevillian tilework, pictures of St Dominic and two carved altarpieces.

A staircase at the back of the courtyard leads down to a small vault, where three saints from Lima are buried: Beato Juan Masias, Santa Rosa and San Martín de Porres. Next to the staircase is the entrance to the chapter house, which contains carved furniture and pictures of scenes from the life of the founder of the Dominican order. The fine mudejar balcony over the entrance is where an emissary from the viceroy sat during the monks' sessions to make sure there were no conspiracies going on.

Casa de Oquendo, Jirón Conde de Superunda 298, is an old eighteenth-century mansion which has some fine rooms with period furniture that may be visited. The look-out tower on top of the building

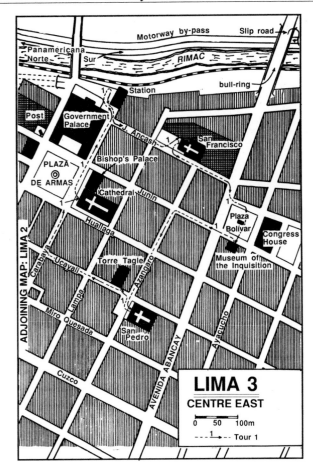

PLACES OF INTEREST ON LIMA MAP 3
- **Estación del Ferrocarril:** Main railway station, with trains to La Oroya and Huancayo.
- **Palacio del Gobierno:** Government Palace, with guards in historic uniforms. Changing of the guards at 12.50pm except Sundays.
- **Convento de San Francisco:** Fascinating monastery with catacombs.
- **Correo Central:** Central Post Office. Historical building with Stamp Museum.
- **Plaza de Armas:** The most beautiful square in Lima. The historic centre of the city.
- **La Catedral:** The Cathedral, containing the tomb of Francisco Pizarro.
- **Plaza Bolívar:** Congress House and Bolívar Monument.
- **Museo de la Inquisición:** Museum of the Inquisition, Plaza Bolívar. Gruesome exhibits.
- **Palacio Torre Tagle:** Palace from the colonial period.
- **Iglesia de San Pedro,** Jirón Azángaro. Luxuriously decorated church.

A view of Miraflores to the south

is one of the few remaining examples of its kind. At one time many of the nobility built their houses with these towers. It seems scarcely credible nowadays that the rich merchants could look through telescopes from these towers and watch their ships coming into port, but no doubt the air was much clearer then than it is now.

Santa Rosa Chapel (Santuario de Santa Rosa), *Bus nos 1, 54a* (*Miraflores*), was built by the Dominicans next to the birthplace of the much-venerated Santa Rosa of Lima. It contains a picture of the Christ Child that the people call *El Doctorcito* or 'The Little Doctor' because it is supposed to have given healing to the sick through the prayers of the saints.

To the left of the courtyard is a tiny hut built by the 28-year-old saint for the purposes of prayer. The 19m (62ft) deep well on the opposite side of the courtyard is where she is supposed to have thrown the key to the heavy iron chain that she wore permanently around her waist as a penance. Nowadays the well is continually surrounded by people throwing in pieces of paper on which they have written prayers to Santa Rosa. The small missionary museum next to the well contains clothing and artefacts from the Indians of the Amazonian region. The colonial mansion in the Jirón Callao has unfortunately fallen down, so visitors should miss this out and carry straight on down to the Jirón Ica.

The ground floor of this eighteenth-century house, the **Casa de Larriva**, Jirón Ica, contains the offices of a women's organisation. There are a few rooms with original colonial furniture. The **Colonial Mansion**, Jirón Ica 323, on the right just past the Municipal Theatre has a very fine courtyard. If the door is open (usually after 11am), it is worth going in to see.

The churrigueresque façade of **St Augustin's Church** (Iglesia San Agustín) is without doubt the most impressive of any in Lima, with stone columns, mouldings and statues that look almost like finely carved wood. The interior has been spoiled by some inept restoration work following earthquake damage, and contains nothing of particular interest. The vestry is worth seeing, but is only rarely open to the public. It consists of two rooms full of beautifully carved furniture and paintings. The colourfully painted mudejar ceiling is one of the finest in Lima. Even more valuable than this is the wooden carving of the Guardian of Death, Lima's finest example of baroque sculpture.

Jirón de la Unión is a busy shopping street in the old city which marks the end of the tour. Visitors staying in hotels to the south can return via at least part of Tour 3 (see below).

Tour 3

Lima Map 2
Length: 2km (1¹/₄ miles)

The only two important buildings along this route are the churches of La Merced and Jesús y María, so it need not be treated as a tour. But it does offer two possible routes between the Plaza de Armas and the main hotel and shopping centre along the Avenida Pierola. The route along the busy Jirón de la Unión is noisier but more interesting, while the route via San Marcelo is rather quieter.

The baroque façade of the **Church of La Merced** (Iglesia de la Merced), which was restored in 1939, presents a fascinating combination of red and green stone. The interior contains some beautifully carved altars. Above the high altar is a magnificent statue of the *Virgen de las Mercedes* or 'Our Lady of Mercies' dressed as the patron saint of the army.

The vestry can be entered by a door to the right of the altar. The beautiful rococo furniture is decorated with mother-of-pearl inlaid work, and is a masterpiece of its kind. The cloister is also to the right of the church. It is decorated in the usual manner with Sevillian tilework and paintings of the founder of the order (San Pedro Nolasco).

The small but very beautiful eighteenth-century **Church of Jesus and Mary** (Iglesia de Jesús y María) belongs to a Capuchin convent and contains some very fine baroque altars.

In the middle of Lima's second great square, the Plaza San Martín, *Bus nos 2, 56, 54b* (Avenida Panamá, Chorrillos), is a statue of the freedom-fighter José de San Martín, who fought for the independence of Argentina, Chile and Peru. The square interrupts the flow of traffic in the Avenida Nicolas de Pierola, which is better known by its former name of La Colmena. Most major airlines have their main offices along here (Lufthansa, Air France, Varig, Aerolíneas Argentinas, Panam, Avianca, KLM, LAN, LAB, Viasa) or around the Plaza San Martín (Braniff, British Airways, Cruzeiro, Aéro Perú).

Although close to the busy Avenida de la Emancipación, the **Church of San Marcelo** (Iglesia de San Marcelo) is in a pleasant little corner that is surprisingly peaceful and redolent of the atmosphere of old times. The church was built by the Augustinians in the mid-sixteenth century, but like many others has been subject to much earthquake damage and subsequent alteration. The most recent restoration was in 1933, when it was given a completely new façade based on a church in the Nazca region. The mudejar doors, the towers and the churrigueresque altars are of particular interest.

MUSEUMS AND OTHER PLACES OF INTEREST

Park of Legends (Parque de las Leyendas)
Lima Map 1 Bus no 48
The park entrance is lined with souvenir stalls selling local artefacts. The park itself is laid out to represent the three natural regions of Peru: the coast (*costa*), the mountains *(sierra)* and the jungle *(selva)*. The park also contains replicas of statues from the Chavín period and a small zoo. Opposite the park entrance is an extensive fairground. This is the site of a large international industrial fair (*Feria del Pacífico*) that is held every other year.

Callao Fortress (Fortaleza del Real Felipe)
Bus no 56 or 48 to Avenida Sáenz Peña, then another 300m on foot
This fort was built in 1776 in order to ward off pirates. In the war of independence it became the last bastion of the king's army. It now houses the **Museum of Military History** (Museo de Historia Militar).

Huallamarca Temple (Huaca de Huallamarca)
San Isidro, Avenida Salamanca, Urb.El Rosario
Bus no 1 to Avenida Belaunde, past the church into Avenida Belaunde, second left into Avenida Salamanca, then one block further on the same corner as Santa Ursula (German) School
Nothing remains of this pre-Inca temple apart from the stump of a pyramid. It is hardly worth visiting, although the small museum contains a few items discovered on the site.

Beaches (*playas*)
Bus no 1 to terminus
Aqua Dulce below the southern suburb of Chorrillos (Lima map 1) is
one of the most popular beaches near the city, and is also one of the
few to offer changing tents for hire. But the beach is extremely
crowded during the high season from December to March, especially
on public holidays.

The scenic coast road goes south from Chorrillos and Aqua Dulce
around a rocky headland into the bay of **La Herradura**, which is also
very popular. The more affluent citizens prefer the more extensive
beaches further south between Chorrillos and Villa on the Panamericana Sur. However, it is very dangerous to bathe there on account of
the heavy breakers.

National Museum of Anthropology and Archaeology (Museo
Nacionale de Antropología y Arqueología) *Lima Map 1*
Plaza Bolívar, Pueblo Libre
*Bus no 12 from Avenida Alfonso Ugarte (accessible on foot from city
centre or by 54b or 56 from Avenida Pierola), or 48 to Avenida La
Marina/Sucre, then 12*
The museum is housed in a modern building, and presents a
chronological history of ancient Amerindian cultures from the Chavín
down to the Incas.

Among the more valuable exhibits is the Raimondi Column that
was found in Chavín. The strange creature seen on this 2m (6$^1/_2$ft)
high stone column has been a subject of much controversy among
scholars. Like many other designs from Chavín, it can be turned
upside down to reveal another figure which shares the same mouth.
In this position it can be interpreted as a strange bird-like creature
with feathers turned up above its head.

The Paracas culture is represented by facsimiles of Paracas
tombs containing genuine mummies. The skulls are often deformed
and show signs of trepanation. But the most valuable exhibits from
this period are the beautiful grave clothes.

The Nazca and Mochica cultures are represented by collections
of exquisite pottery. The highly realistic Mochica vessels are ranged
in glass cabinets according to what they represent: fruits, plants,
animals, human portraits, hunting, agriculture, sexual behaviour,
houses etc. The anatomical deformities section is particularly interesting. The section on the Tiahuanaco or Huari culture is rather less
impressive, consisting mostly of photographs of buildings.

The Inca period, which formed the high-point of ancient Peruvian
culture, was most impressive for its marvellous building techniques.
These are presented in a series of photographs, plus a collection of
scale models of buildings from Ollantaitambo, Machu Picchu and
other Inca cities.

Santo Domingo church

 Gold Museum (Museo de Oro del Perú) *Lima Map1*
Prolongación Avenida Angamos, Monterrico
Bus no 71 from Paseo de la República (Lima Map 4) to Avenida Angamos (then 5min on foot), or Express Line A or B to Avenida Angamos (Stop 8), then minibus 72
The only museum comparable on the South American continent is the Gold Museum in Bogotá, Colombia. There is not only a priceless collection of gold and other ornaments from the Chimú and Inca periods, but also some valuable Indian clothing and a unique collection of weaponry. The weaponry collection includes fifteenth-century crossbows, coats of armour and morning-stars, together with hand weapons from the last four centuries and some particularly valuable oriental exhibits.

The gold collection consists mostly of exhibits from the Chimú period. Among the most valuable items are: a piece of clothing made of 13,000 gold platelets (exhibit no 1906); a Mochica breastplate with chrysoberyl cat's-eyes (nos 1901/2); several Chimú ceremonial knives depicting the god Naimlap (nos 2443 and 2707); a Chimú death mask (no 3049); a gold sacrificial vessel with two spouts (no 4583); various neckchains inlaid with chrysoberyls (no 464); and

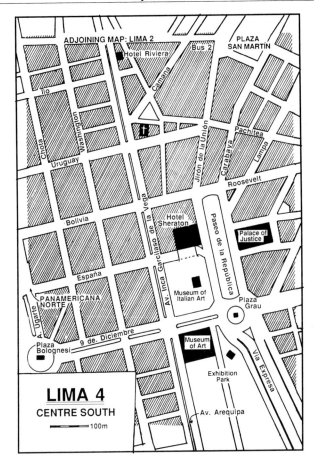

LIMA 4
CENTRE SOUTH
100m

PLACES OF INTEREST ON LIMA MAP 4

- **Avenida Inca Garcilaso de la Vega/Avenida Wilson**: Important thoroughfare in the city centre. The southern continuation forms the Avenida Arequipa, leading to the prestigious suburbs of San Isidro and Miraflores.
- **Hotel Sheraton**: Lima's most modern hotel.
- **Paseo de la República**: Broad square with some interesting bronze statues.
- **Museo de Arte Italiano**: Museum of Italian Art, Paseo de la República. Reproductions of Italian masters.
- **Plaza Bolognesi**: Statue of Francisco Bolognesi, who fell while defending Arica in the Saltpetre War.
- **Plaza Grau**: The hub of the city's traffic system, adjoining a fast dual carriageway (Via Expresa) to the south. Statue of Miguel Grau, a hero of the Saltpetre War against Chile.
- **Museo de Arte**: Museum of Art, Plaza Grau. One of Lima's most varied collections.
- **Parque de Exposición**: Exhibition Park. Location for the International Exhibition of 1863. Statue of Cristóbal Colón (Christopher Columbus).

items of clothing trimmed with feathers and showing jungle birds, thus proving that there were links between the coast and the jungle.

Museum of Art (Museo de Arte) *Lima Map 4*
Plaza Grau
Bus nos A, B, 1, 2, 54a, 66, 71
This museum does not contain the finest works from each period, but provides a good overview of all periods of art, from the ancient Amerindians via the colonial period right down to the present day. The collection includes textiles and pottery from the Indian coastal cultures, excellent furniture and paintings from the colonial period and modern paintings and sculpture.

Museum of the Inquisition — see page 50

Amano Museum (Museo Amano) *Lima Map 1*
Calle Retiro 160, Miraflores
Bus no 59 from Avenida Abancay (Lima Map 3) or Avenida 28 de Julio to Avenida Angamos/Santa Cruz; or A, B or 2 to Avenida Angamos (Express Stop 8), then 59b as above (the road is one block further on the left)
This is one of the finest private collections in Lima, and belongs to a Japanese man called Yoshitaro. Nowhere else is there such a complete collection of textiles from the Chancay period. But apart from textiles there are some exquisite pottery exhibits.

Larco Herrera Museum (Museo Rafael Larco Herrera) *Lima Map 1*
Avenida Bolívar 1515, Pueblo Libre
Bus no 1 or 2 to Avenida Arequipa/Avenida Cuba, then 10a
With as many as 55,000 exhibits, this is by far the largest private collection of ancient Peruvian pottery. There are also some fine gold artefacts and materials, one of which has a record 157 threads per cm. One particular room contains a collection of pottery with erotic designs.

National Museum of Peruvian Culture
(Museo Nacionale de Cultura Peruana)
Avenida Alfonso Ugarte 650
Bus no 56 to Plaza 2 de Mayo (then 50m on foot), or on foot from the Hotel Crillón (Lima Map 2) going west along the Avenida Nicolas de Pierola
The façade is modelled on the ruins of Tiahuanaco, but the collection does not live up to this, since the antiquities to be found here are hardly worth bothering with compared to those elsewhere. However, the folklore section is very interesting, with some Indian costumes

San Marcelo church, Lima

that are still worn today, and a number of pieces of handicraft mainly from Ayacucho.

Museum of Italian Art (Museo de Arte Italiano)
Paseo de las República *Lima Map 4*
Bus nos A, B, 1, 2, 54a, 66, 71
The building stands in the middle of a park between the Hotel Sheraton and the Museum of Art, and is decorated with two mosaics. It was given to Peru by the Italian colony to mark the centenary of Peruvian independence. It is used for temporary exhibitions of contemporary art.

Javier Prado Natural History Museum (Museo de Historia Natural)
Avenidas Arenales 1256
Lima Map 4
Bus no 48 from Avenida Abancay or 54a from Avenida Tacna or Garcilaso de la Vega
The collection is cramped and rather old-fashioned, but provides a good overview of Peruvian fauna, including that of the Amazonian region. Situated behind the main building is a modern collection of minerals.

Museum of National History (Museo Nacional de Historia)
Plaza Bolívar, Pueblo Libre, next to the Archaeological Museum
The building was once occupied by the freedom-fighters San Martín and Bolívar, and houses a collection of furniture and other memorabilia associated with these two national heros. Other rooms contain documents, weapons, flags and pictures connected with the wars of liberation and the history of the republic.

2
EXCURSIONS FROM LIMA

Most of these excursions are shown on the 'Excursions from Lima' map below, though other maps may be indicated where helpful. Distances from Lima are given in brackets.

1 TO THE RUINS OF PACHACÁMAC (half-day excursion)
The quickest route to Pachacámac is via the Via Expresa and the Panamericana Sur (see Lima map 1), but there is a more interesting route through Miraflores and Chorrillos.

This route goes south from the city centre along the broad Avenida Inca Garcilaso de la Vega. Just past the busy crossroads at the end of the exhibition park, there is a square on the right called the Plaza Jorge Chavez, where there is a monument to the Peruvian pilot of that name who was the first person to fly over the Alps. The new international airport is also named after him.

After the crossroads, the road becomes the Avenida Arequipa, which runs straight through the diplomatic quarter of San Isidro to the well-to-do suburb of Miraflores (5.5km, $3\frac{1}{2}$ miles). If you turn right in the main square here, you come out a few hundred metres into the coast road, which runs south along the top of the cliffs. Immediately beyond the bridge there is a viewing point (see Lima map 1) with a fine view across the sea, where even in winter there are always a few surfers doggedly riding the waves.

The road twists and turns along the cliff, with some marvellous views. Then it comes to a ravine, where there is a dual carriageway running down to the sea. It then runs along the beach below the suburbs of Barranco and Chorrillos, passing some of the most popular of Lima's beaches.

The dual carriageway ends just before the ultra-modern buildings of the Lima Regatta Club. Just before that it passes near a fishing harbour, where there some wooden stalls selling local seafood specialities. There are usually a few pelicans hanging around the jetty where the fishermen unload and prepare their catch.

The coast road climbs south over the headland on its way into the next bay, which is called La Herradura. Past a crossroads at the top, there is small road winding up the hillside to **Morro Solar**. At the top of this hill there is a monument to the Unknown Soldier, with a fine view of Chorrillos and Barranco, across the sea and south over the bay of **La Herradura**. Walkers may continue climbing to **Cerro la Chirra**, which is covered with tillandsia plants.

Coming down from Morro Solar, the route goes north again for a while; but this time instead of going back down to the sea, you should go inland to Malecón Iglesias (also accessible by bus no 54 from Avenida Tacna). The first wide road going off to the right past a small park area is the old Panamericana Sur, which runs through this rather poor area to meet the new Panamericana Sur (19km, 12 miles). Just before that, there is a turning to the right for the beach at Villa, which is very dangerous on account of the breakers and the hidden currents. By the time you reach the motorway exit for **Pachacámac** and **Lurín** (26km, 16 miles), the ruins will be visible on the hillside.

Pachacámac was probably a place of pilgrimage even before the Incas, when people came from far and wide to ask advice from the oracle. There is a story of a Spanish helmsman who begged Pizarro for the silver nails which held up the silver wall-dressings and thus obtained 500kg (1,100lb) of silver. This alone will give some idea of the enormous wealth of this temple complex, only a small part of which came into the hands of the conquistadors. Most of their treasure is supposed to have been buried in the desert somewhere between Lima and Pachacámac before the Spaniards arrived.

The small museum at the entrance to the ruins contains samples of material and pottery that were found on the site. But the most valuable exhibit is the carved wooden Idol of the Pachacámac, or Creator God, which once stood in the sanctuary of the great Temple of the Pachacámac (see below). Experts believe that the grooves in the statue were once filled with silver or gold.

At the edge of the car park, just beyond the museum, there is a statue of the Peruvian archaeologist Julio C. Tello. A flight of steps leads down from here to a reconstructed building complex from the Inca period known as the Casa de las Mamaconas. This is thought to have been the home of the *Mamaconas* or 'chosen virgins', who were brought up in seclusion to serve the Inca.

The trapezoid alcoves are typically Inca in form, but their unusually large size has given rise to much speculation. Did the *Mamaconas* stand in them when the Inca came to visit? Or were there idols standing in them? Or did the building serve some completely different purpose such as the worship of the moon, as the German archaeologist Maz Uhle suggests?

The road climbs up from the car park to the great Temple of the Sun. But on the way it passes a small road going down to the site of

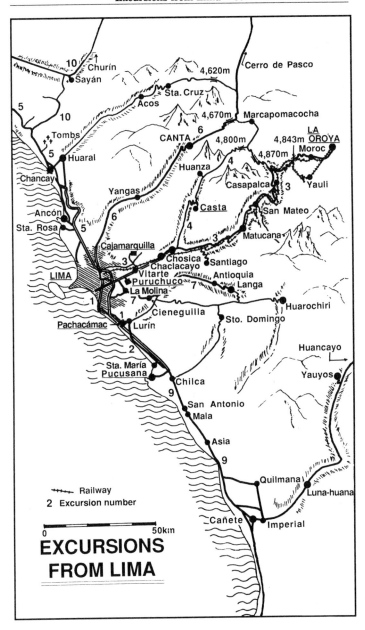

EXCURSIONS
FROM LIMA

Railway

2 Excursion number

0   50km

the great pre-Inca Temple of the Pachacámac, or Creator God. Only a few terraces remain of this vast temple, whose sanctuary lay at the end of a whole labyrinth of corridors. Some of the old paintwork is still visible, however.

The Temple of the Sun stands on the crest of the hill. Unlike the Temple of the Pachacámac, it was built by the Incas after they had conquered this area in the middle of the fifteenth century. The temple consists of a pyramid, of which the most important section was on the side facing the sea, where the massive mud-brick foundations are still visible. From the top of the pyramid there is an impressive view of the whole site. Like all coastal settlements, it was built on the hillside in preference to the fertile valley below, where every bit of soil was needed for the purposes of cultivation. Down towards the sea, between the foot of the pyramid and the motorway, there are two round buildings that are used for bullfights, cockfights and various other local events.

2 TO PUCUSANA HARBOUR (half-day excursion)

This trip is effectively a continuation of the previous one, and the two can easily be combined. The scenery is varied, including some desert, some interesting rocks and a small fishing village.

The route leaves Lima along the Panamericana Sur, which at this point is a motorway. Soon after the exit for Chorrillos (19km, 12 miles) the road starts to run close to the coast, where there are a number of popular bathing beaches. On the left-hand side behind a small refinery, one can see the 78m (26ft) high pyramid of the Temple of the Sun at Pachacámac, which is very much worth a visit (see above).

After crossing the fertile oasis of the Lurín Valley, the road heads out into the desert, and one is led to wonder how anyone can possibly make a living in any of the forlorn little settlements that lie between the road and the sea. Outside the holiday season it is worth coming off the motorway at the San Bartolo exit (46km, 28 miles) and making a short detour to **Santa María**. This small bay surrounded by cliffs has become a holiday village for rich inhabitants of Lima (Santa María Beach Hotel). Each of the many palms along the shore has to be fed by water lorries every day.

If one keeps left through the village, one eventually comes to a second bay. At the point where the road ends, there is a holiday club built on a rocky promontory. The footpath to the club is open to the public outside the season, and makes a fascinating walk. The sea breakers burst through underground passages into rocky basins full of starfish, sea anemones, shrimps and other sea life.

The exit for Pucusana (58km, 36 miles) is not very far beyond that for Santa María. **Pucusana** (66km, 41 miles) is a popular Sunday resort for people from Lima, who flock to the many restaurants along

The Temple of the Pachacámac

the bay. They also row among the brightly coloured fishing boats, which are continually visited by hungry pelicans. One particular point of interest is the nearby **Boca del Diablo**, or 'Jaws of the Devil', a rocky gorge that is filled with the noise and spray of the surf.

3 UP THE RIMAC VALLEY (half- or whole-day excursion)
The Rimac Valley is not the most beautiful of the valleys above Lima, but the road is far better than in the other valleys. So it is a good choice for a short trip for those wishing to get an idea of what the coastal valleys of Peru are like.

It is possible to climb the pass to the height of Mont Blanc (4,884m, 16,019ft) within the space of only 2 to 2½ hours. However, people unused to such heights are advised not to go as far as the top. Even healthy people can be badly affected by mountain sickness, while people with heart or circulatory problems may sometimes be in danger of their lives. So people are advised to turn back at **Chilca** (3,790m, 12,430ft), especially since the scenery is less impressive from there onwards. However, there is much of cultural interest much closer to Lima at **Puruchuco**, **Cajamarquilla** and **Pariache**, although Puruchuco is the only site of great importance. The route is described in more detail in Route 3, Chapter 3.

4 UP THE EULALIA VALLEY (whole-day excursion)

The Eulalia Valley is one of the wildest and most impressive in the Lima region. The route is all the more breathtaking because the road climbs so quickly from the bottom of the valley up to the dizziest heights. The recommended destination is the pretty mountain village of San Pedro de Casta (3,150m, 10,332ft). Take provisions with you.

The route follows the Carretera Central (see Route 3, Chapter 3) along the Rimac Valley as far as 4km ($2^1/_2$ miles) beyond Chosica. The turning off the Carretera Central (38km, $23^1/_2$ miles) is clearly signposted.

At the small village of **Santa Eulalia**, only 2km ($1^1/_4$ miles) from the junction, the road has already passed the 1,000m (3,280ft) mark. The narrow lane is flanked on both sides by irrigated fields of vegetables in the shade of numerous avocado trees. Six kilometres (4 miles) beyond the village, the route leaves the metalled road, which continues for a few hundred yards down to a power station on the right.

Now the road starts to climb in deadly earnest, reaching dizzy heights above the river below. The route passes another power station at **Huinco** (57km [35 miles], 1,880m [6,166ft]) and eventually crosses a bridge over a gorge at **Autisha** (64km, [40 miles] 2,200m [7,216ft]). The more adventurous may care to climb down the gorge to the Río Eulalia below. The road climbs a further 900m (2,952ft) via a series of a dozen hairpins, and eventually comes to a junction (74km, 46 miles) where there is a right turn for San Pedro de Casta (77km, 48 miles).

San Pedro de Casta (3,150m, 10,332ft) is full of the traditional atmosphere of the more isolated villages, with the most amazing views of the barren valleys and slopes. There are various walks along mulepaths providing some breathtaking views.

More adventurous travellers may turn left at the junction for San Pedro and continue across the mountains to Casapalca (see page 95). The route is extremely difficult, but can be covered in one day if the road conditions allow (ie not between December and April). There are two passes to cross at 4,800m (15,744ft) and 4,870m (15,973ft) respectively. But the scenery is fantastic; the road passes high mountain lakes amid the *puna* and runs between the icy peaks of Conchupata (5,275m, 17,302ft) to the right and Raujunte (5,400m, 17,712ft) to the left.

5 ALONG THE COAST TO THE NORTH OF LIMA

(half- or whole-day excursion)

There are a number of popular tourist destinations along the Panamericana Norte. These include the high-class seaside resort of Ancón (45km, 28 miles), the ancient cemeteries of Chancay (87km, 54 miles) and the colourful salt lagoons of Las Salinas (137km, 85 miles). Towards the end of the foggy season (September/October), the *lomas* of Lachay (105km, 65 miles) are also very attractive, as the desert 'comes into bloom'. All these places are described in more detail in Chapter 3, Route1.

6 UP THE CANTA VALLEY (whole-day excursion)

This valley is less heavily populated than the Rimac Valley, and the view is not obscured by long rows of mud-brick huts. But the road stays mostly in the narrow valley bottom, and does not provide any really good views until shortly before Canta.

The route goes north out of Lima along the Avenida Alfonso Ugarte (Lima Map 4), which quickly comes out into dual carriageway (Lima Map 1). The road passes through shanty towns on the edge of the desert before entering the oasis of the Río Chillón, which it now follows.

Five kilometres (3 miles) beyond the small village of **Yangas** (58km [36 miles], 970m [3,181ft]), there is a car park on a sharp left-hand bend. A steep path leads up the mountainside to a broad expanse of cacti, where there are rock carvings of unknown origin (ten minutes on foot). Soon after the road passes the small but very popular sanctuary of **Santa Rosa des Quives**, where there is also a tourist hotel. **Canta** (107km [66 miles], 2,840m [9,315ft]) is a rather insignificant place, where day-trippers are advised to turn back.

The road continues from Canta over the **Viuda Pass** (152km [94 miles], 4,670m [15,317ft]) and eventually to **Cerro de Pasco** (268km [166 miles], see page 96). The route runs for long stretches at altitudes between 4,400m (14,432ft) and 4,750m (15,580ft). Near **Huayllay** (223km [138 miles], 4,310m [14,137ft]) it passes a strange landscape full of weird rock formations that have given it the name **Bosque de Piedras** or 'Forest of Stones'.

7 UP THE LURÍN VALLEY (half- or whole-day excursion)

The Lurín Valley enjoys very similar scenery to the Canta Valley. The route leaves the Carretera Central about 1km (half a mile) from the city ring road, where there is a right turn for **La Molina**. The sunny suburb of La Molina is laid out with several golf clubs and an artificial lake. The road then climbs over a barren pass (600m, 1,968ft) to **Cieneguilla** (32km, 20 miles), which is already on the edge of the Lurín Valley. A left turn here leads down into the valley past a number of hostelries for Sunday trippers.

The road runs through orchards along the valley bottom as far as **Antioquía** (71km [44 miles], 1,550m [5,084ft]). Then it begins to climb steeply in hairpins up to **Langa** (93km [57 miles], 2,860m [9,381ft]). Langa is the largest village in the valley, and is situated in a flat hollow about 350m (1,148ft) above the course of the Río Lurín.

The road deteriorates as it climbs out of the valley up to a height of 3,800m (12,464ft). It then climbs more gently through a *puna* landscape, and crosses a pass at 4,100m, 13,448ft before winding steeply down into **Huarochiri** (3,150m, 10,332ft).

8 RAIL EXCURSION TO HUANCAYO (two to three days)
The highest railway in the world (see map page 97) is an amazing technical feat, rising to 4,781m (15,680ft) over the pass and to 4,817m (15,799ft) along the branch to Morococha, and it is certainly an exciting trip. But a 10-hour rail journey can be very exhausting, especially at such high altitudes; while the Indian market at Huancayo is nothing remarkable. Those who insist on making the trip should take precautions against mountain sickness, and should not rely on obtaining oxygen on the train. The trip is described in more detail in Routes 3 and 3c, Chapter 3.

9 TO THE BAY OF PARACAS (at least two days)
The Bay of Paracas (258km, 160 miles) can be reached from Lima along the Panamericana Sur (map page 109). It is popular on account of its relatively sunny winter climate and the many things to see there. The route from Lima is described in Route 4, Chapter 3, while Paracas itself is described in Chapter 4.

10 TO THE THERMAL BATHS OF CHURÍN (at least two days)
The spa resort of Churín (214km [149 miles], 2,250m [7,380ft]) lies in a coastal valley to the north of Lima (see map page 75). The spa is somewhat primitive by European standards, but for those used to high altitudes it provides a marvellous opportunity to visit the incredible mountain region of Raura. The route is described on page 76.

11 TO THE CORDILLERA BLANCA (at least three days)
The Cordillera Blanca (see map page 75) provides some of the most beautiful scenery in Peru. So the trip is a must for every visitor to Peru, provided he takes precautions against mountain sickness. The route is described in Route 2, Chapter 3, and the region is described in more detail in Chapter 4.

12 ACROSS THE ANDES TO SAN RAMÓN (at least two days)
The route first goes over the Ticlio Pass (4,884m, 16,020ft, see map page 97), and then crosses to the forest zone on the eastern side of the Andes (see Route 3b, Chapter 3). San Ramón (306km [189 miles], 825m [2,706ft]) is the nearest place to Lima providing this kind of scenery. However, tourists who are going to La Paz should forego this trip, and go instead to the much more impressive valleys of the Yungas in Bolivia.

Pucusana harbour

13 AIR TRIP TO THE NAZCA LINES

The Nazcá Lines (about 500km [310 miles] south of Lima) are
becoming increasingly famous thanks to the work of the German
archaeologist Maria Reiche. They are situated on a desert plain,
where the lighter-coloured rock bed is covered by an inch-thick layer
of reddish stone. Parts of the upper layer have been removed to
create enormous mysterious line drawings, about which there has
been much writing and speculation but very little is actually known for
certain.

The bolder geometrical lines are just visible from a jet plane. But
the rather less gigantic drawings of monkeys, birds and spiders are
too small to be made out from a jet but too large to be seen properly
from the ground. They can only be seen from a small plane. There are
various flights available from Lima, about which information can be
obtained at Lima Airport or from various travel agents. Bookings can
be made in the shopping arcade below the Sheraton Hotel. Small
plane flights are also available from Nazca's own little airport.

3

EXPLORING THE COUNTRY

A part from the famous Panamerican Highway (Panamericana) running the whole length of the coast, Peru has very few properly metalled roads. The mountain roads are often narrow and dangerous. Drivers must hoot at sharp bends and give way to climbing traffic. At all events it is advisable to wait at passing places for oncoming traffic.

Lorries and buses frequently use their greater bulk to claim right of way, and besides their brakes are often inadequate. Braking distances are much greater on these loose road surfaces, while cars are all the more likely to skid on bends. It is important to stock up sufficiently with fuel, as there are very few filling stations, especially in the mountains.

When travelling by public transport (buses or *colectivos*), it is vital to take an emergency supply of food. Vehicle breakdowns or landslides in uninhabited areas are not infrequent occurrences. The mountain roads are particularly bad during the rainy season from December to April. The spot heights on maps are often very inconsistent. Those given in this book are taken from Peruvian ordnance maps, the most accurate of these being to the scale 1:100,000. The distances in kilometres given in the margin come either from the Peruvian Automobile Club or from the author's own measurements. The kilometre posts along the roadsides give distances from Lima. However, when new sections of road are built, only some of the posts are replaced, so they do not always correspond to the distances.

Route 1 The Panamericana Norte

Maps: pages 75 and 77
Overnight accommodation: Barranca, Huarmey, Chimbote, Trujillo, Cajamarca (1b), Chiclayo, Piura, Zorritos, Tumbes
Public transport: numerous buses and *colectivos* along the coast and to Cajamarca; travelling times from Lima: Trujillo (9 hours), Piura (2 hours), Tumbes (17 hours).

MAP SHOWING THE
VARIOUS ROUTES

The route north to the Ecuadorean border runs mostly through the coastal desert, though this is frequently interrupted by green valley oases. There is not very much scenery apart from rocky mountains, a few dunes and the occasional view across the Pacific. But there are some fascinating archaeological sites along the way. These include Sechín near Casma and the Chimú and Mochica remains around Trujillo. A detour via Huaraz and the beautiful Cordillera Blanca is also highly recommended.

0   **Lima**. The junction of the Panamericana (ring road) with the Carretera Central. Avenida Alfonsa Ugarte (Lima map 4, page 59) is the best way out of the city centre onto the Panamericana Norte. The motorway leaves Lima through the poor area of San Martín de Porres and the industrial area to the east of the airport.

35   Turning along a dual carriageway for Ventanilla (oil refinery), leading back down the coast via the Jorge Chavín International Airport to Callao.

44   Turning for **Ancón** (2km, 1¼ miles). This most prestigious of Peru's seaside resorts lies in a bay that is protected from the wind. Ancón is proud of its fine promenade (hotel). Buses and lorries leave the motorway here and take a short cut along the old road (8km, 5 miles shorter), which runs along a dangerous sandy slope above the sea. Though very impressive, the route has been closed to private cars since the building of the new motorway. However, foreigners without any Spanish are usually allowed through without a fine, although this is only possible from the northern end because of the tollbooth!
     The new motorway forms a wide loop, bypassing these dangerous sandy slopes. This road climbs to 400m (1,312ft) through areas covered in cloud during the damp season, when it is often surrounded by vegetation. In clear weather there are fine views of Ancón and the coast, and of the Chancay Valley inland.

71   Turning for **Huaral** (12km, 7½ miles), a small town in the Chancay Valley surrounded by cotton fields.

75   Northern end of the short cut along the sand slopes (see above), which is closed except to heavy vehicles.

77   Turning for **Chancay**, a fishing port that is of little interest to tourists.

82   Turning for **Huaral** (11km, 7 miles, see above).

86   The **ancient cemetery of Chancay**. One of the major pre-Inca cultures left a vast cemetery here which, although it has been robbed of its treasures down the centuries, has still retained some for posterity. The cemetery can be reached via a path to the right of the Panamericana Norte. After 2km (1¼ miles) it arrives at a series of barren hills. The path to the left here goes down to the cemetery itself, which is covered with crater-like diggings. The ground is strewn with

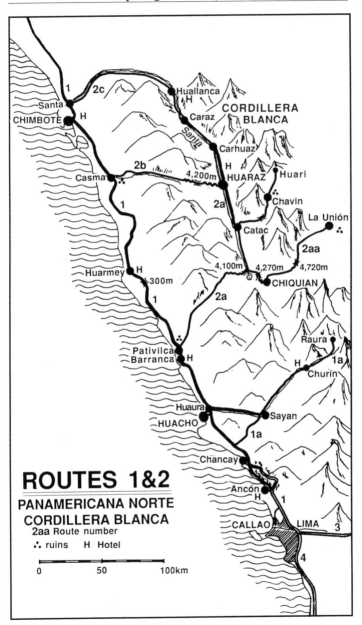

ROUTES 1&2

PANAMERICANA NORTE
CORDILLERA BLANCA

2aa Route number

∴ ruins   H Hotel

0   50   100km

human bones and hair, and bits of pottery rejected by the grave robbers. Just beyond the turning for the cemetery, there are a few buildings to the right of the motorway, where items from the diggings are on sale, together with a variety of antiques, all of them forgeries.

103   Turning for **Sayan** and **Churín**.

1a EXCURSION TO SAYAN, CHURÍN AND RAURA

The route goes from the Panamericana Norte via the thermal baths of Churín to a mine surrounded by wild mountain scenery. The road follows a dry valley up to a green oasis that is irrigated by water channelled from the Huaura Valley nearly 50km (31 miles) away. The road becomes unmetalled as it turns right to climb over a pass (700m, 2,296ft). It later comes down among the sugar cane plantations of the Huaura Valley. **Sayan** (50km [31 miles], 680m [2,230ft]) is situated to the right of the road across the river. This is the last place on the route where fuel is available.

Further up the valley (108km, 67miles), there is a turning along a very bad road to **Chiuchin** (136km [84 miles], 2,700m, [8,856ft]), where there is a hotel with thermal springs and a primitive spa.

Churín (111km [69 miles], 2,250m [7,380ft]) is a small village with several second-class hotels. There are hot springs to the right above the village, which provide water for the thermal baths. Past Churín the scenery becomes much more exciting. The journey to Raura runs along the foot of an enormous glacier that comes down steeply from the icy peak of Santa Rosa (5,700m, 18,696ft).

The small mining community of **Raura** (176km [109 miles], 4,600m [15,088ft]) has a population of some 6,000. It is in an extraordinarily beautiful situation next to a lake surrounded by mighty ice-covered peaks. There is a road going up to where the glacier ends at 5,000m (16,400ft).

---

103   Turning for **Sayan** and **Churín**.

105   Turning for the *lomas* of **Lachay**. At the highest point of the Panamericana Norte there is a rough sandy track going off to the right. About 5km (3 miles) along here is an area where in September and October the desert turns into green pastures. There have been attempts at afforestation, and these have shown that vegetation helps store up water in the ground, which encourages yet more vegetation once a critical point has been reached.

The Panamericana crosses another dry valley, and then runs in a straight line for 30km (18^1/$_2$ miles) across a somewhat flatter area of desert.

130   Turning for **Las Salinas** (7km, 4 miles). It is worth a short trip down to the salt pans of Las Salinas, which are about a kilometre outside the village along a road to the right. They consist of a series of

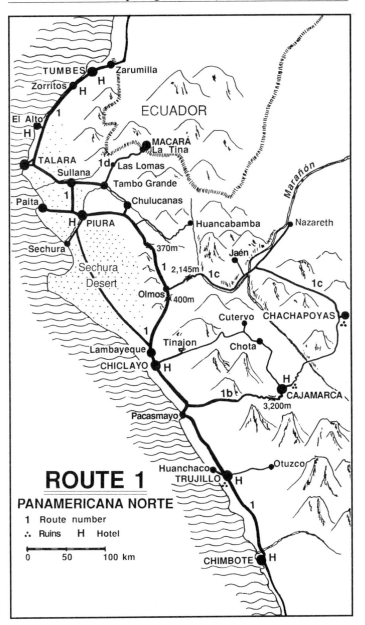

ROUTE 1
PANAMERICANA NORTE

1 Route number
∴ Ruins   H Hotel

0   50   100 km

beautifully coloured lakes supplied by thermal springs of varying temperatures. As the water evaporates, the chalk and gypsum deposits create a whole medley of colours, ranging through every shade from pure white to deep russet.

148 **Huacho** (population about 50,000). The new motorway ends just before this busy town, which possesses little of interest to tourists. The Panamericana passes to the east of the town centre.

152 **Huaura** is the home of a special drink called *guinda*, a very sweet liqueur made from sour cherries, which is sold at stalls all along the roadside. There is another turning here for Sayan and Churín (see excursion 1a above).

186 **Supe** is a rather unsightly collection of mud-brick huts, sadly typical of the Peruvian coast. The atmosphere is made yet more unpleasant by the pungent stench of the nearby fishmeal plant.

195 **Barranca** is a very busy little town offering various categories of overnight accommodation (Hotel Chavín).

203 **Pativilca** is the centre of a prosperous sugar cane region. On the left-hand side of the main street is a building known as Bolívar's House (Casa de Bolívar, No 253). History relates that during the short time Bolívar lived here, he was suffering from fever and plagued by bad tidings of his army's defeats. When asked what he would do after such news, he replied with just one word: 'Triumph!'

205 Turning for **Cajatambo.**

207 Turning for **Huaraz**. From here it is possible to make a detour through one of the most beautiful parts of the Andes, the **Cordillera Blanca**, returning to the Panamericana at Casma.

211 **Paramonga Fortress**. Though ruined, the site is impressively situated on a mound above the valley. Archaeologists are still uncertain as to whether it was built as a fortress or whether the building served some kind of religious purpose. What is certain, however, is that the Chimús fought back Inca attacks at this point. There is a path to the top of the pyramid from the car park to the right of the Panamericana. From the summit is a view of the valley, with its sugar plantations.

North of Paramonga the Panamericana runs through one of the longest stretches of uninterrupted desert along the whole of this route. However, the scenery is varied, thanks to the amazing variety of colours and the more mountainous nature of the scenery.

239 **Pass** (300m, 984ft). The road descends from the pass and crosses a series of dunes before running for a short stretch along the shore, where bathing is possible.

292 **Huarmey**. The tourist hotel to the right of the Panamericana offers overnight accommodation. The desert section which follows is again

The Paramonga Fortress

fairly mountainous. The road reaches 400m (1,312ft) over two passes at 322km (199 miles) and 358km (222 miles) from Lima respectively.

Turning for **Huaraz** (see page 90) and for the ruins of **Sechín** (2km, about a mile), which are described in detail in Chapter 4.   370

Casma was almost completely destroyed in the 1970 earthquake, but has now been substantially rebuilt.   373

Pass (420m, 1,377ft). The road descends into the valley oasis of the Río Nepeña, which was once an important centre of Mochica culture. However, any structural remains have been mostly destroyed.   399

With a population of nearly 250,000, **Chimbote** is Peru's sixth-largest town. It has grown especially fast in recent years thanks mainly to industrial expansion. This in turn has been made possible by the building of a vast hydroelectric plant in the Cañon del Pato. Apart from the older fishmeal plants, whose smell fills the air during the fishing season, there is a highly developed steel industry, which is based on ores mined in Marcona near Nazca and shipped north from San Juan. The Panamericana goes sharp right in the square next to the Gran Hotel Chimú. As the road leaves the town it goes up into a narrow cutting that leads across into the Santa Valley.   429

442 Turning for **Santa** and **Huaraz** (see page 91).

444 Bridge over the **Río Santa**, the most prolific river along the whole of the Peruvian coast.

476 **Pass** (410m, 1,344ft). The road descends through a stony desert surrounded by reddish mountains into a region full of crescent dunes that continually threaten to swamp the road. It is inadvisable to stop next to the road, as the sand is extremely soft and dangerous.

514 Turning for **Virú** (3km, nearly 2 miles). About a kilometre to the left of the road there is a giant crescent dune that is reputed (no doubt wrongly) to be the largest in the world.

554 Turning for **Salaverry** (4km, 2¹/₂ miles), Peru's most modern sugar cane port. About 2km (a mile) to the right of the road is the enormous silhouette of the **Huaca del Sol**, a great pyramid from the Mochica period.

561 **Trujillo** (population 350,000) is Peru's fourth-largest city. There is much here that is of interest to tourists, including the ruins of **Chan Chan**, the largest mud-brick city in the world, and the great **Huaca del Dragón** (Temple of the Dragon). The city is described in more detail in Chapter 4. There are several good hotels offering accommodation.
    The Panamericana crosses an especially bleak stretch of desert before entering Peru's largest sugar cane producing region.

594 **Chicama** is the first of a series of towns and villages inhabited mainly by sugar cane workers, whose houses are crowned by a forest of aerials. The sugar cane is planted and harvested using all the latest technology. There are several factories in the area, where the cane is processed to make sugar, rum, paper and animal feed.

604 **Chocope.**

616 **Paiján.** Soon after the last of these sugar cane towns, the scenery changes abruptly back into the desert.

659 **San Pedro de Lloc** is an old village among the sand dunes, with narrow streets and a large church.

668 **Pacasmayo** makes its presence known from a great distance because of the smoke that goes up from its cement factory. This small port once had a railway going inland towards Cajamarca. The town centre lies at the bottom of a deep valley.

669 Turning for **Jequetepeque**, a small oasis around a river of the same name that the Panamericana crosses after another stretch of desert.

683 Turning for **Cajamarca**.

1b EXCURSION TO CAJAMARCA

The metalled road runs up through the Jequetepeque Valley, which is one of Peru's fastest-growing tourist regions. **Tembladera** (45km [28 miles], 420m [1,377ft]) means 'place of trembling', and is so named because it was once a notorious place for malaria. **Chilete** (88km [54¹/₂ miles], 870m [2,853ft]) was formerly the terminus of the railway from Pacasmayo.

Beyond **Magdalena** (112km [69 miles], 1,300m [4,264ft]) the road climbs steeply in hairpins up the side of the valley. It eventually climbs over a pass called the Abra del Gavilán (3,200m, 1,049ft).

From the pass there are views across the valley of Cajamarca, into which the road now descends. In **Cajamarca** (177km [110 miles], 2,750m [9,020ft]) there are many interesting things to see from both the Inca and colonial periods. The town is described in detail in Chapter 4.

Turning for **Cajamarca**. 683

Guadalupe is an old town at the foot of a steep hill, and is famous for its annual fair on 8 December. 692 ❄

Mocupe is a village on the edge of the Saña Valley oasis. 733

Turning for **Saña** (14km, 8¹/₂ miles), which in the seventeenth century was famous for its legendary wealth, and was compared with the Bolivian town of Potosí. But a pirate raid in 1686, followed by a catastrophic flood in 1720, brought the town's prosperity to an end. There are still remains of monasteries and churches from that period. 734

Reque is on the edge of a large valley oasis formed by the rivers Reque and Chancay. 758

Chiclayo (population 324,000) is Peru's fifth-largest city, but has little of interest to tourists. However, there are several hotels offering overnight accommodation. The road from Chiclayo up to Chongoyape runs past the vast **Tinajonas Reservoir** (52km [32 miles], then 2km [a mile] off to the left) that was built with German aid. Water is brought there through a tunnel from the other side of the Andes, and it is planned to irrigate whole swathes of the desert to the north of Chiclayo. 769

Lambayeque. The Panamericana bypasses the centre of the town, but tourists are recommended to go straight on into the centre, where the Brünning Museum is housed in a modern building to the right of the main street. It is named after a German businessman who spent much of his life studying the Chimú and Mochica cultures. Exhibits here include pottery, materials and some beautiful gold ornaments. 781

Junction of the old and new Panamericana. The new Panamericana goes straight across the Sechura Desert, and is 57km (35 miles) 784

Clay brick wall, Chan Chan

shorter than the old road. The old Panamericana runs along the foot of the mountains through a variety of savanna and dry woodland landscapes, providing an interesting contrast to some of the previous coastal scenery. But being both longer and slower, it can only be recommended to travellers with plenty of time. However, those wishing to visit the Marañón region must follow the old road.

THE OLD PANAMERICANA

784 Junction of the two roads.

799 **Mochumi** is the first of a long series of villages scattered along the road. The desert becomes greener at this point, and the unirrigated areas are covered with algarrobo trees that are typical of this region. There are two reasons why these trees flourish here: firstly it is close to the Andes, where the water table is higher; and secondly, the Andes are much lower at this point, allowing more moisture to penetrate from the Amazonian region.

816 **Jayanca**. The road runs through dry savanna towards mountains covered in dry woodlands.

845 **Motupe** lies beneath a mountain called Chapan (1,820m, 5,970ft). From now on the changed scenery is reflected in the houses, which are made of wood instead of mud bricks.

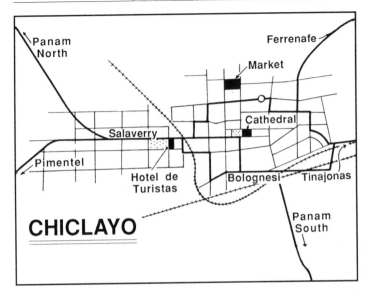

Panam North

Ferrenafe

Market

Cathedral

Salaverry

Pimentel

Hotel de Turistas

Bolognesi

Tinajonas

Panam South

CHICLAYO

Pass (400m, 1,312ft). The dry forest is made up of cactuses and thorn bushes, and only comes into leaf during the rainy season. It becomes progressively sparser as the road descends into the Olmos Valley.

866

Turning for the **Marañón**.

869

1c THE ROAD TO THE MARAÑÓN

This road was built by the military. It runs alongside the Amazon-Pacific Pipeline over the lowest of the Andean passes and down into the jungle to meet the upper reaches of the Amazon (Marañón).

The road crosses the watershed at the Abra de Poculla (2,145m, 7,035ft), and drops down into the valley of the Río Hualabamba, which enters the larger Río Huancabamba at **Tambo** (75km [46$^1/_2$ miles], 1,200m [3,936ft]). **Pucara** (125km [77$^1/_2$ miles, 900m [2,952ft]) is the first place of any significance along the route.

Further down the valley (188km, 116 miles) there is a turning for **Jaén** (16km, 10 miles), where there is overnight accommodation and a small airport with regular flights to Lima.

The main route continues in the direction of Moyobamba, crossing the Marañón, already an impressive river, via a 200m (656ft) long suspension bridge.

Shortly afterwards (214km, 132 miles) there is a turning for **Nazareth** (another 109km, 67$^1/_2$ miles), an old colonial settlement next to the Marañón in the region of the Aguaruna Indians, who until recently were still making genuine shrunken heads. The main route leaves the valley of the Marañón and instead follows the course of a tributary called the Río Utcubamba.

At **Pedro Ruiz Gallo** (303km, 187 miles) there is another junction. The road to **Moyobamba** (another 195km, 121 miles) and **Tarapoto** (another 306km, 190 miles) is usually only navigable by lorry. (There is a good tourist hotel at Tarapoto.)

Chachapoyas (354km [219 miles], 2,330m [7,642ft]) is the capital of the department of Amazonas. The old town's main charm lies in its sheer isolation, seemingly unaffected by the new road, which is often cut off by landslides. Overnight accommodation is available here.

869   Turning for the **Marañón**.

874   Turning for **Olmos**, a small town surrounded by orange groves. The Panamericana runs to the east of the town.

880   **Cascajal**. After the oasis the road runs back into dry savanna.

923   **Ñaupe**. A cluster of wooden huts in the desert, whose inhabitants live on the trade from travellers on the Panamericana, who stop here for refreshments.

931   **Las Animas** (370m, 1,213ft). Another pass provides a little variety, after which the road runs in a straight line towards a cone-shaped mountain called Vicus (469m, 1,538ft), where some important pottery finds have been made.

987   Turning for **Chulucanas** (8km, 5 miles). The poor road from here to Tambo Grande (37km, 23 miles) cuts off a corner for those wishing to use the mountain route to Ecuador (see Route 1d below), saving a total of 87km (54 miles).

From this junction (275km, 1,705 miles) the road drops gently towards Piura (35m, 115ft), passing through the northern part of the Desierto de Sechura, which means 'desert of dryness'. The oil drums in front of the wooden huts at the roadside are for storing drinking water that is brought here by lorry.

1,038   **Piura**. The old and the new Panamericana converge.

THE NEW PANAMERICANA

784   Junction of the two roads near Lambayeque.

801   **Mórrope**. At this point the road enters the Desierto de Sechura, which is well known to be the hottest desert in Peru.

886   Turning for **Bayovar** (63km, 39 miles), the Peruvian oil port at the end of the Amazon-Pacific pipeline.

997   Turning for **Catacaos** (6km, 4 miles), a rather nondescript little place

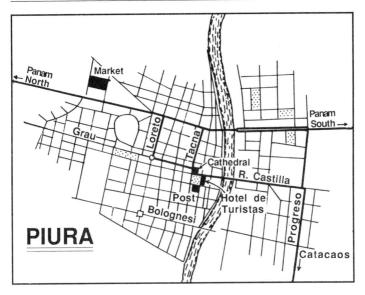

that tries to attract tourists with straw hats and other items of interest.

Piura. The old and the new Panamericana converge. The city is popular on account of its warm climate. It has recently undergone a considerable expansion thanks to the development of new industries and the creation of more reliable water supplies by means of new reservoirs. The main item of interest is the carved pulpit in the Cathedral, which stands next to a pretty square. There are several hotels providing overnight accommodation.   981

Turning for **Paita** (48km, 30 miles), where Peru's largest and most modern fishing port was opened in 1975.   988

Turning for **Tambo Grande**.   1,019

1d MOUNTAIN ROUTE TO ECUADOR

The road to Tambo Grande continues across the mountains to Loja in Ecuador, and eventually to Quito. It was in fact the original Panamericana, but because of its poor condition and the difficult mountain passes, it has lost out to the coastal route, which is both shorter and faster. The section between Las Lomas and the border village of La Tina is often impassable during the rainy season, but the continuation on the Ecuadorean side is considerably better.

The newly metalled road from Sullana to Tambo Grande runs through an area criss-crossed by irrigation channels. Thanks to reservoirs near the border, this region has been turned into fertile land. From the **Tambo Grande** turning (44km, 27 miles) it is another 2km (about a mile) to the town itself, while the Panamericana turns sharply northwards towards Las Lomas.

Las Lomas (76km, 47 miles) is at present no more than a collection of wooden huts. But the building of the San Lorenzo Reservoir 7km (4$\frac{1}{2}$ miles) to the east has created better conditions for developing the area, which is planned as a tourist region. The scenery becomes extraordinarily beautiful as the road climbs through forests of trees that are bare during the dry season. Of particular interest are the bottle trees, which store up water for the dry season in their bulbous trunks.

At the turning for **Ayabaca** (103km, 64 miles), the Panamericana swings north again towards **Suyo** (115km, 72 miles), which is the last place of any significance before the border.

The Peruvian border post of **La Tina** is no more than a few primitive huts basking in the tropical heat. The road crosses the Río Macará, which forms the border, to the Ecuadorean town of Macará, where there are airport facilities. The border is open only until 6pm.

1,019   Turning for **Tambo Grande**.

1,021   **Sullana** (population 68,000) is the busy commercial centre of the fertile Chira Valley, which the route now crosses.

1,049   **San Jacinto** is the last village before the road leaves the valley oasis. It is characterised by pleasant coconut plantations and houses made of wattle and daub.

1,081   Turning for **Talara** (8km, 5 miles). Although surrounded by waterless desert, the town of Talara is growing fast thanks to the surrounding oilfields and a fast-developing petrochemical industry, including a fertiliser plant (population 75,000).

1,103   Turning for **Talara** and **Lobitos**. The new Panamericana turns to the right, while the old road continues to Lobitos, which is now almost deserted but was once the centre of a now-exhausted oilfield.

1,137   Turning for **El Alto**. A short detour is recommended to the end of the village (2km, about a mile), where there is a fine view of the sea 275m (902ft) below. The cliff looks almost white from out at sea — hence the popular name **Cabo Blanco** or 'White Cape'. Below is the Fishing Club Hotel, which is now open to everyone but shows clear signs of its former exclusiveness in more prosperous days. Cabo Blanco was once famous on account of the wonderful sea fishing to be found here, attracting rich anglers from all over the world. It is supposed to have cost $10,000 for the Fishing Club entry fee alone. The dining hall contains photos and models of the largest fish to have been caught here, including several swordfish (*pes espada*) over a metre long and a black marlin (*merlin*) weighing 710kg (1,552lb). This place is supposed to have inspired Hemingway to write his novel *The Old Man and the Sea*.

The Panamericana continues through a rather messy region full of large petroleum-pumping machines.

Los Organos. A settlement built by the national oil company. 1,152

Mancora is the first of a series of fishing villages, where the landing of the fishing catch provides an interesting spectacle, especially in the afternoon. The fish are loaded straight onto refrigerated lorries. 1,165
※

Cancas. From here onwards the road runs along the shore, where there are a number of white beaches with bathing and camping facilities. 1,191

Zorritos. This seaside resort offers hotel accommodation, and is popular with day-trippers from Tumbes. The wooden towers of the old petroleum wells are a reminder of the fact that this was the first oilfield to be opened up in the whole of South America. 1,243

La Cruz is where Francisco Pizarro is supposed to have landed when he first arrived in Peru. 1,253

Tumbes (population 56,000) is the capital of Peru's northernmost coastal department. There is little of interest to tourists here, but overnight accommodation is available. 1,270

Turning for **Puerto Pizarro** (4km, 2½ miles). There are boat trips from the motel on the beach to the mangrove swamps around the delta of the Río Tumbes, where the land area is constantly growing. 1,280

Zarumilla. Near the border the vegetation undergoes a remarkable change. The dry savanna, with its thornbushes and algarrobos, gives way to dry woodland made up of cactuses and bottle trees, which are scarcely visible beneath a thick layer of creepers. Within the space of only 40km (25 miles) there is a dramatic transition from arid desert to lush tropical forest. 1,292

Aguas Verdes forms the border with Ecuador. The border posts are only open until 6pm. The roads beyond the border are good, leading eventually to Guayaquil (316km, 196 miles) and Quito (709km, 440 miles). 1,296

Route 2 To the Cordillera Blanca

Map: page 75
Overnight accommodation: Huaraz, Barranca, Huarmey, Chimbote
Public transport: Lima-Huaraz several buses and *colectivos* a day (8 hours); Casma-Huaraz 1 service a day (7 hours); Chimbote-Huaraz 2 services a day

The Cordillera Blanca is the most spectacular mountain range in the whole of Peru. Below it is the Santa Valley, parts of which are known as the Callejón de Huaylas. This forms a deep trench between the Cordillera Blanca and the Cordillera Negra. The former is covered with glaciers (*blanca* means 'white'), while the latter is mostly free of snow (*negra* means 'black'). The town of Huaraz is the main tourist centre of this mountainous region.

There are three possible routes from the coast, the most southerly of which is from Pativilca (2a) via the Conococha Pass. This is not only the shortest route, but also has the best (ie metalled) road surface.

The route from Casma (2b) goes through some spectacular scenery, but is narrow and much more difficult to drive. There are many narrow sections along steep slopes that require skilful drivers with nerves of steel! Travellers from Lima should preferably follow this route on the way back, as the steep drops are then mostly to the left of the road, forcing the oncoming traffic to go nearer the edge.

The route from Chimbote to Huaraz (2c) is not recommended, as the road is in poor condition and the scenery is less impressive. The most interesting part of the route, the Cañon del Pato (or 'Duck Canyon'), is best visited on a day trip from Huaraz.

2a LIMA • PATIVILCA • CONOCOCHA • HUARAZ

0   **Lima**. The first part of the route from Lima along the Panamericana Norte is described on page 72.

203   **Pativilca**. See page 78.

207   Turning for **Huaraz**. The route leaves the Panamericana and runs along between large sugar cane plantations. Later the road begins to climb through the more arid regions of the Fortaleza Valley.

253   **Chasquitambo** (780m, 2,558ft). This rather unprepossessing little village was once a relay station for the *chasqui* messengers of the Inca empire. At this point the valley becomes steeper and narrower.

283   **Raquia** (2,160m, 7,084ft). Valley slopes with little more than cacti become less steep for a while, allowing enough room for maize fields and a few villages, which the road climbs up through.

293   **Cajacay** (2,600m, 8,528ft). The road climbs up the side of the valley, which eventually becomes a gorge. The road crosses the gorge twice before beginning the final climb with many hairpins to the top of the pass.

324   **Conococha** (4,100m, 13,448ft) is a small village situated 70m (230ft) above a lake of the same name. There is a turning here for **Chiquian**, leading eventually to Huánuco on the Carretera Central (see map page 97).

2aa Conococha • La Unión • Huánuco

The road goes off to the right and down past the lake, then climbs gently over another pass (4,270m, 14,005ft), with views of the Río Pativilca in the valley 1,000m, 3,280ft below. Across the valley is the mighty **Cordillera de Huayhuash**, whose cliffs and jagged peaks make it one of the wildest mountain ranges in Peru. The highest peak is Yerupajá (6,620m, 21,713ft), which is famous among mountaineers as one of the most difficult mountains in the world.

The road winds down to **Chiquian** (32km, 20 miles), which is still high above the valley bottom. Further clusters of hairpins lead eventually to the bottom of the valley (3,080m, 10,103ft), which the road follows upstream as far as **Aquia** (48km [29 miles], 3,370m [11,053ft]). It then climbs over the spectacular but very difficult Yanashalla Pass (4,720m, 15,480ft) and eventually arrives at **La Unión** (136km [84 miles], 3,200m [10,496ft]).

To the right of the village is a narrow road leading up to the Inca ruins of **Huánuco Viejo** (another 11km, 7 miles), which deserve much more interest than their extremely isolated location allows.

The road leads downstream from La Unión along the uppermost reaches of the Marañon, and then climbs up over the Ayapitag Pass (3,750m, 12,300ft) to **Huánuco** (273km, 170 miles) on the Carretera Central (see map page 97).

Conococha (4,100m, 13,448ft). The road to Huaraz runs gently downwards through the *puna* landscape of the upper Santa Valley. The horizon is dominated by the long chain of snowy peaks that form the Cordillera Blanca. The cliffs and glaciers of Jeulla Rajo (5,680m, 18,630ft) seem almost close enough to touch.   324

Turning for the **Puya Raimondii National Park** (see Chapter 4). A new road has been opened up beyond here, providing an interesting alternative route to **La Unión** (see above). The road goes over the Huarapasca Pass (30km [18¹/₂ miles], 4,800m [15,744ft]), and joins the other route (85km, 53 miles) at a point 16km (10 miles) above Aquia and below the Yanashalla Pass.   361

Catac (3,540m, 11,611ft) is the first village in the Santa Valley. A road to the right goes up to fascinating ruins of **Chavín de Huántar** (see Chapter 4). The road to Huaraz continues across the Río Santa. The mountain chain of the Cordillera Blanca becomes visibly closer, with Huandoy to the left and next to it the mighty double peak of Huascarán, which at 6,770m (22,205ft) is the highest mountain in Peru.   367

Ticapampa (3,430m, 11,250ft).   373

Recuay (3,390m, 11,119ft). A new metalled road bypasses the village, which is the only place in the valley where enough has survived the great 1970 earthquake that one can see what the other   377

Indian woman with child in Chiquian

places were like before it. The next part of the valley is very narrow, and only seldom affords a view of the snowy peaks above.

402 **Huaraz** (3,090m, 10,135ft) is the main town of the region. It is described in Chapter 4, together with a number of excursions into the area around.

2b LIMA • CASMA • HUARAZ

0 **Lima**. The first part of the route along the Panamericana Norte as far as **Casma** is described on page 72ff.

370 Turning for **Huaraz** (see page 79). The road first runs up the Sechín Valley, and then crosses over a barren pass (700m, 2,296ft) into the valley of the Río Casma, which it then follows upstream.

403 **Yaután** (806m, 2,643ft) is perched on a ledge above the Río Casma. From this point onwards the road becomes narrower and the surface deteriorates.

423 **Pariacoto** (1,240m, 4,067ft). The road begins to climb steeply in hairpins, with terrifying drops, so deep that the Río Casma is often scarcely visible at the bottom.

475 Turning for **Pira** and **Cajamarquilla** (3,450m, 11,816ft). The road climbs through a set of hairpins as it approaches the top of the pass.

Ruins at Huánuco Viejo

Punta Callán (4,200m, 13,776ft). Immediately beyond the pass, the horizon opens up into a breathtaking panorama of the whole chain of the Cordillera Blanca. The closer the road comes to these ice-covered giants, the more fantastic the view becomes, until it reaches its best at a point 12.5km (7¹/₂ miles) from Huaraz (see Chapter 4).   487

Huaraz (3,090m, 10,135ft) is described in Chapter 4, together with a number of excursions into the area around.   517

2c CHIMBOTE • HUARAZ
NB Always check before setting out, as the Cañon del Pato is often closed to traffic.

Chimbote. The route first runs northwards for a few kilometres along the Panamericana Norte.   0

Turning for **Santa** (442km [274 miles] from Lima, see page 80). A right turn leads up into the Santa Valley.   13

Tablones (250m, 820ft). From this point onwards the road runs along the narrow track formed by the old railway, which was destroyed in 1970 by a catastrophic flood that had been triggered by the great earthquake.   64

Huallanca (1,450m, 4,756ft) is where the most interesting and varied   138 section of the route begins, as the road runs through the Cañon del Pato in the direction of Huaraz. This whole section is described in detail in Excursions from Huaraz, Chapter 4.

254 **Huaraz** (3,090m, 10,135ft). See Chapter 4.

Route 3 The Carretera Central

Maps: pages 65 and 97
Overnight accommodation: 3a Huánuco, Tingo María, Pucallpa; 3b Tarma; 3c Huaychulo, Huancayo
Railway: Lima • La Oroya • Huancayo
Bus transport: Lima-Huancayo several services a day (10 hours); Lima-La Merced various *colectivos* (10-11 hours); Lima-Huánuco-Pucallpa bus service (24 hours to Pucallpa)

The Carretera Central is a fairly good road by Peruvian standards, linking Lima with the central Andean region and the tropical jungles to the east.

The first part of the route climbs to 4,843m, 15,885ft over the Ticlio Pass, and the sudden steep climb makes heavy demands on the human organism. Anyone with heart or circulatory problems should not undertake the journey, while even healthy people should take careful precautions.

The best method is to travel non-stop from Lima to La Oroya. It is not usually advisable to rest near the top even for the purposes of acclimatisation, because the oxygen level in the blood takes some time to reduce and does not normally reach the critical phase on a fast trip over the pass. The rail journey is much slower, and is therefore more difficult for the body to cope with.

At La Oroya the route divides. The most important route (3a) goes north to the mining town of Cerro de Pasco and continues northwards through breathtaking scenery to the forest regions of Tingo María and Pucallpa, where there are sporadic boat services down the Ucayali and the Amazon to Iquitos. The second route goes from La Oroya to La Merced (3b), and is the shortest and quickest route from Lima to the tropical jungle.

The third route goes south to Huancayo (3c). The road is much better than on the other routes, but the scenery is less interesting. More adventurous travellers may wish to continue from Huancayo along the slow and difficult route through the mountains to Ayacucho and Cuzco (see page 126ff).

0 **Lima**. This route begins 7km (4¹/₂ miles) from the city centre at the point where the Carretera Central comes off motorway ring road, this being the easiest way out of Lima (see Lima map 1, page 45).

5 Turning for **Puruchuco** (1km, half a mile). These fascinating ruins

Huaraz three years after the 1970 earthquake

are well worth a short trip. There is a museum (closed on Mondays) showing some of the best finds discovered on the site, including textiles, pottery and musical instruments. A few hundred metres beyond the museum is a reconstruction of the original mud-brick castle, which was probably the home of the local prince. The reconstruction gives a good impression of the labyrinthine nature of such buildings.

Vitarte (350m, 1,148ft) is an unsightly collection of mud huts, and is sadly typical of the many shanty towns that cluster around the Peruvian capital.

Turning for **Huachipa**. The road to the left goes up to the ruined pre-Inca city of **Cajamarquilla** (5km, 3 miles). Although the site is very extensive, it is not particularly interesting. The route to Cajamarquilla is somewhat complicated. One must go straight on at the point where the metalled road bends sharply to the left, then take the first right turn for a farm called the Hacienda Niveria. The ruined city lies about 1km (half a mile) beyond the farmstead. A path going to the right off the main road leads to another ruin with underground grain stores.

11 Turning for **Granja Azul** (2km, 1$\frac{1}{4}$ miles to the right). The complex includes a luxurious restaurant and one of the finest hotels in the whole of Peru. The site also includes bungalows to let, set in beautiful gardens, and some of them with marvellous views across the valley.

13 **Hacienda San Juán.** There is a path between two buildings on the right-hand side of the road leading to the ruins of **Pariache** (1km, half a mile). These have been restored in a similar way to those of Puruchuco (see above).

19 **Nana.** This is the point where in winter the thick cloudbank over the coast forms a layer of fog on the ground. People in Lima find it difficult to imagine that areas above the cloud can enjoy a clear sky with temperatures about 10°C (50°F) warmer.

24 **Chaclacayo** (670m, 2,197ft) is the first of a series of towns and villages where the rich people of Lima build winter villas so that they can enjoy the sunshine while Lima is covered in cloud.

29 **Bosque Club** (790m, 2,591ft). This holiday club set in beautiful woodland surroundings is a popular winter weekend resort.

34 **Chosica** (850m, 2,788ft) is the largest and most prestigious of the winter resorts in the valley. Day trippers attracted here by the sunshine can enjoy facilities of all kinds, including restaurants, amusement arcades, camping and picnic sites.

38 Turning for the **Eulalia Valley** (see page 68).

53 **Cocachacra** (1,430m, 4,690ft). There is a turning to the right here for **San Bartolomé.** If one keeps right through this village, one eventually comes out along a narrow road that zigzags up the mountainside through the cactuses. There are some wonderful views along the way until it finally arrives at **Santiago de la Tuna** (20km [12 miles], 2,900m [9,512ft]), a village surrounded by groves of peach trees.

Shortly after San Bartolomé the railway makes the first of many zigzags, where the trains have to stop and go backwards. The difficult terrain means that they cannot climb in loops but instead must go forwards and backwards in zigzags up the mountainside.

68 **Surco** (2,010m, 6,592ft). Below the first of the hairpins, which start just before the village, there is a hydroelectric plant that is powered by water brought through tunnels from the eastern side of the Andes. The massive drop of nearly 5,000m (16,400ft) is enough to power a whole series of stations along the valley.

76 **Matucana** (2,380m, 7,806ft). The road bypasses the village, where landslides have several times carried away whole rows of buildings. The Rimac Valley now becomes steeper and narrows into a gorge.

The gorge widens at the point where the Río Parac comes in, making enough room for two zigzags on the railway. The road effectively imitates the railway, making two long hairpins as it climbs

Band, including a portable hand harp

up through the eucalyptus woods below San Mateo.

San Mateo (3,140m, 10,299ft) is a somewhat down-at-heel village   95
with an unattractive hotel that rejoices in the name of *Danubio Azul*
or 'Blue Danube'. After San Mateo the gorge narrows again to form
a deep canyon known as **Infernillo** or 'Little Hell', where both road
and railway cross over each other several times via a series of
superimposed bridges.

Chilca (3,790m, 12,431ft) is an ugly mining settlement where the   106
railway climbs the steep slope by means of another pair of zigzags.
The landscape becomes less interesting as the vegetation becomes
sparser.

Turning for **Casapalca** (4,050m, 13,284ft). The road climbs steeply   114
up the mountainside, passing high above the copper, lead and silver
mines of Casapalca. It enters a high mountain valley, at the end of
which (4,350m, 14,268ft) is a road going up to the left. This road
crosses a very lonely and dangerous stretch of mountains and comes
back down into the **Eulalia Valley** (see page 68).

  The road conditions deteriorate considerably as the road climbs
a final series of hairpins up to the Ticticocha Lagoon. At this point the
railway takes a different route. It plunges through a tunnel at 4,780m,
15,678ft and comes out into the Yauli Valley, which it then descends

by means of two further zigzags. The road meanwhile follows a more interesting route close to the Morococha branch line, which is used mainly for the ore mines.

132 **Ticlio Pass** (4,843m, 15,885ft). Provided it is not shrouded in fog or blizzards, as is often the case, the pass is a gift for photographers. The subject can stand in front of a sign saying 'The highest railway in the world, 4,818 metres, 15,806 feet', with the snow-covered peaks of the Nevado Anticona (5,250m, 17,220ft) in the background. The road then descends through a *puna* landscape with many lakes. The mountainsides take on a variety of hues where they have been gouged out by mines.

141 Turning for **Morococha** (4,560m, 14,956ft). The roofs of the miners' cottages are painted in loud colours, which contrast sharply against the uniform redness of the mine-pocked mountain that rears up behind the town.

174 **La Oroya** (3,730m, 12,234ft) lies in a narrow valley between white chalk cliffs, and has a population of 57,000. Its prosperity relies partly on its copper and lead smelting works and partly on its important position on a road and rail junction. All the ores mined in the central mountains, from Cerro de Pasca in the north to Huancayo and Huancavelica in the south, must be transported via La Oroya.

3a LA OROYA • HUÁNUCO • TINGO MARÍA • PUCALLPA

174 **La Oroya** (3,730m, 12,234ft). The road climbs gradually upwards through the Mantaro Valley, which forms a shallow gorge.

195 Turning for **Tarma** (see Route 3b). The road crosses the pass (4,200m, 13,776ft) almost imperceptibly and comes out into a vast plateau called the Pampa de Junín. This region was the scene of bitter fighting on 6 August 1824 during the independence struggles. An obelisk was erected to commemorate this bloody event. It is visible from the road about 5km (3 miles) from Junín, across the plateau about $2^1/_2$km ($1^1/_2$ miles) to the left.

230 **Junín** (4,130m, 13,546ft). The main square in this rather godforsaken little town is to the left of the main street. The church is interestingly crooked, and its carved baroque altar possesses a number of very Indian features.

The road carries on past Lake Junín, which is badly silted up, but which is famous on account of its great flocks of wild ducks and giant edible frogs.

289 Turning for **Huayllay** and the road over the Viuda Pass and down the Canta Valley to Lima (see page 69).

296 Turning for **Cerro de Pasco**. A 9km ($5^1/_2$ mile) detour is possible to this mining town (with a hotel), which was famous even in colonial times. Situated at 4,330m (14,202ft), and with a population of 25,000

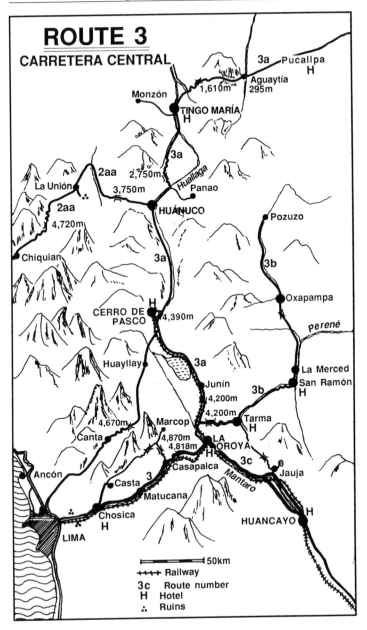

ROUTE 3
CARRETERA CENTRAL

3a Pucallpa H

Aguaytía 295m

1,610m

Monzón

TINGO MARÍA H

3a

2aa 2,750m

La Unión

3,750m Huallaga Panao

2aa

4,720m HUÁNUCO

Chiquian

3a Pozuzo

3b

Oxapampa

H

CERRO DE PASCO 4,390m

Perené

Huayllay 3a

La Merced

Junín 3b San Ramón H

4,200m

4,200m Tarma H

4,670m Marcop

Canta 4,870m LA

4,818m OROYA 3c

Ancón H

Casapalca Jauja

Casta 3 Mantaro

Matucana

HUANCAYO H

Chosica H

LIMA

|══════|50km
+++ Railway
3c Route number
H Hotel
∴ Ruins

in 1975, it must be one of the highest towns in the world. It lies at the edge of a large chasm, where miners have scratched for copper, lead, zinc and silver since time immemorial.

Opinions are sharply divided as to the town's aesthetic value. There are still a few romantic old streets with crumbling Andalusian-style balconies. But the old town is soon to be sacrificed to the cause of industry as the mining is extended, while a new town is already being built 3km (2 miles) away to the north. The road begins to drop steeply into the valley of the Río Huallaga, which develops from a few small mountain tarns to one of the largest tributaries of the Amazon.

329 **Chicrin** (3,550m, 11,644ft), a bleak mining settlement.

360 **San Rafael** (2,690m, 8,823ft). This is the first place where there are proper plants in the main square. The valley becomes broader, with a rich covering of epiphytes, cactuses, thorny algarrobos and other succulents.

415 **Huánuco** (1,910m [6,264ft], population 64,000). This provincial capital on the upper reaches of the Huallaga is a popular holiday resort on account of its pleasant climate (there is a tourist hotel), but has little of interest to foreign visitors. There is a turning here for **La Unión** (144km [89 miles], see page 89) and the Inca ruins of Huánuco Viejo.

438 Turning for **Panao** (1,750m, 5,740ft). The road crosses the Huallaga and climbs steeply out of the valley.

460 **Carpish Pass** (2,750m, 9,020ft). The road crosses the mountains to avoid a wide loop in the Río Huallaga. The forest begins just below the top of the pass — a phenomenon known to the locals as the 'eyebrow of the mountains'. The road itself crosses the pass via a tunnel, and comes out into a completely different landscape on the other side. All the mountain slopes are now covered with a moist green covering of tropical forest. The road climbs down in a series of broad loops to the valley floor 2,000m (6,560ft) below. It continues along a gorge covered in green vegetation, and eventually comes back into the Huallaga Valley.

513 **Huallaga Bridge** (790m, 2,592ft). A short way beyond the bridge there is a collection of wooden stalls selling freshly picked papayas and other delicious tropical fruits.

536 The town of **Tingo María** (670m, 2,196ft) has all the primitive charm of a pioneer town in the American Wild West. It is surrounded by rich plantations of coffee, tea, sugar cane, bananas and other tropical crops. The limestone mountains emerge from the forest like sugar loaves. The lush greenery of Amazonian forest, combined with the equable climate, has made Tingo María into a popular holiday resort. There is a tourist hotel.

Tropical vegetation near Tingo María

To the left as you approach the town is an interesting botanical garden, with a massive thicket of giant bamboos up to 60m (197ft) tall. The market is fascinating, with everything on sale from magic herbs to jaguar skins. Also worth visiting are the tea plantations on the Pucallpa road and the nearby Cueva de las Lechuzas National Park.

To get to the **Cueva de las Lechuzas** or 'Owls' Cave', one turns left at the entrance to the town and crosses a suspension bridge over the Huallaga. After another 4km (2¹/₂ miles), the road ends at another river, which can be crossed by means of dug-outs with outboard motors (there are several on hand). A 15-minute walk along the old road (keep left!) leads to a cliff with a marvellous view of the surrounding forest. Visitors are advised not to go into the cave. The air inside is full of fungal spores that cause an obscure illness leading to fever and in some cases to death.

Turning for **Aucayuco.** The road climbs up into the mountains through banana plantations, with some marvellous views. The tea plantations are briefly glimpsed in the valley below. 550

La Divisoria Pass (1,610m, 5,280ft) through the Cordillera Azul or 'Blue Mountains'. 578

Boquerón del Padre Abad (470m, 1,540ft). The road now enters one of the most exciting parts of the whole journey as it runs through 607 a wild canyon dripping with moisture. Its vertical walls are covered with hosts of flowering orchids. The canyon was named after the Franciscan missionary who in 1757 was the first to discover this route through the Cordillera Azul, which until then had been thought completely impassable.

630 **Aguaytía** (295m, 967ft). The road crosses the Río Aguaytía via a long suspension bridge. Bananas are brought here by dug-out and transferred to lorries to be transported away. The road continues the long journey through the Amazon jungle, which is by no means as flat as one might think when seeing it from an aeroplane. As the road approaches Pucallpa, the secondary forest gradually gives way to grassland. But the stumps of the old forest are still visible from when it was burned down to make way for cattle pasture.

790 **Pucallpa** (200m, 656ft). The road terminates at this point. There are plans to extend it across the Brazilian border, but this is only one of many projects that will probably take some years to achieve. The only way to go further inland is to take a boat trip to Iquitos. The boats are very primitive and the journey very slow, taking 5-6 days down to Iquitos and 6-9 days for the return journey upstream. The town of Pucallpa and its environs are described in Chapter 4.

3b LA OROYA • TARMA • LA MERCED • OXAPAMPA

174 **La Oroya** (3,730m, 12,234ft). The road climbs gradually upwards through the Mantaro Valley, which forms a shallow gorge.

195 Turning for **Junín** and Cerro de Pasco (see Route 3a). The road goes right and continues to climb.

202 **Abra Cochas** (4,240m, 13,907ft). After crossing the pass, the road begins the long descent into the tropical forest.

228 **Tarma** (3,050m, 10,004ft) is the first town along the route (there is tourist accommodation). It is surrounded by hardy green eucalyptus trees and the scent of wild flowers. In Holy Week there are glorious processions over beautiful carpets of flowers.

237 **Acobamba** (2,940m, 9,643ft). There is a turning here for the pilgrimage chapel of **Muruhuay** (3km, 2 miles), whose impressive modernistic design won a prize for the architect. The site commands a fine view of the whole valley, and is the scene of great festivities in May.

248 **Palca** (2,730m, 8,954ft) is the last village in the more populated region around Tarma, since from here onwards there is no room for even the smallest of fields, as the road begins its steep and winding descent across near-vertical slopes that are subject to landslides.

294 **San Ramón** (825m, 2,706ft). This small town on the edge of the broad Chanchamayo Valley offers tourist accommodation, making it a good base for trips into the pineapple, orange, coffee and cocoa

plantations in the area around.

La Merced. The main commercial centre of the Chanchamayo Valley is perched on a small hill above the forest to the left of the road. There is some basic hotel accommodation.   305

Turning for **Satipo**.   318

Excursion to Satipo
The new road to Satipo was built by the military. It mainly follows the course of the Río Perené, which is effectively the continuation of the Chanchamayo. The road has enabled the development of rich tropical fruit plantations over land that originally belonged to the Campa Indians. The biggest Indian settlement is **Marankiari** (14km, 8¹/₂ miles), which is situated to the right above the road. These Indians have long since become assimilated, but their individual character is still reflected in the construction of their wooden huts and in the dark clothes worn by the women.

Turning for **Satipo**. The road to Oxapampa climbs up through a valley covered with cloud forests.   318

Paucartambo Bridge. Near the crossing of the Río Paucartambo, there is a turning for **Villa Rica** (19km, 12 miles), a coffee-growing centre that was originally founded by German colonists. The subsequent climb through the tropical fruit plantations and forested slopes is one of the most beautiful parts of the whole journey.   336

Oxapampa (1,780m, 5,838ft) is blessed with a pleasant mountain climate and provides basic hotel accommodation. It is the centre of an important forestry industry, which employs about 70 per cent of the population. The wooden houses are strikingly smart and untypical of Peru. These and the wooden church with its onion-shaped dome are a stark reminder of the fact that Oxapampa was founded in 1890 by Germans and Austrians who moved here from Pozuzo, 68km (42 miles) further into the jungle.   382

Pozuzo is a remarkable village of Tirolean farmhouses, and some of the people even speak the Tirolean dialect of German. It was completely cut off from the outside world until 1975, when a road link was built from Oxapampa.

The foundation of Pozuzo goes back to 1854, when 200 people from the Austrian Tirol, together with 100 from the German Rhineland, were persuaded by the Peruvian government to set up a colony in the jungle. They were promised a road link and financial support, but in the event they were left with absolutely nothing. They were forced to make their own way through the wilderness to the designated area, which they managed in the face of appalling conditions. A hundred and fifty of them survived the 2-year trek through the jungle to set up the colony here. And it was 1975 before the Peruvians at last fulfilled their promise to build a road link to Pozuzo.

3c LA OROYA • HUANCAYO

174   **La Oroya** (3,720m, 12,201ft). The road to Huancayo is mostly fairly decent. It crosses the Río Mantaro in front of the smelting works, which occupy the whole of the valley bottom. It then follows the valley downstream parallel to the railway.

253   Turning for **Mito**. From this point onwards there are two roads running parallel along the broad green plateau of the Huancayo Basin. The present route follows the road to the left (east) of the river. Though 5km (3 miles) longer, it is more interesting than the other.

255   Turning for **Jauja** (3,410m, 11,184ft). This old town was Pizarro's capital for the short period until the founding of Lima. Beyond it is the legendary **Laguna Paca**, where after the announcement of Atahuallpa's death 10,000 llamas are supposed to have been driven into the lake laden with gold and silver. There is a tiny tourist hotel next to the lake.

273   Turning for **Ocopa**. There is a left turn along a metalled road to Ocopa (6km, 3$^1/_2$ miles) just beyond the first houses of the village of Mata-huasi. Santa Rosa de Ocopa is a Franciscan monastery that was built between 1724 and 1744 in order to train missionaries for the jungle.

     The monastery now houses a museum with mementos of that period. But its main attractions are the Santa Rosa Altar with its alabaster (*piedra de Huamanga*) engravings, the gallery full of paintings in the Cuzco style, and the library with its priceless collection of old books written in many different languages.

277   Turning for **Huaychulo** (2km, 1$^1/_4$ miles).

298   The bustling city of **Huancayo** (3,270m, 10,725ft, population 190,000) is famous for its Sunday Indian market, where virtually everything is available that can be bought anywhere else in Peru. The carved gourds are a local speciality, but like everything else they are similarly available in Lima. What is more, the market is not particularly Indian! Travellers to the Cuzco region will find much better markets that are genuinely Indian.

     Huancayo is also a hotbed of thieves, who make a particular point of robbing tourists, and will find cash in the most obscure of hiding places. They will even tear handbags apart and cut cameras open.

     Some travellers may wish to continue south-eastwards through the mountains on the long and difficult journey to Ayacucho and eventually to Cuzco (see page 126ff). Others might try the rough journey down to the coast via Yauyos; the road is narrow and unmetalled, and goes through deep gorges, eventually coming out near Cañete (303km, 188 miles, see page 104).

Tropical forests near Oxapampa

Route 4 Lima to Arequipa

Map: pages 109 and 113

Overnight accommodation: Pisco, Huancavelica (4a), Ayacucho (4a), Paracas, Ica, Nazca, Abancay (4b), Chala, Camaná

Public transport: numerous buses and *colectivos* along the coast Lima-Nazca (7-8 hours); 1-2 services a day Pisco-Huancavelica (13 hours), Pisco-Ayacucho (12 hours)

The Panamericana Sur, like its northern counterpart, runs through long stretches of desert. But there are far fewer valley oases than along the northern part of the coast. Just before Arequipa there is a major fork, with one branch going south to Chile (see Route 5) and the other inland towards Bolivia (see Route 6).

Lima. Distances are counted rather illogically from the junction of the Carretera Central with the motorway ring road. But there is a better route from the city centre along the Via Expresa (see Lima Map 1, page 45). Of the two exits along the Avenida Javier Prado, the second (signposted Monterrico) leads directly to the Panamericana.

11   Exit for **Miraflores**.

26   Exit for **Pachacámac**. These famous ruins are visible on the hillside above the motorway, The entrance to them is 1km (half a mile) from the motorway along the road to Lurín (see page 63).

58   Turning for **Pucusana**, a small fishing port with interesting rock formations (see page 66).

64   **Chilca** (17m, 56ft) is small town that depends mostly on the products of the local salt pans. The motorway climbs over a pass (160m, 524ft) through the desert before dropping steeply again.

83   **San Antonio** is on the edge of the fruit-growing region of the Río Mala valley oasis.

86   **Mala**. Travellers are easily lured by the many fruit stalls along the roadside, which offer a rich variety of fruit for sale.

102   **Asia**. The new motorway bypasses the village. The old Panamericana is falling into decay, but past the village it runs along the shore. The rock pools along the beach are full of red starfish, black sea urchins and scuttling crabs. The main road begins to climb again, and there are numerous paths across the dunes to the 130m (426ft) high cliffs, which command some fine views of the sea.

145   **San Vicente de Cañete**. The motorway ends at this point. Cañete lies at the centre of a broad oasis that is mostly planted with cotton. Just past the town one can see a small castle across the fields to the left. This was formerly the viceroy's country residence, and is now being turned into a museum.

198   **Chincha** (120m, 393ft). After a short stretch along the shore past some beautiful beaches, the road climbs inland again to the town of Chincha (population 40,000). Chincha is a centre for the production of a special Peruvian brandy called *pisco*, which is available at numerous stalls along the roadside.

228   Turning for **Tambo Colorado**, **Castrovirreyna**, Huancavelica and Ayacucho. The ruins of Tambo Colorado (see below) are only 38km (23$^1/_2$ miles) inland, and are the best-preserved Inca ruins along the whole of the coast.

4a PISCO • HUANCAVELICA • AYACUCHO

This route goes through some delightful scenery, but includes long sections over 4,000m (13,120ft) or even 4,500m (14,760ft). Altitude precautions are therefore essential. The appalling road conditions and the many unsignposted junctions make the route even more difficult. Also, the mountain regions around Huancavelica and Ayacucho have become increasingly subject to terrorism in recent years. Anyone contemplating going this far should make enquiries beforehand to see if it is safe to travel.

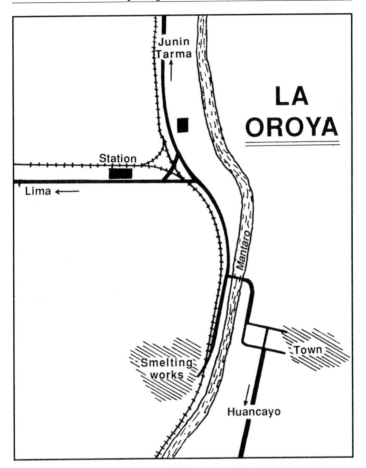

The road from the coast runs right through the middle of the ruins of **Tambo Colorado** (38km, 23¹/₂ miles), which is so named because of the residual red, yellow and white paint on the walls. The trapezoid design of the windows and doors leaves one in no doubt as to the site's Inca origins. But archaeologists are not yet agreed as to its actual purpose. Some say there was a pre-Inca temple down the slope to the right. As for the main site on the hillside above, some see it as the remains of an Inca sun temple, while others think it served a military purpose, securing the stability of this conquered region.

At **Pampano** (81km [50 miles], 1,300m [4,264ft]) there is a right

The Panamerican Highway through the desert

fork up to the mining area of Huaytará, where there are further Inca remains. The narrow road to the left for Castrovirreyna leads up a steep narrow gorge and climbs via a series of hairpins to **Ticrapo** (110km [68 miles], 2,184m [7,163ft]) and to Castrovirreyna.

Castrovirreyna (151km [94 miles], 3,890m [12,760ft]) is the provincial capital of this desperately poor region. After another series of hairpins, the road comes out into a bleak *puna* region with lakes and snow-covered mountains. Three lakes follow in close succession: Lake Pacococha (4,416m, 14,484ft), where there are some mines along a road to the left, the San Francisco Reservoir (4,630m, 15,186ft) and Lake Orcococha (4,530m, 14,858ft).

There is a road junction near the last of these three lakes (189km, 117 miles). The road to the left is for Huancavelica. It runs along past the lake, then climbs up over the **Chonta Pass** (4,850m, 15,908ft) before descending gradually along a valley towards the departmental capital of **Huancavelica** (267km [165 miles], 3,500m [11,480ft]). This town is described in more detail in Route 9a.

The right-hand road from the junction near Lake Orcococha is for Ayacucho (see Route 9a). It drops down to **Pilpichaca** (209km [220 miles]) and then climbs over the Alpacheta Pass (4,750m, 15,580ft) to **Ayacucho** (355km [220 miles], 2,670m [8,757ft]), which is described in detail in Chapter 4.

228 Turning for **Tambo Colorado** and **Castrovirreyna**.

232 Turning for **Pisco** (6km, 3¹/₂ miles). Travellers are recommended to make a 25km (15¹/₂ mile) detour via the fishing port of Pisco (simple hotel) and the bay and peninsula of **Paracas** (luxury hotel), but only provided there is enough time for a museum visit and/or a boat trip to the Islas Ballestras (the Sealion Islands). All this is described in more detail in the section on Paracas, Chapter 4.

Turning for **Paracas** (12km, 7$\frac{1}{2}$ miles). The Panamericana now turns inland, passing through a dry oasis with the only date palms in Peru. The road then runs through a long stretch of stony desert. Shortly before Ica this gives way to cotton fields, with an impressive array of sand dunes beyond them. 246

The busy town of **Ica** (440m, 1,443ft, population 128,000) is the centre of Peru's most important wine-growing region. There are two important places to visit here: the Archaeological Museum and the beautiful Huacachina Oasis. Both of them can be reached easily from the modern tourist hotel. The Archaeological Museum has recently been moved to a new building. It contains many excellent examples of textiles and pottery from the Nazca and Tiahuanaca periods, and some beautifully carved oars. The Huacachina Oasis (2km, 1$\frac{1}{4}$ miles) is a small collection of villas, hotels and palm trees clustered round a tiny lake surrounded by high sand dunes. The setting is magical, but the lake is sadly drying up because of a series of deep wells that have recently been sunk in the nearby Ica Valley. 304

Santiago (370m, 1,213ft). The Panamericana first goes through the villages and cotton fields of the Río Ica Valley oasis. But these gradually peter out as it turns back towards the coast, giving way to a flat expanse of grey desert. 319

Santa Cruz (500m, 1,640ft). This small oasis is continually subject to water shortages. 386

Pass tunnel (650m, 2,132ft). The road crosses the pass via a tunnel and comes out into the valley of the Río Grande (350m, 1,148ft). 388

Palpa (320m, 1,049ft) is in the centre of an oasis covered with extensive cotton fields and numerous orange plantations. 397

Illipata. The road crosses the fertile valley of the Río Ingenio that has been irrigated since time immemorial. It then enters a flat stone desert called the **Pampa Colorado**, which has become famous on account of the **Nazca Lines**. The road runs through the middle of the site. There is a lookout tower to the right of the road, from which one can just make out some of the figures and long geometrical lines. But the majority of the lines and figures can only be seen from a small plane. There are flights from the airport on the opposite side of Nazca — provided the plane is capable of flying! 402

Nazca (590m, 1,935ft) is at the centre of the Nazca Oasis, which was the home of one of the most important ancient Indian coastal civilisations. The Nazca people excelled both in their pottery designs and in their irrigation techniques, which involved building underground channels. 445

4b NAZCA • CUZCO

The mountain road from Nazca forms the shortest overland route from Lima to Cuzco. The road is mostly in very poor condition, but even so it is still better than any of the other routes between Cuzco and the coast. The road immediately climbs out of the valley, and runs along the crest of the mountains onto a high plateau (4,140m, 13,580ft) before dropping steeply into the valley of the Río Acari.

After **Puquio** (160km [99 miles], 3,210m [10,528ft]) the road begins a long and twisty ascent to the **Yauriviri Reservoir** (4,390m, 14,399ft). It continues across a gently undulating *puna* plateau covered with lakes and swamps. The highest point of the route is 4,550m, 14,924ft.

The road then drops steeply via a series of hairpins into the gorge-like valley of the Río Chalhuanca. The turning for Antabamba (335km [208 miles], 3,100m [10,168ft]) is soon followed by **Chalhuanca** (350km [217 miles], 2,900m [9,512ft]), which is the main town in the valley. After Chalhuanca the valley narrows down into a deep gorge. The Río Chalhuanca is joined by the Río Antabamba and becomes the Río Pachachaca.

The road eventually comes to the junction (458km, 284 miles) with the Central Andean Highway from **Ayacucho** (see page 128). It then climbs out of the Pachachaca Valley up to the town of **Abancay**, and continues along the Central Andean Highway to **Cuzco** (see page 126).

445 **Nazca**. The Panamericana now runs through long stretches of dry, uninhabited desert.

484 Turning for **San Juán** (39km, 24 miles). San Juán is the main port for the export of iron ores from the mines at Marcona, which is situated half-way along the same road.

519 Turning for **San Juán** (33km [20 miles], 280m [918ft]). There is a fine view of the sea from the car park at the junction with a small road that is often swamped by sand dunes.

527 Turning for **Puerto Lomas** (7km, 4 miles).

530 Turning for **Acari** (24km, 15 miles).

553 **Chaviña**. The road passes the small oasis around the Río Acari, and then enters a very windy desert region where the road traffic is often badly affected by driving sand.

566 Turning for **Yauca**. After crossing another small oasis full of gnarled old olive trees, the road is again at the mercy of the wind and the sand. A nearby mountain is piled up with sand, and is appropriately called the Cerro la Arena or 'Sand Mountain' (920m, 3,017ft).

577 **Tanaca**. The road climbs to the *lomas* of Atiquipa, where it is often

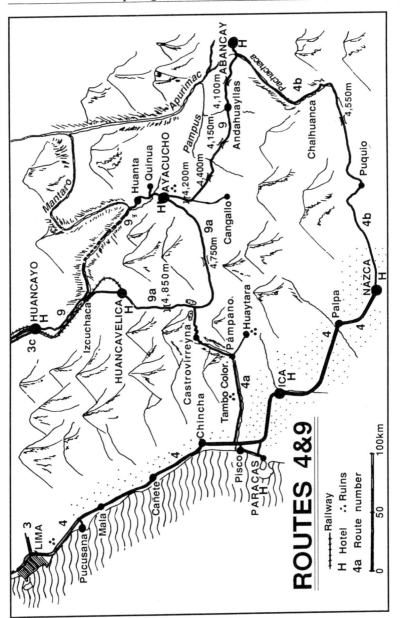

ROUTES 4&9

—+—+— Railway   ∴ Ruins

H Hotel   4a Route number

swathed in fog. But the result of this is a colourful green carpet of vegetation, particularly during the month of September.

595 Turning for **Atiquipa** (230m, 754ft).

614 **Chala**. This old port (with a tourist hotel) was where the Incas landed their fish, which were then carried up to their capital in Cuzco by runners (*chasquis*) working in relays. Right up until the last century, goods for Cuzco were landed here and carried by mule caravan up through the Andes. But with the building of the Mollendo-Cuzco rail link, the port of Chala soon fell into disuse.

After Chala the Panamericana runs for some considerable distance along the coast, which at this stage falls steeply into the sea.

703 **Atico**. There now follows one of the most beautiful stretches along the whole of the Peruvian coast, with steep sandy slopes and rocky bays surrounded by cliffs. Shortly before Ocoña the road climbs to 350m, 1,148ft, and runs inland towards the deep valley of the Río Ocoña.

778 **Ocoña** is a collection of mud-brick huts on the edge of the valley oasis. The road climbs out over a pass (280m, 918ft) straight back into the pathless coastal desert.

835 **Camaná** is in the centre of a broad valley oasis (it has a tourist hotel). Soon after Camaná the road leaves the coast again and climbs 1,000m, 3,280ft through a dry valley up to a bleak barren plateau.

895 Turning for **Aplao**.

4c EXCURSION TO TORO MUERTO AND THE VALLEY OF THE VOLCANOES

The trip to the rock carvings of Toro Muerto is highly recommended, and takes about three or four hours. The more adventurous traveller may like to continue to the Valley of the Volcanoes, but the route is slow and difficult; it requires a pioneering spirit, a sturdy vehicle, an overnight tent (unless sleeping in the car) and plenty of food and fuel.

The route follows a good metalled road for the first 20km (12½ miles), running in a straight line across the monotonous grey desert. But then a sudden sharp bend is followed by an abrupt descent of some 1,000m (3,280ft) into a deep valley, where the Río Majes runs through green fields towards the sea. At **Punta Colorada** (37km, 23 miles) the road crosses the Rio Majes, whose upper reaches are known as the Colca.

A short way further on is the turning for **Toro Muerto** (45km, 28 miles). The warden's hut (3km, 2 miles) is at the very edge of the valley oasis, and from it there are several tracks leading up a sandy slope scattered with about 5,000 rocks. Many of these rocks, especially those towards the top, are carved with primitive drawings of hunters, llamas and pumas. The origin of these ancient petroglyphs

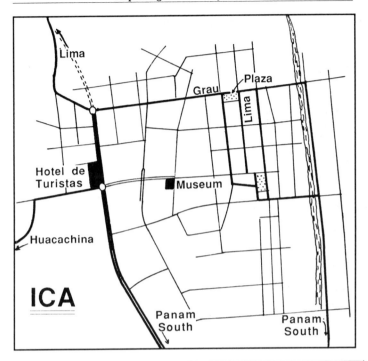

has baffled the experts for many years — though the odd space ship or astronaut is no doubt of more recent origin!

The road continues up the valley via the village of **Corire** (47km, 29 miles), where there is a simple hotel, to **Aplao** (67km, 41$^1/_2$ miles), where the last filling station is located. From here onwards the road conditions deteriorate rapidly. There is a left turn (72km, 44$^1/_2$ miles) for **Chuquibamba**, and the road to the Valley of the Volcanoes goes down to the right.

The **Albergue Turístico Nacional** (74km, 46 miles) is a small hotel that forms the last bastion of civilisation. The owners organise dinghy trips along the river, either downstream in safety for the more anxious visitor, or upstream for the more ambitious, leading to the narrows and rapids along the deepest part of the mighty **Cañon de Colca**. At this point the river has cut a 3,000m (9,840ft) deep canyon through the mountains.

Travellers with sufficient food and fuel (and preferably an over-night tent) may now undertake the trip through the Valley of the Volcanoes. The whole journey is dominated by the snow-covered cone of the Nevada Coropuna (6,613m, 21,690ft), which becomes a beacon of hope for travellers battling with the enormous ruts, the sand and stones, the terrifying climbs and all the other obstacles that conspire to thwart the vehicle's progress.

The track goes via **Tipan** (132km, 82 miles) and **Machaguy** (148km, 485 miles) and eventually comes to a crossroads (188km, 116 miles). A right turn here leads down a steep zigzag track to **Andagua** (208km, 129 miles). This little village exists in total isolation, but the broad square offers plenty of shade. The large church provides a glimpse of some of the volcanoes in the valley far below. A difficult track makes the final descent into the valley itself, where a dozen or so volcano cones rise some 100-200m (330-660ft) above the cactuses that cover the valley floor.

895   Turning for **Aplao**. There is a sudden and dramatic change from grey desert into green fields. This is the result of a massive irrigation project in which the Río Majes (Colca) is channelled through a vast system of tunnels and canals.

915   Turning for **Huacán**, **Chivay** and the Colca Valley (see Chapter 4, Excursions from Arequipa). The Panamericana climbs almost imperceptibly to 1,450m (4,756ft), then there is a sudden and unexpected view of the canyon of the Río Sihuas.

919   **Tambillo** (1,250m, 4,100ft). The road crosses the Río Sihuas gorge, then climbs up again to cross another level plateau before descending the even deeper canyon of the Río Vitor (Chile).

950   **Río Vitor Bridge** (1,160m, 3,804ft).

968   **Repartición** (1,750m, 5,740ft) is situated at a major fork where the Panamericana divides into two branches, one to Chile (see below) and one to Bolivia via Arequipa and Puno (see Route 6). There are two roads from here to Arequipa. The older road is longer (48km, 30 miles) and more difficult, and goes via a 2,700m, 8,856ft high pass and the copper mines of Cerro Verde. The new road goes over a lower pass (2,350m, 7,708ft) and drops down into the Chili Valley.

993   **Uchumayo** (1,950m, 6,396ft) lies on a valley plain covered with volcanic ash, dominated by the majestic cone of the Volcán Misti.

1,010   **Arequipa** (2,360m, 7,740ft) is a unique and fascinating city that is well worth a longer visit. Both the city and its environs are described in detail in Chapter 4.

Route 5 Arequipa to the Chilean Border

Map: page 118
Overnight accommodation: Mollendo, Moquegua, Ilo, Tacna
Railway: Tacna-Arica (Chile) four services a day (except Sundays)

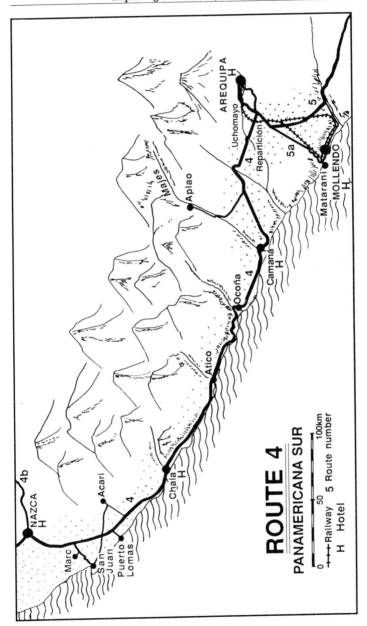

ROUTE 4
PANAMERICANA SUR

0   50   100km

+++ Railway   5 Route number
H Hotel

Bus transport: two services Lima-Tacna (23 hours); numerous buses and *colectivos* Arequipa-Tacna (6-8 hours); *colectivos* Arequipa-Mollendo (2 hours), Mollendo-Tacna, Tacna-Arica (border closed on public holidays)

The southernmost section of the coastal route runs at a considerable distance from the coast across a series of dull arid plateaux. The seaside resorts of Mollendo, Ilo and Boca del Río are served by good roads, but their facilities are mostly geared to the rather modest needs of Peruvian visitors.

0   **Arequipa** (2,360m, 7,740ft). The route retraces the previous route for the first 42km (26 miles) as far as Repartición, from where distances are given from Lima.

968   **Repartición** (1,750m, 5,740ft). The route rejoins the coastal Panamericana Sur at the edge of the mountains. This road then runs in a straight line across a dull plateau that slopes towards the sea.

982   Turning for **Mollendo** (1,350m, 4,428ft).

5a EXCURSION TO THE COAST

The road down to the coast goes through some beautiful scenery. One can take a different route back to the Panamericana along a very poor road going from Mejia to the Tambo Bridge; the resulting detour adds 54km (33 miles) to the overall distance.

Immediately on leaving the Panamericana the scenery starts to become more interesting, with grey crescent dunes forming over the reddish bedrock. The road suddenly leaves the plateau (1,150m, 3,772ft) and enters a dry valley that drops steeply towards the sea.

Mantarani (51km, 32 miles) consists of a few delapidated huts inhabited by dock workers and railway employees. The road to the right leads down to the newly built port (2km, $1^1/_4$ miles), which handles goods destined for Arequipa and much of the trade for Bolivia.

Mollendo (64km, 39 miles) has just one good hotel, which stands on a cliff high above the sea, surrounded by numerous old wooden houses. Many people from Arequipa spend their summer holidays in Mollendo. But European visitors prefer the rather quieter resort of **Mejia** (80km, 50 miles), which has a particularly fine beach.

The road from Mejia via La Curva (91km, 56 miles) and Cocachacra (101km, 63 miles) is narrow with a very poor surface, but it eventually leads back into the Panamericana at the Tambo Bridge.

982   Turning for **Mollendo** (1,350m, 4,428ft). The Panamericana goes to the left and runs close to a series of crescent dunes.

987   **La Joya** (1,270m, 4,165ft) is where the Ministry of Agriculture have created a huge irrigation project in the middle of the desert. The plateau extends for another 37km (23 miles) until the road drops

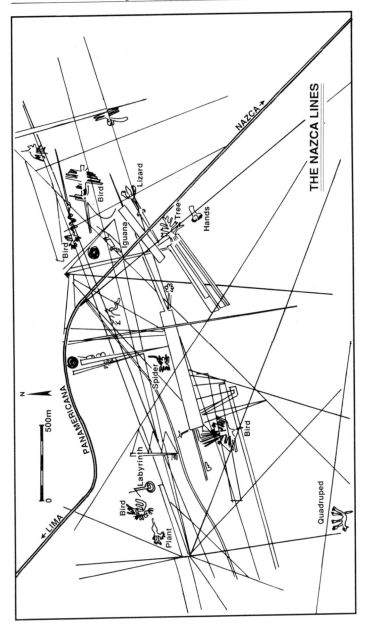

THE NAZCA LINES

down steeply into the Tambo Valley.

1,041   **Tambo Bridge** (140m, 460ft). Just before the road crosses the Río Tambo, there is a right turn along a poor road that leads eventually to **Mollendo** (see above). The following newly built section of the Panamericana climbs through a series of gorges with interesting erosion patterns. It returns to another flat plateau that is only once interrupted by a gully. The road runs in a straight line for 23km (14 miles) before a dry valley provides welcome relief, with a steep climb from 1,450m (4,756ft) down to 1,220m (4,000ft). The road climbs up again to 1,500m (4,920ft) and crosses another dry valley, before it finally approaches the green Moquegua Valley.

1,139   Turning for **Moquegua** (1,250m, 4,100ft). The town of Moquegua lies just 5km (3 miles) upstream at an altitude of 1,430m, 4,690ft. It has recently enjoyed a boom thanks to the opening up of copper mines at nearby Toquepala (see below). Three kilometres beyond the town is one of the finest tourist hotels in Peru, perched on a hill with some beautiful views. The Panamericana runs for a short distance through the green valley, then climbs up again into the desert via a series of beautifully eroded cliffs, with the green of the valley bottom forming a stark contrast to the barrenness of the mountains.

1,185   Turning for **Ilo** (1,120m, 3,673ft).

5b EXCURSION TO ILO

The metalled road descends a dry valley in company with the new Toquepala Railway. At about 600m (1,968ft) there is a view of the sea. The town of Ilo (47km, 29 miles) is in an unlikely location in the middle of a waterless desert. It owes its existence to a sea-water purification plant and a large copper smelting works on the coast 16km (10 miles) to the north, which is based on ores from the Toquepala mines. There is a new tourist hotel at Ilo.

1,185   Turning for **Ilo** (1,120m, 3,673ft).

1,203   Turning for **Toquepala** (64km, 40 miles), Peru's largest copper mine.

1,212   **Camiara** (390m, 1,279ft). The road crosses the Río Locumba and then enters the most monotonous section of the whole coastal route, running in a completely straight line across the desert for two stretches of 21km (13 miles) and 33km (20 miles) respectively.

1,292   **Tacna** (570m, 1,869ft). The town of Tacna has an air of smartness and tidyness, but offers nothing of special interest to tourists. However, it does make a good resting point for travellers going on into Chile, with plenty of Chilean currency available from stalls along the palm-lined avenue next to the tourist hotel.

1,302   Turning for **Boca del Río** (47km, 29 miles). A metalled road leads down to a primitive seaside resort with a fine sandy beach.

Border post. From here it is only another 20km (12½ miles) to **Arica**,   1,328
Chile's most northerly city, where accommodation is available.

Route 6 Arequipa to Puno (Lake Titicaca)

Map: page 118
Overnight accommodation: Juliaca
Railway: 9pm daily, 7.40am Mon, Wed, Fri (10 hours); seats bookable in buffet car, tickets available from travel agents
Bus transport: buses and *colectivos* to Arequipa-Juliaca (9-10 hours), with connections to Puno

Road and rail follow completely different routes for this difficult journey through the mountains. The railway climbs to 4,490m (14,727ft), while the road goes even higher to 4,700m (15,416ft). It is therefore vital to take precautions against altitude sickness, although a short stay in Arequipa (2,360m, 7,740ft) will be of some help in getting used to the altitude. Most travellers prefer the more comfortable rail trip to being jolted and twisted along the rather inferior road link. However, the journey takes at least nine hours in both cases.

6a THE RAIL JOURNEY

Arequipa (2,360m, 7,740ft). The first part of the journey goes through some quite spectacular scenery. The track runs along the foot of Chachani (6,075m, 19,926ft), with wide vistas across the coastal desert and to the snow-covered peak of Ampato (6,310m, 20,697ft).

Yura (30km [18.6 miles], 2,750m [9,020ft]) is famous for its thermal baths (see Chapter 4), but little can be seen of it from the railway apart from a rather ugly cement works. After Yura the railway starts to twist and climb up the valley below the western slopes of Chachani.

Pampa de Arrieros (71km [44 miles], 3,750m [12,300ft]). Soon after this station the landscape levels out somewhat. The track runs along the edge of a *puna* plateau grazed by llamas, alpacas and vicuñas (these have recently been re-introduced). It then begins to wind its way upwards between a series of round-topped mountains covered with grass.

Sumbay (113km [70 miles], 4,137m [13,370ft]). There is a view of the north-eastern side of Misti, which is free of snow.

Vincocaya (154km [95 miles], 4,430m [14,530ft]). The railway crosses the broad level plateau of Imata.

Crucero Alto (187km [116 miles], 4,477m [14,684ft]). The highest

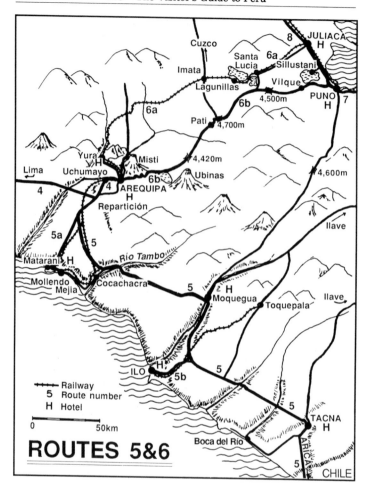

ROUTES 5&6

point in the whole journey.

Lagunillas (207km [128 miles], 4,360m [14,300ft]) is a small mining village next to a lake, which is visible to the left of the track. The section which follows goes through some beautiful scenery. For more than half an hour one can look down into the silvery waters of this irregularly shaped lake enclosed by grassy round-topped mountains.

Saracocha (4,220m, 13,841ft). The railway winds downhill to Lake Saracocha, where it meets the road to Juliaca.

Santa Lucia (238km [147 miles], 4,033m [13,228ft]). From here onwards both road and rail follow the valley of the Río Cabanillas, which flows down into the great plateau known as the Altiplano.

Juliaca (304km [188 miles], 3,830m [12,562ft]). There is a long stop at this important railway junction, where the night train from Arequipa connects with the train to Cuzco.

Puno (350km [217 miles], 3,380m [11,086ft]). The town of Puno and Lake Titicaca are described in Chapter 4.

6b THE ROAD JOURNEY

Arequipa (2,360m, 7,740ft). The best route out of the city is along the Calle Mercaderes (see Arequipa, Chapter 4), turning left in front of the hospital and then right after about 700m.   0

Jesús (2,620m, 8,593ft). The metalled section of the road ends at the thermal baths of Jesús. It then becomes narrow and very rough, but is usually kept up sufficiently to enable cars to get through. During the rainy season, however, there can be problems crossing the Río Andamayo, sometimes leading to severe delays. The road climbs steeply across the slopes of Pichu Pichu (5,660m, 18,564ft), with marvellous views across the valley to the volcanic cone of Misti (5,820m, 19,089ft). After a short tunnel the road crosses the first pass (4,380m, 14,366ft).   9

Laguna Salinas (4,308m, 14,130ft) is a salt lake situated in a mountain basin with no outlet. Flocks of flamingoes wade around along the banks and shallows. The lake is surrounded by snowy peaks on all sides. One of the most impressive of these is a volcano called Ubinas (5,670m, 18,597ft), whose symmetrically shaped cone towers above the right-hand shore of the lake. The road continues from Laguna Salinas over another pass (4,420m, 14,497ft).   64

Pati (4,280m, 15,809ft) is a godforsaken little village with a steep slope behind it, which the road proceeds to clamber up.   119

Turning for **Imata** (4,600m, 15,088ft).   124

Toroya Pass (4,700m, 15,416ft). The road reaches its highest point, then descends gradually through the *puna* landscape.   150

Río Tincopalca (4,150m, 13,612ft). The road crosses the river valley and then climbs over another pass (4,350m, 14,268ft).   164

Turning for **Juliaca** (4,300m, 14,104ft). The road to Juliaca (86km, 53 miles) is often impassable in the rainy season. It runs down to Lake Saracocha and then parallel to the railway along the valley of the Río Cabanillas. The road to Puno crosses one final pass (4,500m, 14,760ft) before descending into the Altiplano, the vast plateau where Lake Titicaca lies.   187

244 **Mañazo** (3,930m, 12,890ft) is the first place of any size since Arequipa.

254 **Vilque** (3,860m, 12,660ft). The church next to the main square has a beautifully carved stone façade. The cross to the right of the west door is typical of this region; it is decorated with a sun and a moon — signs of ancient Amerindian gods.

263 **Tiquillaca** (3,880m, 12,726ft). The road crosses a shallow pass (4,080m, 13,382ft) and then descends towards Lake Titicaca.

283 Turning for **Juliaca**. The road at last meets the metalled road that runs from Juliaca to Puno.

288 **Puno** (350km [217 miles], 3,380m [11,086ft]). The town of Puno and Lake Titicaca are described in Chapter 4.

Route 7 Puno to Bolivia

Map: page 121

Overnight accommodation: Copacabana

Bus transport: Through bus services are infrequent and expensive (Transturin Puno, Jirón Tacna 201), but *colectivos* are to be found everywhere. The best routes are also the cheapest ($US10-20 Puno to La Paz). Passengers must change vehicles at the Bolivian border; Copacabana is preferable to Desaguadero, where a missed connection can leave passengers stranded. Promises to wait at sightseeing spots are only honoured if the driver is paid afterwards!

Boat transport: The combined bus and boat trip offered by Crillón Tours is simple, comfortable and well organised, but it is not cheap (about $US80, lunch inclusive). The boat goes from from Juli to Huatajata, with short stops on the Island of the Sun and at Copacabana, and connects with a bus to La Paz.

The route via Copacabana is longer but much more scenic, and the roads are much better, being metalled throughout. The Desaguadero route is less desirable, for although it passes the famous ruins of Tiahuanaco, there is rarely enough time for bus passengers to see them properly. The road is metalled all the way to the Bolivian border, and bypasses all the towns along the route. But the beautiful churches of Juli, Pomata and Zepita are well worth a short detour from the main road.

0 **Puno**. The road runs close to the low shores of the lake. The Hotel Tambo de Titicaca stands on a rocky promontory just before Chucuito.

21 **Chucuito**. The large church is surrounded by a galleried courtyard, where mass baptisms were once held.

54 **Ilave**. There is a turning here for Tarata (231km, 46 miles) and Tacna

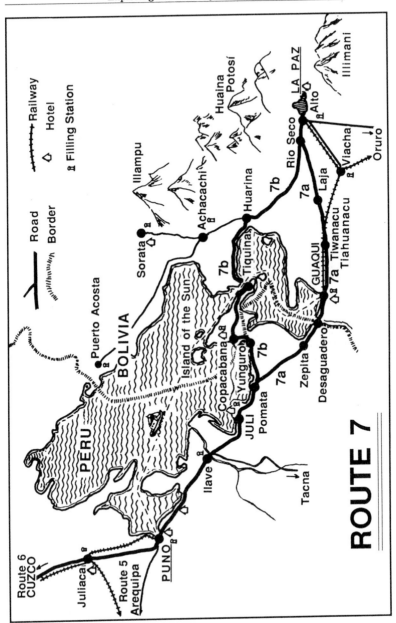

ROUTE 7

La Paz, the Bolivian capital

(320km, 198 miles) on the Pacific coast, forming the best road link between central Bolivia and northern Chile.

79 **Juli** (3,890m, 12,759ft). The new road bypasses this interesting little town, which is famous for its four large sixteenth- and seventeenth-century churches. They were built at a time when Juli was a centre for the training of Jesuit missionaries for the jungle. All are within easy reach of the main square.

San Pedro is the main church in the town. It stands in the square opposite an old colonial house that once belonged to the Inquisition. The four beautifully carved plateresque side altars are particularly impressive. The Mother and Child to the right of the entrance show Indian influence, both in the painting technique and in the way the child is swaddled.

San Juan is the most interesting of the churches, and has now been turned into a museum. The walls are covered with large paintings with highly carved gilt frames. But the most impressive feature is the fine Indian-style stonework around the columns and windows, the vestry door and the side altars.

Santa Cruz stands next to a remarkable Jesuit cemetery from which there is a remarkable view across the lake. In clear weather the white peaks of the Cordillera Real or 'Royal Mountains' are visible high above the lake.

122

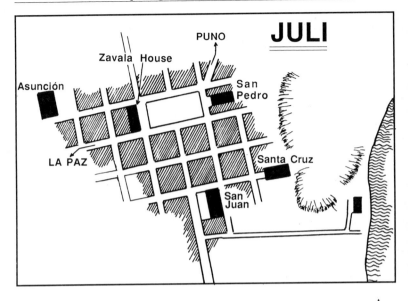

The Church of the Assumption is sadly almost completely destroyed. But the door arch and the remains of the tower show that it was a remarkably large and elegant church for a town of this size.

Pomata. The large village church is yet another good example of the rather ponderous Andean baroque style. The marvellous interior stonework is particularly impressive. 104

7a POMATA • DESAGUADERO • TIAHUANACO • LA PAZ

Turning for **Copacabana**. The road forks soon after Pomata. The right fork leads along the shortest route to La Paz via Desaguadero. 110

Zepita. This poor little village is remarkable for its unusual church. The grass on the roof shows that the church is continuing to decay. But the carvings inside are a wonderful expression of Indian piety amid the great poverty of the Altiplano. 137

Desaguadero border station. 146

Guaqui is a port at the southern end of Lake Titicaca. Up until the great floods of 1986, it was the landing place for both freight and passengers, who then travelled on to La Paz by train. 166

Tiahuanaco. The ruins of Tiwanacu, as the Indians call it, are situated immediately beyond the village. This is probably the most important pre-Inca site in the whole of the Andean region. The great 188 monolithic statues are particularly famous, together with the massive Gate of the Sun that is hewn out of one block of stone.

The road climbs a little after Tiahuanaco, giving a good view of the long chain of the Cordillera Real. The mighty Illimani (6,462m, 21,195ft) forms a separate block.

248 **El Alto** (4,082m, 13,388ft). This outer suburb of La Paz is perched high up on the edge of the plateau, looking down over the capital spread out across the valley below.

261 **La Paz** (3,577m, 11,732ft). The Bolivian capital.

7b POMATA • COPACABANA • LA PAZ

110 Turning for **Desaguadero**. The road forks very soon after Pomata. The road to the left is for Copacabana.

133 **Yunguro** is closely followed by the **Bolivian border**.

144 **Copacabana**. This popular place of pilgrimage has a number of hotels. But these are usually fully booked well in advance for the first week in August, when the town's main attraction, the great festival of the Dark Virgin of the Lake, takes place. There are folk dancers from all over the Altiplano region, making it a truly unforgettable experience. The road from Copacabana runs along a steep cliff above the shore, with marvellous views of the Cordillera Real.

186 **Tiquina**. Ferries carry vehicles across the 800m (2,624ft) wide channel that links the two main parts of Lake Titicaca.

209 **Huatajata** is the landing point for boats from Puno. The road leaves the lake soon afterwards, and continues across the Altiplano along the foot of the Cordillera Real.

284 **La Paz** (3,577m, 11,732ft). The Bolivian capital.

Route 8 Puno to Cuzco, the Inca Capital

Map: page 129
Overnight accommodation: primitive hotel in Sicuani
Railway: Mon-Fri via Juliaca (10 hours); seats bookable in buffet car (slightly dearer than 1st class), tickets available from travel agents
Bus transport: frequent *colectivos* to Juliaca; several services a day to Cuzco

Large sections of the road are very poor. It follows the same route as the railway over the La Raya Pass. The scenery is less interesting than on other routes through the mountains, but gives a good impression of the *puna* landscape of the central Andes. Car travellers should not miss the ruined temple near Raqchi and the beautiful church at Andahuaylillas.

0 **Puno** (3,830m, 12,562ft). The road is metalled as far as Juliaca. It

climbs to about 200m (656ft) above the level of Lake Titicaca, giving a fine view over the town with the lake and the modern university quarter.

Juliaca (3,830m, 12,562ft) is an important road and rail junction between Puno, Arequipa and Cuzco, and is well known for the alpaca knitwear that is available from the local market. The road to Cuzco runs in a straight line from Juliaca across a level plateau that was once covered by Lake Titicaca. 19

Pucará (3,900m, 12,792ft) is famous for its local pottery, most of which is made in the nearby village of **Santiago de Pupuja** (8km, 5 miles) on the road to Azangaro. This is the home of the brightly coloured china bulls that are available throughout the country, and that are almost the trade mark for Peruvian handicraft skills. Santiago de Pupuja also has one of the most beautiful churches in the whole of the Altiplano. 103

Ayaviri (3,910m, 12,824ft) is an important market town. 135

Santa Rosa (3,990m, 13,087ft). From here onwards the valley becomes gradually narrower. The snow-covered peak of Cunurana (5,440m, 17,843ft) becomes visible ahead to the right. The road climbs gently through the *puna* among the grazing alpacas. 177

La Raya Pass (4,313m, 14,146ft). The road crosses the watershed between the Lake Titicaca and Amazonian basins. The glaciated slopes of Çhimboya (5,490m, 18,007ft) are visible across a nearby valley to the right. 206

Sicuani (3,650m, 11,972ft) is the largest town along the route, but has little of interest to tourists. 246

San Pedro (3,540m, 11,611ft). 266

Raqchi. The little church about 100m to the right of the road is typical of the plateau region. Not far from here are the substantial ruins of the famous Temple of Viracocha, which was built in the fifteenth century. The walls are up to 12m (39ft) high, and are built of polished stone blocks topped with sun-dried bricks. 269

Checacupe (3,430m, 11,250ft). The massive church with its rich interior decorations forms a stark contrast to the extreme poverty of this small mountain village. 288

Urcos (3,150m, 10,332ft) is situated next to a small heavily silted lake. There is a small Sunday market here that is so far unspoilt by tourism. 339

Andahuaylillas (3,090m, 10,135ft). This small village conceals one of the finest churches in Peru (see page 183). The road climbs out of the Urubamba Valley via a modest pass. To the left of the road are the remains of fortifications that once guarded the Inca capital (see 346

Rumicalca in Chapter 4).

354   Turning for **Piquillacta**. This major pre-Inca site is situated 1km (half a mile) to the right of the road (see page 183).

356   Turning for **Paucartambo** (77km, 48 miles) and also for Pisac in the Urubamba Valley.

361   Turning for **Oropesa**, a small village across the valley with a fine church (see page 183).

386   **Cuzco** (3,400m, 11,152ft). The former capital of the Inca empire is described in detail in Chapter 4.

Route 9 Cuzco to Huancayo

Maps: pages 109 and 129
Overnight accommodation: Abancay, Andahuaylas, Ayacucho, Huanta, Huancavelica
Public transport: no through connections; 5-7 days needed to get through; twice weekly buses Cuzco-Ayacucho (40 hours according to timetable); Cuzco-Abancay-Nazca-Lima (Nazca 27-30 hours, Lima 45-60 hours)

The roads to Ayacucho are often closed due to the activities of the *Sendero Luminoso* or 'Shining Path', who are variously dubbed as criminals, terrorists or liberation fighters depending on the speaker's point of view. The army keep tight security, but attacks are nonetheless an everyday occurrence. At all events car drivers should ask local lorry drivers for exact information on road conditions and whether the *guerrilleros* are 'under control'. No one without a knowledge of Spanish should even attempt the road journey between Abancay and Huanaco.

The road is extremely narrow and rough from Abancay onwards, and there are so many twists that the average speed is never more than 30km/h (20mph). The route should be avoided during the rainy season between December and April, as it is often blocked by mud or landslides, while the view is often restricted by fog.

The direct road link between Ayacucho and Huancayo along the Mantaro Valley was destroyed by a natural disaster in 1977. A massive landslide caused a dam to burst, turning the valley into a large lake. An enormous flood wave swept down the valley, reaching a depth of 200m (656ft) at the narrower points. The reconstruction work has not yet been finished, and traffic is diverted via a different route that is given below. The alternative route via Huancavelica is very much longer.

0   **Cuzco** (3,400m, 11,152ft). The road climbs steeply out of the city (see map page 161) and crosses a pass into the Anta Valley.

16   Turning for **Chinchero**, a small village with an Inca ruin and a Sunday

market.

Izcuchaca (3,340m, 10,955). There is a turning here for Urubamba (see page 177). Afterwards the road becomes fairly straight as it climbs gently up the valley. 25

Huillque Pass (3,900m, 12,792ft). The road begins a steep and twisty descent into the next valley. 51

Limatambo (2,650m, 8,692ft). The road climbs down along the Limatambo Valley into the deep gorge of the Río Apurímac. 78

Apurímac Bridge (1,800m, 5,904ft). The road climbs precariously up the opposite side of the gorge, with magnificent views of the snowy peaks of Amparay (5,290m, 17,351ft) and Salcantay (6,270m, 20,565ft). 98

Curahuasi (2,680m, 8,790ft). 123

Turning for **Saihuite**. Only 500m (1,640ft) down from the road is the little explored archaeological site of Saihuite (Saywite). The most interesting find here is a stone block about 4m (13ft) across that has been carved out to show hills, houses, cultivation terraces and irrigation channels. Some experts see it as a kind of Inca map, while others think it is an altar belonging to some unknown cult. 152

Socchaccasa Pass (4,020m, 13,185ft). The innumerable hairpins along the steep descent into Abancay provide some marvellous views of the town and across to the usually snow-covered peak of Amparay. 158

Abancay (2,460m, 8,068ft). The capital of the department of Apurímac has nothing of particular interest, but is one of the few places along the route with overnight accommodation. 197

Turning for **Chalhuanca** and **Nazca**. See page 205. 205

Pachachaca Bridge (2,030m, 6,658ft). The narrow road climbs steeply out of the gorge in a never-ending series of hairpins. As many as 60km (37 miles) from Abancay, the town is still visible far below across the valley. 212

Huayllaccasa Pass (4,100m, 13,448ft). 297

Andahuaylas (2,900m, 9,512ft) is a small town in a valley full of eucalyptus trees. 333

Talavera (2,800m, 9,184ft). After crossing the Río Chumbao, the road begins to climb another pass. 338

Soraccocha Pass (4,150m, 13,612ft). 382

Chincheros (2,800m, 9,184ft). The road climbs down into the deep gorge of the Río Pampas. 421

Pampas Bridge (2,010m, 6,592ft). The road runs for a short distance 451

Detail from the altar in San Juan church, Juli

along the bottom of the gorge, where it is hot enough for sugar cane, bananas and enormous cacti. It then climbs quickly back up into the mountains where llamas and alpacas graze.

527 **Huamina Pass** (4,420m, 14,497ft). The highest point of the whole route.

549 **Tocto Pass**.

593 **Ayacucho** (2,760m, 9,052ft). The old departmental capital with its many churches is described in Chapter 4, together with some trips into the area around. There is overnight accommodation available.

607 Turning for **San Miguel** and **Quinua** (see page 150). The road continues through a landscape of deep limestone gorges.

641 **Huanta** (2,600m, 8,528ft) is a busy little town offering simple overnight accommodation. Further down the valley the vegetation becomes increasingly sparse until it soon consists of nothing more than cacti, algarrobos and other thorny succulents.

669 **Mayoc** (2,200m, 7,216ft). The road enters the Mantaro Valley, which forms a deep and difficult gorge further upstream. This was the site of the great flood disaster of 1977. The road now bypasses this section by climbing up the opposite side of the valley.

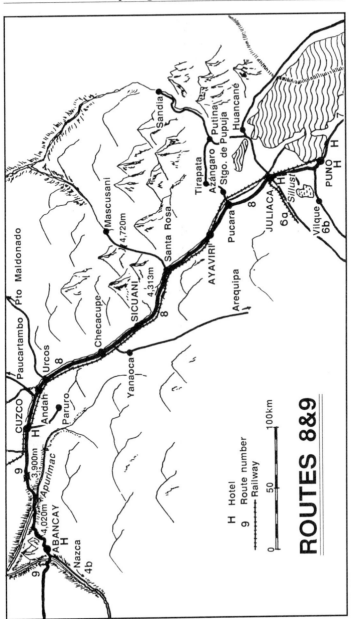

ROUTES 8&9

694 **Churcampa** (3,260m, 10,692ft).

722 Turning for **San Pedro de Coris**.

824 **Pampas** (3,270m, 10,725ft). After this small town the road crosses another pass (3,940m, 12,923ft) before finally descending into the broad Huancayo basin.

893 **Huancayo** (3,270m, 10,725ft). This major market town is described in Route 3c. There is overnight accommodation available. There is a good road link to Lima (298km, 185 miles) via the Carretera Central.

9a AYACUCHO • HUANCAVELICA • HUANCAYO

0 **Ayacucho** (2,760m, 9,052ft). The road crosses a pass (3,400m, 11,152ft) into the valley of the Río Apacheta, which it then follows upstream.

98 **Apacheta Pass** (4,750m, 15,580ft).

146 **Pilpichaca** (4,090m, 13,415ft).

166 Turning for **Castrovirreyna** and **Pisco** (see Route 4a). The road crosses the **Chonta Pass** (4,850m, 15,908ft), then descends gradually along a valley towards Huancavelica.

214 **Huancavelica** (3,500m, 11,480ft). The departmental capital is an old mining town that flourished during the colonial period on account of the nearby mercury mines. The mercury was needed for extracting silver, and was carried by mule and llama through the mountains to the famous silver mines of Potosí in what is now Bolivia. The churches from this period contain some beautiful baroque altars, but they are sadly falling into decay. There is tourist accommodation available. The road to Huancayo runs across to the steep slopes above the Mantaro Valley, which it climbs down via a series of hairpins.

322 **Izcuchaca** (2,830m, 9,282ft). The road crosses the Río Mantaro via a remarkable old bridge, and continues towards Huancayo via another pass (3,800m, 12,464ft).

390 **Huancayo** (3,270m, 10,725ft). See Route 3c.

4

THE MAIN TOURIST CENTRES

Arequipa

Altitude: 2,360m (7,740ft)
Population: 386,000
Air links: Lima, Cuzco, Puno
Rail links: Cuzco 641km [397 miles] (16 hours), Puno 350km [217 miles] (9 hours)
Road links: Lima 1,010km [626 miles] (Route 4), Tacna 393km [243 miles] (Route 5), Puno 283km [175 miles] (Route 6); bus not recommended to Lima (18 hours), Tacna, Puno or Cuzco (24 hours)

Misti (5,830m, 19,122ft) may not be as famous as Fujiyama, but it is at least as beautiful, especially after the January-March rains, when its perfect white cone seems almost to hover over the 'white city' of Arequipa. But as soon as the rains are over, the sun gets to work and the snow disappears — not only from Misti with its sulphurous clouds, but also from the neighbouring volcanoes, Pichu Pichu (5,660m, 18,564ft) and Chachani (6,075m, 19,926ft). These three giants in a cloudless blue sky are part of Arequipa's unique atmosphere.

Arequipa was founded by the Spaniards as early as 1540, so impressed were they at the greenness of this oasis in the desert, whose existence was assured by the water stored in the nearby snow caps. They called the city the *Villa de Nuestra Señora de la Asunción del Valle Hermoso de Arequipa*, or 'City of Our Lady of the Assumption in the Beautiful Valley of Arequipa'. Only the last element of this title has been preserved; it probably came originally from an Aymará expression meaning 'behind the mountains'.

The mountains and desert are not the only features that determine the city's unique character. The architecture is probably its most distinctive feature of all, due to the shortage of timber; the frequency of earthquakes, which have several times destroyed the city; and the extreme isolation due to poor transport links across the surrounding mountains and deserts, though this has since been ameliorated by the building of the railway in 1870.

In the absence of timber, most buildings are constructed out of a light-coloured material called tuff that was spewed out of the crater of Chachani during the Tertiary Period. This material is easy to work with, and its light colour gives the 'white city' an air of smartness and beauty.

In order to minimise the earthquake danger, the walls of the buildings are supported by massive buttresses, while the few remaining doors and windows are relatively small. The large expanses of wall are decorated with garlands, figures, coats of arms and other ornamentations. This fascinating mixture of Spanish and Indian elements is also to be found on some of the modern buildings.

Arequipa enjoys a delightful climate thanks to its moderate altitude, which also makes it the ideal place for acclimatising oneself to higher altitudes before going on to visit places such as Cuzco or La Paz. One or two whole days are needed to do justice to this fascinating city. The most important things to see are the Santa Catalina Convent and La Compañía.

TOUR 1
Length: 1.5km (about a mile)
Map: page 133

This suggested itinerary gives a good impression of the city's strange architecture and its unusual situation. All the major colonial buildings are included, while still leaving enough time for a wander among the souvenir shops. (The numbers in brackets correspond to those on the map.)

The Jesuits in the seventeenth century spared no effort to ensure that their church, **La Compañía** (1), would outshine the others, both in its beauty and in its ability to withstand earthquakes. How well they achieved this was amply demonstrated in the severe earthquakes of 1958 and 1960, which did very little damage to the structure. But the artistic aspects were never compromised, and the gorgeously carved façade is one of the most remarkable of its kind. The naively drawn figures and leaf-like scrollwork show a strong Indian influence, while the overall concept is pure Spanish baroque.

The interior has sadly fallen victim to the classical ardour of the nineteenth century. Only some of the altars have retained their original baroque decorations, especially the main altar, whose beautiful gilt carvings are typical of their period. The rich wall paintings, on the other hand, are now obscured by a thick layer of plaster. The 1960 earthquake led to the fortunate rediscovery of the old vestry. This was restored in 1969 by two Spanish painters, and now provides a colourful impression of the church's original decorations. The vestry

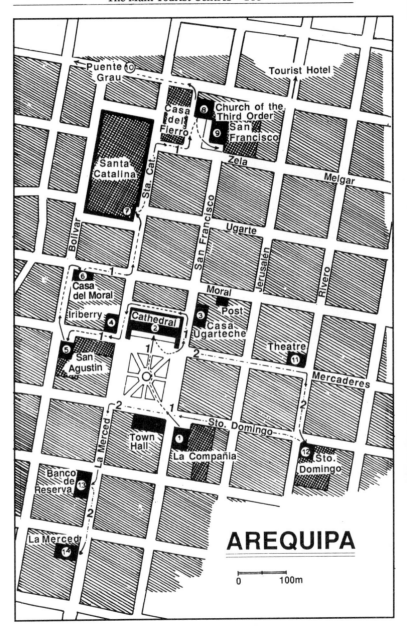

AREQUIPA

0   100m

Painting in the vestry of La Compañía

is only open for short periods during the day, but it should on no account be left out of the visit.

Next to the church in the Calle Santo Domingo is the entrance to the former Jesuit Monastery (Convento La Compañía), which was renovated in 1974. The tuff in the columns, arches and friezes has been beautifully ornamented in the distinctive Arequipa style. The many courtyards are occupied by restaurants and souvenir shops.

The large **cathedral** (2) occupies the whole of the north side of the colonnaded Plaza de Armas, framed by the snowy cap of Chachani. It is a classical structure built in the last century, and the only items of interest are the carved choirstalls and a few statues of saints.

Casa Ugarteche (3) (Ricketts House), Calle San Francisco 108, is one of the finest examples of Arequipan architecture. The carving above the entrance includes the badge of the Jesuits, who built it as a seminary in the eighteenth century. A quick glance along the passage to the right of the house will reveal a solid buttress that affords protection against earthquakes. Immediately opposite the house is a rather romantic passageway leading along the back of the

Santa Catalina
Convent, Arequipa

cathedral. It is usually lined with artists' and souvenir stalls.

 Casa Iriberry (4), Calle Santa Catalina 101, built in 1793, is simpler in design than the Casa Ugarteche, but its elegance is beyond dispute. It is a marvellous period example of a well-to-do Arequipan residence.

 Across the Calle Mercadores from the Casa Iriberry is **San Agustín** (5), the old Augustinian monastery, which now houses the University of Arequipa. The church is at the opposite end of the monastery. Its beautiful carvings are comparable with those of La Compañía, but have unfortunately been damaged by earthquakes. However, the glorious façade has been preserved and is a masterpiece of *mestizo* architecture.

 Casa Moral (6), Calle Moral 318 was named after the old mulberry tree growing in the courtyard (*moral* is Spanish for 'mulberry'). It is one of the finest houses in the city, with a perfect blend of baroque architecture with Indian elements. The carved door lintel depicts a puma with snake tongues that is reminiscent of Tiahuanaco, while the Spanish baroque is fully expressed in the white tuff walls, the coat of arms above the doorway and the windows with their iron grills and double arches. The interior is open to the public. The rooms are filled with heavy colonial-style furniture, while the walls are hung with old paintings from the Cuzco school.

NB It is worth noting at this point that the next port of call, Santa Catalina, is in an area frequented by gangs of young thieves, so visitors who are alone should take a taxi at this stage.

Santa Catalina Convent (7), Calle Santa Catalina 301, was finally opened to the public in 1970, following heavy restoration work, and the mysteries behind those high white tuff walls were at last unveiled to the outside world. What was revealed was a complete walled city from the sixteenth and seventeenth centuries, which had preserved its original character thanks to its total seclusion.

The long windowless walls, the narrow streets with their buttresses and the beautiful cloisters are all reminiscent of Moroccan towns — a sign of the Moorish influences which the Andalusians brought across to South America. The colours of the walls are gloriously contrasted, with some being of dazzling white tuff, while others are covered with plaster painted in brown, ochre or light blue.

The route is marked out by arrows, and leads from the entrance into the visiting room (*locutorios*), which shows how strict the closed orders were. No outside visitor was allowed to see any of the nuns, and it was a great privilege even to have a short conversation through a wooden grill. The route continues through a cloister with ochre-coloured walls to the white-walled novices' cloister (*claustro de novicias*), which was kept separate from the rest of the convent. This was where the novices spent their probationary period, testing their vocation and preparing for full acceptance into the order. The next port of call is the orangery (*claustro de los naranjos*), where the light-blue walls are covered with paintings with mystical themes. This is followed by the Calle Málaga, where the infirmary (*enfermería*) once was. Among the exhibits in the small museum are two valuable paintings by the famous Cuzco painter Diego Quispe Tito: the *Archangel Michael* and the *Nativity of Christ*.

Returning to the orangery, one then enters the lovely Calle Córdoba with its colourful flower decorations. This leads out of the cloistered part of the convent into the older more town-like area. The buildings here presumably existed before the convent was founded and were taken over for the nuns' quarters. Immediately to the left is the closed new cloister, where the remaining nuns still live in seclusion. There follow a series of little brown houses, mostly consisting of no more than a bedroom and a kitchen, though some had a servant's room too. The Calle Toledo is the longest street inside the convent, and leads to the washing area (*lavandería*). Here beneath the shade of a long-needled Chile pine is a stone channel that once fed water into the earthenware washing troughs either side.

The Calle Burgos is lined with larger houses and a garden, and must therefore have been a wealthier quarter before the foundation of the convent. The next street, Calle Granada, is even wider and more stately, and is overshadowed by the white dome of the church. The last building on the left is particularly interesting since it was used by the nuns as a large kitchen for preparing special feasts. Pots, pans, pastry moulds and other cooking utensils are on display here.

The Plaza Socodobé is named after the famous square in Toledo in Spain. The well in the middle once supplied a whole network of water channels leading to all parts of the convent. The corner building was the nuns' bath-house.

The guided tour now leads back into the cloistered area, past the large dining hall (*refectorio*) and back into the ochre-walled main cloister (*claustro mayor*). The side passages are hung with numerous paintings depicting the life of the Holy Family. The tiny cells along the side of the church were where the nuns made their confessions. The cloister is surrounded by long halls full of museum exhibits. Most of the paintings on display are by unknown masters from the Cuzco school and depict scenes from the life of St Catharine (Santa Catalina).

Plaza San Francisco (8), lined with jacaranda trees is one of the finest in the city and shows remarkable architectural harmony. The north side is occupied by the rather sparsely decorated white walls of the **Church of the Third Order**. The long building along the west side is the **Casa Del Fierro**. Originally founded as a school by a rich Arequipan called Del Fierro, it now houses a local handicrafts shop.

The white-walled church of **San Francisco** (9) to the east of the square is similarly sparsely decorated. It has been continually rebuilt after earthquakes, and the result is rather shabby, especially inside.

Some visitors may wish to break off the tour at this stage, while others may care to walk the 400m to the **Puente Grau** (10). This bridge was named after the great naval commander who was the hero of the Saltpetre War. The Puente Grau is not particularly interesting in itself, but it does provide a marvellous view of the city and the mountains around.

TOUR 2
Length: 1km (half a mile)
Map: page 133

The second tour goes along the major shopping streets past some interesting new buildings, whose design was inspired by the old colonial traditions of Arequipa. They are indicative of a very distinctive modern trend in local architecture. Apart from these new buildings, there are still a number of old colonial churches, monasteries

Casa Ugarteche

and private mansions to be seen.

The starting point is the Plaza de Armas, turning right in front of the cathedral along a busy shopping street called Calle Mercadores.

Situated two blocks along on the left, the **theatre** (11) together with the bank next to it are typical examples of modern Arequipan architecture. The florid tuff carvings have been revived, but the solid stone façades have been broken up to allow more light in. This change has been made possible thanks to modern earthquake-proof building techniques.

Santo Domingo church (12), Calle Santo Domingo, was badly damaged in the great 1958 and 1960 earthquakes, but has now been largely restored. The typically florid carvings on the façade are especially fine. Also of interest are the choir and the palm-lined cloister, which can be viewed from the street.

When returning to the Plaza de Armas along the Calle Santo Domingo, it is worth glancing at the bank premises along the first side street (Calle de San Juan de Dios), which are typical of the new Arequipan style. The tour continues south from the Plaza de Armas along the Calle La Merced.

The **Banco de Reserva** (13) (Casa Goyeneche) building has been carefully restored, and provides a unique opportunity of seeing what a rich colonial residence used to look like from the inside. Two of the rooms adjoining the inner courtyard have been turned into museum pieces filled with valuable period furniture.

La Merced (14), the oldest church in the city has not been spared the ravages of the many earthquakes. But it has frequently been restored, and has thus preserved much of its original appearance. The altar is covered with rich baroque gilt carving. The adjoining monastery is remarkable for its Moorish-style entrance and the chapter house.

Excursions from Arequipa

No visit to Arequipa is complete without a trip to Yanahuara, which requires no more than an hour to visit and can even be reached on foot. There are further opportunities for walking in the park at Selva Alegre near the tourist hotel, and also at Yura only 30km (18 miles) away by rail. The nearby salt lake (Laguna Salinas) is a must for all car travellers with time to spare who are able to withstand altitudes — unless of course they will be passing it on the way to Puno.

Much is made these days of the trip to the 'deepest canyon in the world', the Cañon del Colca. But it is only one of many such canyons that are to be found in the Andes. The scenery is undoubtedly very impressive, but cannot compare with that of the Cordillera Blanca and the Cañon del Pato (see page 185ff), and it would be a pity to miss that trip for the sake of this one.

The desert tour, on the other hand, is much to be recommended for those without any experience of the desert. The local travel agents may advise against it, but the desert for them is an everyday experience.

Travellers with a taste for adventure should try a trip to the Majes Valley, possibly culminating in a Grand Canyon-style dinghy ride up the rapids of the Río Colca.

Apart from the trip to Mollendo, these excursions are hardly possible by public transport. But travel agents offer a number of excursions, some of which are package deals with overnight accommodation and/or an English-speaking guide. However, a taxi may be cheaper for a party of several people. Anyone hiring a vehicle should make sure it will run properly at altitudes over 4,000m (13,120ft), and should be prepared for driving under difficult conditions without proper signposts.

1 TO THE CHURCHES AT THE FOOT OF CHACHANI

The whole trip takes no more than an hour by car, while Yanahuara is only half an hour's walk away from the Plaza de Armas. There are some beautiful sights along the way, with wide panoramas, old streets full of Andalusian charm and two churches that are among the finest in the region.

The road to Yanahuara turns right off the main road about 500m beyond the bridge over the Río Chili (Puente Grau). **Yanahuara** has long since become a suburb of Arequipa, and there are modern estates as well as some delightful old Andalusian-style streets with wrought-iron lampstands and baskets of flowers. The palm-lined main square is particularly fine, and the adjoining terrace commands a magnificent view of the 'white city'. The old tuff church rivals La Compañía down in the city with its decorative carvings.

To get to Cayma by car, one should return to the main road, continue out of the city and take a later right turn for Cayma. **Cayma** is known as the 'balcony of Arequipa' because of the marvellous city views. The main square is less impressive than that of Yanahuara, but the church is another jewel of Arequipan architecture.

From Cayma it is possible to extend the journey to the thermal springs of Yura (see below).

2 TO THE LAGUNA SALINAS

A day trip to the salt lake in the *puna* is one of the most memorable of the many short excursions that are possible from Arequipa. But it is only worth undertaking if the weather is clear. The lake is on the road to Puno, so the journey is described in Route 6b, Chapter 3.

Close to the lake there is a right turn along a track leading to the foot of a volcano called Ubinas, which can be climbed in about four to five hours.

3 TO THE THERMAL SPRINGS OF YURA

The earth's crust is very thin in the area of Arequipa's three great volcanoes. This means that there are many cracks in the surface where warm water full of minerals bubbles up from the ground. Of the few thermal baths that are open to the public, the best are at Jesús on the Puno road (see Route 6b, Chapter 3) and at Yura. But neither of them have facilities that match up to normal European standards.

The road to Yura leaves Arequipa via the Puente Grau in the direction of the airport. It runs along the foot of Chachani, but there are no steep climbs along the way.

The thermal baths of Yura (30km, $18^1/_2$ miles) are situated in a narrow valley on the opposite side of the town next to the state-run tourist hotel. The road up to the springs is signposted La Calera, and runs through a series of strangely eroded rock formations.

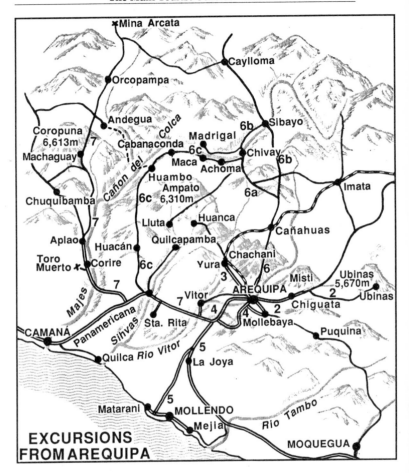

EXCURSIONS FROM AREQUIPA

4 THE DESERT TOUR

The coastal region of Peru is characterised by barren mountains interspersed with green valley oases. Any visitors to Arequipa who have missed this should take the opportunity of a short trip into the desert around. The desert tour from Arequipa is much better than the equivalent from Lima. The visibility is much better, and there is a much greater variety of scenery within a very small area.

The route out of the city is along the continuation of the Calle La Merced, which eventually comes out into the suburb of Tingo (5km, 3 miles). There is a small lake here that is popular with Sunday visitors from Arequipa. To the right just across the bridge over the Río Chili is the German School (Colegio Max Uhle), which is situated in spacious grounds.

Tiabaya (9km, 5 miles) is a village surrounded by green birch groves and forests of prickly pears (a kind of cactus with edible fruits). It is yet another popular Sunday resort, with numerous hostelries full of local atmosphere. After Tiabaya the road climbs steeply up to Cerro Verde, which means 'green mountain'. Cerro Verde is famous for its rich copper deposits. It is possible to visit the copper mines by applying in advance to Minero Perú in the Avenida Alfonso Ugarte.

The road climbs to 2,700m (8,856ft) and crosses a pass via a tunnel before dropping down to **Repartición** (see Route 4, Chapter 3). One can then return to Arequipa along the new road via Uchumayo.

5 DOWN TO THE COAST FOR BATHING

The two seaside resorts of **Mollendo** and **Mejia** are both within easy reach of Arequipa, and the road conditions are also good (see Route 5b, Chapter 3). The beach at Mejia is more to European tastes, but does not have a decent hotel.

6 TO THE CAÑON DEL COLCA

Map: page 141

The journey to the Cañon del Colca has much to recommend it. There are amazing views of deep gorges and mighty volcanoes, barren plateaux and snow-covered mountains; quaint villages that have not changed for centuries and cultivation terraces from the Inca period; Indians in traditional costume and processions of llamas. But the Colca Canyon is a deep gorge rather than a canyon in the strict geographical sense, and is nothing like the Grand Canyon of Arizona, where the horizontal strata are visible in the shelved erosion patterns.

At least two days are needed for the whole journey. Overnight accommodation is available at the Aldea Turística, where a former building site has now been turned into a hotel that is quite decent by local standards. Travel agents in Arequipa can book rooms here via a radio link.

Of the three possible routes from Arequipa, the first (6a) is probably the best choice. It is not only shorter but goes through even better scenery than the longer route via Sibayo (6b). However, the latter is a good return route for travellers who can cope with appalling road conditions at high altitudes.

A further trip to the Cruz del Cóndor (6c) is highly recommended, being only 24km (15 miles) further on from the hotel. The more adventurous often continue from here along the difficult and lonely route down to the coast (6c), but this can be a risky enterprise as there will be no other vehicles on the way. And this road should on no account be attempted between December and March. One advantage of the route is that it can be linked with a trip to the rock carvings of Toro Muerto (see Route 4c, Chapter 3), and this in turn is not far from the tourist hotel that organises dinghy trips up the wildest part of the Colca Canyon.

6a AREQUIPA • CHIVAY • ALDEA TURÍSTICA

Arequipa. The route out of the city is along the Yura road, which leaves the centre via the Puente Grau. About 1km (half a mile) further on there is a right turn up the Avenida Cayma. The metalled road climbs up the slopes of Chachani in a never-ending series of hairpins. The city soon disappears in a sea of haze, while the black ash slopes of Misti become ever closer.   0

At about 4,000m (13,120ft) the road winds up through a gap between Chachani and Misti and comes out onto a broad plateau covered in *puna* grass. About 400 vicuñas were introduced here with the help of the World Wildlife Fund (now called the Worldwide Fund for Nature). These animals had previously died out here, but are now doing so well that small herds of them are often visible from the road.

Cañahuas. Immediately beyond this sorry collection of mud-brick huts, the road begins to climb again. It also crosses the Arequipa-Puno railway (there is a storage depot at this point).   64

Turning (4,300m, 14,100ft) for **Sumbay** (4km, 2¹/₂ miles). This village has a station on the railway. There are some fascinating animal drawings in a nearby cave. The only problem is finding someone with a key to show the way and open them up.   77

Viscachani. Even though the road carries on, this village seems like the end of the world.   83

Right turn for **Pulpera** and **Sibayo** (see 6b below). Though it scarcely seems credible, the road becomes even lonelier as it continues to climb. To the left are the peaks of snow-covered Ampato (6,318m, 20,723ft) and Sabancaya (5,798m, 19,017ft), while Chucura (5,360m, 17,580ft) rises up to the right. The road reaches its highest point over the **Patapampa Pass** (4,900m, 16,072ft).   86

Mirador del Mismi. This viewing point offers a truly breathtaking panorama of the Colca Valley and the peaks of Mismi (5,597m, 18,358ft) beyond.   144

Left turn for **Achoma** and **Aldea Turística**. Before carrying on to the hotel, a short trip to Chivay (2km, 1¹/₄ miles) is strongly recommended.   151

Chivay (3,651m [11,975ft], population 5,000). The church here is unusually large, just like all those in the Colca Valley. The reasons for this go back to the great wealth of the early colonial period. In 1540 Gonzales Pizarro, brother of the conquistador, began the so-called *Corrigimiento Colahuas* in this area. This involved resettling the Colahua Indians in villages to make them more accessible to missionaries and to provide labour for the rich mines in the district.

The region later fell into obscurity, and remained cut off from the outside world until the 1970s, when a new road link was built. The reason for this was a massive irrigation project that involved diverting the Río Colca through a 100km (62 mile) long system of underground tunnels.

The long period of isolation has meant that the local Indians have preserved their traditional costumes from as far back as the colonial period. One can watch the women at the market in Chivay as they embroider their beautiful robes.

There are more places to visit beyond Chivay. Only 2km (1¹/₄ miles) to the north there are yet more thermal baths (La Calera). The road out of the village to the north crosses the so-called Inca Bridge (though only the foundations are of precolonial origin). Over the bridge one can turn right for Sibayo (see 6b below) or left for the villages downstream along the Colca Valley — Corporaque (8km, 5 miles), Ichupampa (16km, 10 miles), Lari (28km, 17 miles) and Madrigal (35km, 22 miles) — though they are only worth visiting if there is plenty of time.

151   Turning for **Achoma** and **Aldea Turística**.

160   **Yanque** (3,413m, 11,195ft). The village is perched on a broad

terrace overlooking the river, and its church is one of the finest in the valley. Towards evening there are always llama caravans passing through, bringing supplies to outlying communities.

166   **Achoma**.

170   **Aldea Turística**. The hotel is situated down below the road to the right. There is a small museum with mementoes of the building of the great Majes irrigation system (Río Majes is the name given to the lower reaches of the Colca). The workers lived here during that period. The result of their efforts was that 60,000 hectares (148,200 acres) of desert was reclaimed for cultivation, while 200,000 people were resettled in the region near the coast.

6b AREQUIPA • SIBAYO • CHIVAY • ALDEA TURÍSTICA

0   **Arequipa**. The route is the same as 6a above for the first 86km (53 miles).

86   Left turn for **Chivay** (direct route, see route 6a). The present route is along the road to the right, which climbs up past Lake Lancocota.

97   Right turn for **Imata.** The Sibayo road goes straight on and continues

to climb steeply.

Ventana de Colca. The 'Window of Colca' is so named because of the breathtaking view that opens up here along the Colca Valley. 112

Turning for the **Mollepunco Caves**, which contain rock drawings. Further down to the right there are two rock columns known locally as the Castillos Encantados or 'Enchanted Castles'. 130

Sibayo (3,880m, 12,726ft). More adventurous drivers may wish to tackle the dramatic 6-hour journey (including several fords) to the silver mines at **Arcata**. The road climbs through the mountains to Caylloma (4,200m, 13,776ft) and eventually to Arcata (4,600m, 15,088ft), which is supposed to have the largest silver mine in Peru (there is a guesthouse). However, most people will take the road to Chivay, which crosses the Río Colca and runs down along the north side of the valley. 143

Tuti (3,804m, 12,477ft). At this point there is a dam across the river from which water is diverted into the Majes irrigation system. 153

Pumunuta. These rather unimpressive ruins may possibly be remnants of the 'copper palace' which Inca Mayta Cápac is supposed to have built for his wife, who originally came from here. 158

Chivay (see 6a above). The first filling station. 174

Aldea Turística. See 6a above. 194

6c ALDEA TURÍSTICA • CABANACONDE • HUAMBO • PANAMERICANA

Aldea Turística.The road runs down along the south side of the valley, high above the Río Colca. 0

Maca (3,225m, 10,578ft). To the left of the road is a simple but impressive church. 4

Mirador Antahuilque. This viewing point is the best place for seeing the enormous cultivation terraces built during the Inca period. These served the dual purpose of assisting irrigation and preventing soil erosion. 10

Pinchollo. The character of the valley changes dramatically, and from this point onwards it turns into a deep gorge. 15

Cruz del Cóndor. A cross to the right of the road marks the point for obtaining the best view of the spectacular Colca Canyon, where the river has cut a gorge through the mountains as much as 1,500m, 4,920ft deep. In the early morning the condors rise up on warm air currents to the height of the surrounding peaks, and then in the evening they glide gently back down to their eyries. 24

Turning for **Cabanaconde** (3,230m, 10,594ft). The village is perched 33

The Colca Valley

on a hill below the road. From here it is possible to climb down the side of the gorge to a suspension bridge over the river. The 6-hour climb follows the 1-2m (3-6ft) wide Inca road, parts of which have been carved out of a vertical cliff.

After Cabanaconde the journey becomes very rough and lonely as the road climbs up through bleak, uninhabited mountains, then drops steeply down towards Huambo, which is visible in the valley below.

77 **Huambo.** The tiny village is followed by yet another steep climb, which goes almost to the very foot of the snow-covered peak of Ampato (6,318m, 20,723ft). After a never-ending journey through the mountains, the road then begins a steep descent of some 3,500m, 11,480ft.

160 **Huacán.** The journey becomes less steep after this small mission station, while the presence of sand marks the beginning of the coastal desert. But then suddenly the road is surrounded by green fields — living evidence of the success of the Majes irrigation project.

195 **Panamericana.** The rest of the journey back to Arequipa is described in Route 4, Chapter 3.

7 TO THE ROCK CARVINGS OF TORO MUERTO
Map: page 141

This excursion can be easily combined with the desert tour (see 4 above). Beyond Repartición it runs along the Panamericana in the direction of Lima. Twenty-four kilometres (15 miles) after Tambillo there is a turning for Aplao. Toro Muerto is another 48km (30 miles) along this road. The site is scattered with rocks covered in strange carvings. Overnight accommodation is available further up the valley beyond Aplao. The same hotel organises dinghy trips up the rapids along the bottom of the Colca Canyon. The whole trip is described in more detail in Route 4c, Chapter 3.

Ayacucho

Altitude: 2,760m (9,052ft)
Population: 37,000
Air links: Lima, Cuzco
Road links: Lima 583km [361 miles] (Route 4a), Cuzco 593km [367 miles], Huancayo 258km [160 miles] (Route 5)

Ayacucho was founded in 1539 by the Spanish conquistadors to guard the vital trade route between Lima and Cuzco. Since then it has fallen into obscurity, but the consequent isolation has helped to preserve much of its old folklore. This, however, is of far greater interest than the many famous colonial churches and mansions, which are disappointing when compared with the great baroque masterpieces of Cuzco. Ayacucho is also well known for its local handicrafts, especially the alabaster (*piedra de Huamanga*) figures and brightly painted house shrines.

During Holy Week Ayacucho must be the liveliest town in the whole of Peru. The festivities include glorious processions that attract Indians from far and wide, turning the streets of the town into one large fair that has so far remained unspoiled by too many tourists.

TOUR OF THE TOWN
Length: 1.5km (1 mile)
Map: page 151

The best time for sightseeing is in the early hours of the morning, because most of the churches are only open between 6am and 8am. The suggested tour begins in the main square (Plaza Mayor), which is surrounded by the colonnades of old colonial mansions. In the middle is a statue of General Antonio Sucre, one of the heroes of the liberation struggles. (The numbers in brackets correspond to those on the map.)

The **Cathedral** (1) was founded in 1672 during the period of greatest prosperity. It possesses some particularly fine churrigueresque altars. The **Colonial Mansion** (2), Jirón 2 de Mayo 204, was the family residence of one of the twenty Spanish nobles who founded the city in 1539. Both the entrance and the balcony are very fine. Further along across the street is the church of the Mercedarian order, which was founded in 1540.

Apart from a few large paintings, the most interesting feature of **San Francisco de Asís** (3) church is the carved altar in the left aisle. The angels look rather fearsome, showing the strong Indian influences on the art of the colonial period. The old convent church, **Santa Clara** (4), looks rather shabby from the outside, but is in fact one of the most interesting in the town. The nuns' area is separated from the rest of the church by an iron grill rather like the women's chamber in a mosque. The beautiful Moorish panelled ceiling and carved 'cedarwood' pulpit are the finest in Ayacucho.

Colonial Mansion (5), Jirón 28 de Julio 197, the house of the Marquez de Mozobamba goes back to the mid-sixteenth century, and is probably one of the oldest colonial buildings in the whole of the American continent. The columns around the courtyard are each carved out of one stone, and bear the snake insignia that was the trademark of the local Indian stonemasons.

La Compañía (6), the Jesuit church, was founded in 1605. The main altar is a fine example of churrigueresque art. The church is also the home of the much-revered painting of the *Agony of Christ* (*Jesús *de la Agonía*) that is the focus of the Good Friday ceremonies, when it is carried in pomp to the Cathedral. The **Museum** (7) is housed in the former side chapel of La Compañía but it contains little of particular interest to foreign visitors.

The **Prefecture** (8) or the provincial headquarters are housed in a large colonial mansion across the main square from the Cathedral. The entrance door is secured with heavy bronze mountings, and leads through into a very fine courtyard.

The church of **San Francisco de Paula** (9) was founded in 1713. It has a classical façade and one of the finest pulpits in the town while **Santo Domingo** (10) church was built between 1548 and 1562 in a very unusual style with colonnades along the west front. The Inquisition are supposed to have stood here to watch the execution of condemned heretics, who were hanged from the detached bell tower in such a way that the last thing they saw was the stone cross opposite.

San Agustín (11) is the last of the churches to be included in this tour, which are only a few of the thirty or so old colonial churches still remaining in Ayacucho. Those who wish to see more of them should at least visit **Santa Teresa**, which is situated off the bottom of the map in the sixth block of the Jirón 28 de Julio.

EXCURSIONS FROM AYACUCHO

1 To Huari and La Quinua (31km, 19 miles)

The route follows the road to Huancayo (see Route 9, Chapter 3) down to the bottom of the valley 500m (1,640ft) below Ayacucho (14km, 8^1/$_2$ miles), where there is a right turn for San Miguel. This road climbs steeply until after another 10km (6 miles) there is a left turn along a rough track to **Huari** (pronounced Wari, another 5km, 3 miles). This village was once the centre of an important pre-Inca empire, though very little remains of it on this site.

The village of **Quinua** (28km, 17 miles) is further along the road to San Miguel. It is famous throughout Peru for its weird pottery 'Ayacucho Churches' that have roofs blown askew by the wind. Every roof is decorated with strange talismans of Indian origin that are supposed to ward off evil spirits. Even the village church has them.

Three kilometres (2 miles) beyond La Quinua is the battlefield site where on 9 December 1824 the 6,000-strong liberation army under Sucre routed 10,000 of the viceroy's troops. A vast monument was erected here in 1974 to commemorate the 150th anniversary of the last decisive battle of the liberation struggle. The monument commands a marvellous view across the valley to the town of Ayacucho.

2 To the Inca Ruins of Vilcashuamán (110km, 68 miles)

The route follows the Abancay road as far as the turning for Cangallo (47km, 29 miles). At Condorcocha (64km, 39^1/$_2$ miles) on the Can-

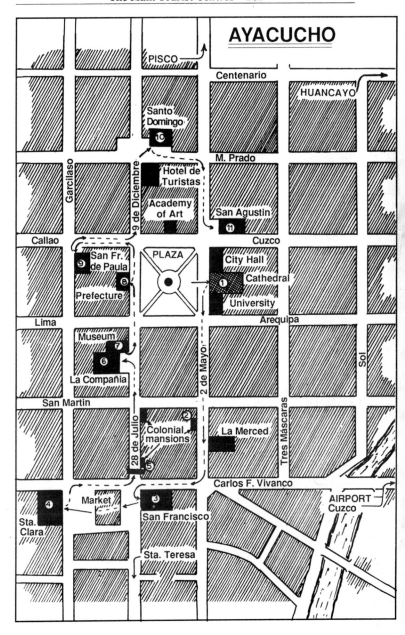

AYACUCHO

gallo road there is a left turn for Vilcashuamán. The extensive remains include the walls of the old fort (*ciudadela*) and the sun temple.

Cajamarca

Altitude: 2,750m (9,020ft)
Population: 40,000
Air links: Trujillo, Lima
Road links: Trujillo 299km [185 miles], Lima 860km [533 miles], Chiclayo 263km [163 miles] (Route 1b)

Cajamarca is a popular holiday resort for Peruvians, thanks to the warm hospitality, the many interesting excursions and the thermal baths that go as far back as the Incas. Items of interest to foreign visitors include some remarkable churches and a number of precolonial remains.

TOUR OF THE TOWN

The suggested tour begins in the **Plaza de Armas**, which is unusually large and well kept. Immediately next to the colonial-style tourist hotel is the **Cathedral**. The west front, though incomplete, is a masterpiece of baroque stonemasonry and shows a remarkable unity of style. The whole façade is carved into a carpet of leaves, flowers, angels, cornices, and decorative gables. The columns are carved with rows of vines decked with grapes to symbolise the Eucharist. The interior is much more simple in design, but has a remarkable gilt pulpit.

San Francisco on the opposite side of the square has a façade rivalling that of the Cathedral. There is a door inside the church leading through to the old Franciscan monastery, part of which has been turned into a museum of religious art. Guides will also take visitors down to see the catacombs, which were only discovered a few years ago.

To the right of San Francisco is the **Capilla de la Dolorosa** or Chapel of the Sorrows of Mary, which is one of the jewels of Peruvian colonial architecture. The walls, cornices, window frames, columns and ceiling vaults are all covered with filigree carvings. The two large stone reliefs either side of the main altar are particularly remarkable, one showing the Last Supper and the other the Washing of the Feet. At window height there are representations of Christ's Nativity, the Three Kings, the Flight to Egypt and other events from the Bible.

Directly opposite the chapel in the Avenida Amalia Puga is the **Cuarte del Rescate** or Ransom Chamber, which is the sole surviving Inca building in Cajamarca. This room must originally have been part of the sun temple, and is closely associated with the fall of the Inca empire. Cajamarca was where the Spaniards met the Inca ruler Atahuallpa, who was still recuperating from injuries sustained during the recent civil war. The Spaniards ambushed and captured the unsuspecting Inca, even though he was guarded by several thousand troops. Atahuallpa then promised that if they freed him he would give them enough treasure to fill the room they had kept him in three times over, first with gold and then twice with silver. He kept his promise, and soon the Spaniards were carrying off the Inca's treasures. But Atahuallpa they simply condemned to death.

The first turning on the right along the Avenida Amalia Puga leads up to a church called **Belén**, which was founded by the Bethlehemite order in 1774. The elegant façade is covered with a rich display of carvings, while the interior decorations are very colourful and original. The naively formed angels depicted under the domes are typically Indian features.

If one goes right after the church this takes one back in the direction of the Plaza de Armas. The fine gateway on the corner was part of the Bethlehemite School, which is now in ruins. About a hundred metres or so along on the left there is a flight of steps leading up to the **Capilla de Santa Apolonia**, from which there is a marvellous view of the town. Above this chapel and almost at the top of the hill is a carved stone that is known as the **Inca's Throne**.

One block below the Plaza on the same side as the tourist hotel is a small **Archaeological Museum** (Avenida Arequipa 289). Apart from the usual pottery, it contains models of the old Inca temple and the water channel of Cumbe Mayo (see below).

EXCURSIONS FROM CAJAMARCA

1 Baños del Inca (6km, 3¹/₂ miles)
The former Inca baths can be reached via a metalled road from the roundabout on the Lima road. The hot springs are now encased in concrete and surrounded by a large bathing complex. This includes a swimming pool that is refilled at the beginning of each week — though the water is usually too hot for bathing until the Thursday.

2 Ventanillas de Otuzco (7km, 4¹/₂ miles)
The 'Little Windows of Otuzco' are a series of holes carved out of the rock, and are probably part of a pre-Inca burial site that goes back about 1,400 years. They can be reached via the continuation of the Avenida 2 de Mayo, which goes from the San Francisco side of the the Plaza de Armas (this road also goes to the airport).

3 Cumbe Mayo (25km, 15¹/₂ miles)
To get to Cumbe Mayo one must first go up the Avenida Arequipa from the tourist hotel and take the third turning on the left. The road is only passable in dry weather. After a long climb up the slopes of the

San Francisco church, Cajamarca

Cerro Apolonia, it eventually goes up through a pass (3,500m, 11,480ft). It continues uphill along a valley with strange rock formations until there is a left turn for Cumbe Mayo.

π   The archaeological site includes cave sanctuaries with rock carvings and a water channel, and is estimated to be some 3,000 years old. The best way to see everything is to hire one of the young guides that advertise their services in the Plaza de Armas.

The water channel is the most interesting feature of all. In places it runs through a tunnel hacked out of the rock, and with a gradient of only 1.5 per cent it is a remarkable feat of ancient engineering. The purpose of the right-angled bends is still the subject of some debate. Some experts suggest these were simply to slow down the water and help preserve the channel, while others think the channel was used for extracting gold and that the gold dust was precipitated out at the corners.

Chavín de Huántar

Altitude: 3,150m (10,332ft)
Road links: Huaraz 109km [67 miles], Lima 441km [273 miles] (Route 2a)

Chavín is a fascinating pre-Inca site set in beautiful mountain

Cajamarca

scenery, and the trip is highly recommended. The best starting point is Huaraz (see page 185). The poor road surfaces and the unusually high altitude make the journey an extremely exhausting one. It is therefore advisable to spend the night at the hotel in Chavín (pre-booking is essential in July and August). The journey takes four to five hours each way.

The Journey
The route from Huaraz follows the road for Pativilca and Lima as far as Catac (35km [22 miles], see Route 2a, Chapter 3), where there is a left turn for Chavín. The road climbs up to Lake Querococha (3,980m, 13,054ft), with a continuous view of the icy peaks of Yanamarey (5,260m, 17,252ft). It crosses the Cahuish Pass (73km [45 miles], 4,510m [14,792ft]) via a rather strange tunnel, then begins a hair-raising descent along the gorge of the Río Mosna, which is a tributary of the Amazon. The road reaches the bottom of the valley near the small village of Machac (101km, 62 miles). The ruins are clearly visible immediately before the village of Chavín (109km, 67 miles).

The Ruins

The site was built in several phases between 1000 and 300BC, and was originally thought to have been a large palace or fortress. But recent excavations have led to the inevitable conclusion that it was a vast temple complex that attracted pilgrims from the whole of the Andean region. It has yet to be established whether Chavín was merely the spiritual centre of a bloodthirsty cat-god cult, or whether it was also the capital of a mighty empire, as is sometimes thought. Such is the flood of literature on the subject that it is difficult to extract hard scientific evidence from a web of speculation, fantasy and wishful thinking.

There is no doubt that the ruins of Chavín are the oldest stone buildings in Peru to have been discovered so far. But their technical perfection, together with evidence of detailed pre-planning, suggests that their design must have been developed over a much longer period of time. The most puzzling feature is a complicated system of underground passages that are reminiscent of bunkers. They include tiny tomb-like chambers and long corridors that sometimes end in a blank wall. There are no windows at all, but the horizontal and vertical shafts suggest a highly developed ventilation and water system.

Tour of the Site

The route goes from the entrance along the northern edge of the site to a square arena that was probably used for religious ceremonies. Like the other arena it is sunk into the ground and would have required an accurate system of drainage. The outflow openings are still visible in the corners. Like the rest of the site, the arena was buried under a massive mudslide. A remnant of this can be seen on the southern terrace overlooking the arena, showing how deep the mud must have been.

The steps on the opposite side of the arena lead past the remains of houses built by later inhabitants to the so-called *castillo*, a vast structure measuring 72sq m (775sq ft) that must have originally been in the form of a three-layered pyramid. The walls were once covered with polished stone slabs and decorated with sixty-eight carved stone heads (*cabejas clavas*) shaped like strange human or animal heads. These are thought by some experts to have represented the heads of conquered enemies, suggesting a practice similar to that once used in the jungle whereby enemies' heads were used as war trophies.

The gateway to the *castillo* is particularly interesting. The variegated colours on the staircases and the carvings on the round columns either side symbolise the duality of sun (left) and moon (right) that is used all over the site. The sun represented light, day and masculinity, while the moon symbolised darkness, night and femininity. The stone beam that spans the columns is decorated with seven

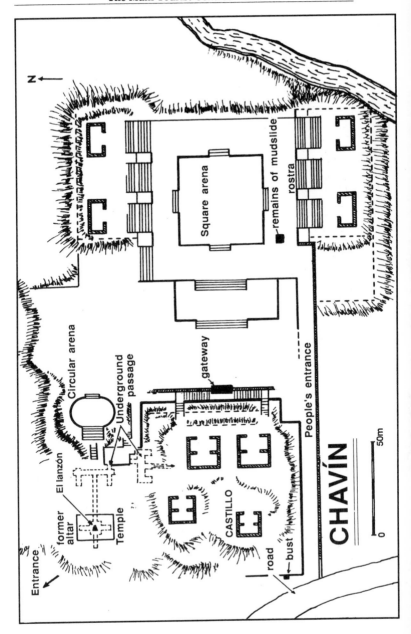

A street in Chavín

bird-like creatures facing towards the middle. To the north of the *castillo* is the round arena, which has only recently been excavated. This is decorated with fine carvings of the cat-like deity.

The path leads finally up to the oldest part of the temple, where there are the entrances to two of the eighteen underground tunnel systems that have so far been discovered on the site. The right passageway leads to the so-called *lanzón*, a stone shaped like a giant dagger sticking into the ground. The face carved in the granite shows a typical combination of humanoid features with those of a snake, an eagle and a jaguar. This monolith no doubt represented an important deity, but it is not known how it was worshipped or why it was hidden in an underground passage. The story that the altar above it was regularly bathed with blood cannot be proved.

Cuzco

Altitude: 3,400m (11,152ft)
Population: 205,000
Air links: Lima, Arequipa, Ayacucho, Puerto Maldonado, Iquitos
Rail links: Main Station: Puno 381 km [236 miles] (10 hours), Arequipa 641 km [397 miles] (16 hours), Santa Anna
Station: Machu Picchu 112km [69 miles] (4 hours)

Remains of the large temple at Chavín

Road links: Puno 386km [239 miles] (Route 8), Abancay-Ayacucho 593km [367 miles] (Route 9),
Abancay-Nazca-Lima 1,108km [688 miles] (Routes 9 and 4b)

Cuzco is not only the most important tourist centre in Peru, it is without doubt the most fascinating city in the whole of South America. There is everything to be found here, from impressive Inca ruins to priceless colonial treasures, from ancient costumes and folklore to breathtaking mountain scenery. Such is the Andean city which the Incas called Cuzco or 'navel' because it formed the centre of their mighty empire.

According to legend, the first Inca Manco Cápac and his sister Mama Ocllo came to the Cuzco region from Lake Titicaca. They carried with them the golden staff which their father the sun god had given them with the command that they should go and settle in the place where the staff sank deepest in the ground. And there they were to found a city that would become the capital of a mighty empire, where people would at last enjoy the benefits of civilisation under the blessing of the sun god.

Those first Incas fulfilled that command. The empire flourished, and each ruler built even richer palaces than the last one — until on 15 November 1533 Francisco Pizarro marched into Cuzco with his band of adventurers. They tore the gold and silver from the walls, melted down the idols, demolished the palaces and dismantled the skilfully matched stonework for building their churches.

Important Things to See

The list of things to see in and around Cuzco is virtually endless. At one end of the scale there is the Indian mother breast-feeding her baby on the church steps or weaving a brightly coloured poncho on the outskirts of the city. At the other end there are the mighty Sacsayhuamán Fortress and the Santo Domingo Monastery, the two most outstanding surviving examples of Inca architecture. The riches and artistry of the colonial period are best shown in the Cathedral, the Archbishop's Palace and churches such as La Compañía and San Blas. The Sunday markets at nearby Pisac and Chinchero provide a glimpse into the brightly coloured world of Indian costumes, traditions and handicrafts. But the high-point of any stay in Cuzco is a visit to the Inca city of Machu Picchu and the breathtaking mountain scenery that surrounds it.

A Suggested Timetable

Most travel companies allow their customers only three days in Cuzco, although a whole week would be more suitable, especially since no exertion is advisable on the first day. Anyone who is unaccustomed to high altitudes should allow at least half a day's rest for acclimatisation. Nine days is the ideal length of time, including two Sundays for visiting the Sunday markets at Pisac and Chinchero. But there are ways of economising on time. If only one Sunday is available, for example, one can set off very early for Chinchero and go on to Pisac, while still leaving the afternoon free for visiting Ollantaitambo.

It is best to go to Machu Picchu on a Sunday, a Wednesday or a Thursday so as to avoid the worst of the crowds. This is because most travel companies arrange a weekend stay in Cuzco for the sake of the Sunday markets, followed by Machu Picchu on the day after (usually Monday).

An overnight stay in Machu Picchu is highly recommended. Then it is possible to take a short walk through the area. The Inca site is also particularly beautiful in the morning or evening. Rooms at Machu Picchu should be booked well in advance, and at the very latest on arrival in Cuzco (at the Hotel Cuzco). There is, however, emergency accommodation available for visitors with sleeping bags.

CITY TOUR 1
Length: 1km (half a mile)
Map: page 165

The route begins in the Plaza de Armas, the large square in the centre of the city, whose unchanging character is determined by the beauty of the colonial churches around it. At the time of the Incas it was

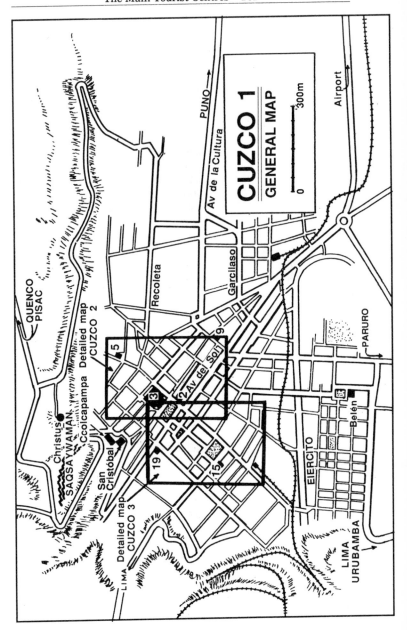

Indian woman shopping at the market

surrounded by elaborate palaces, temples and government buildings, and was filled with sand to a depth of half a metre. It is thought
that the sand was brought here by visitors from the coast as a tribute
to the superiority of the Inca. At the time of the winter equinox (21
June) this was the location for the great Inti Raymi Festival, in which
the people prayed to the sun god to return and not to abandon them.

The numbers in brackets on this tour and on other tours correspond to those on the maps. **The University** (1) was originally part of
the Jesuit monastery, and it was the Jesuits who founded the first
university on this site in 1622. The baroque façade includes two
figures over the entrance whose Indian features are typical of all
colonial buildings in Cuzco.

The Jesuit church **La Compañía** (2), is undoubtedly one of the
finest in Cuzco. The façade is even more elegant and harmonious
than that of the Cathedral. The Jesuits' deliberate attempts to rival the
Cathedral earned them displeasure of the Church authorities, who
even complained to the Pope. But the dispute went on for so long that
the church was finished in the meantime according to the Jesuits'
wishes. The interior includes several carved gilt altars with cork-
screw-like columns and paintings that are mostly by the *mestizo* artist
Marcos Zapota. They show scenes from the life of Ignatius Loyola,
the founder of the Jesuit order. The two large pictures hanging on

The Plaza de Armas and La Compañía, Cuzco

opposite walls near the entrance are of particular historical significance. The one on the left shows a Spanish nobleman marrying an
Inca princess. The other one also shows a wedding, and both of them
depict costumes that were typical of sixteenth-century Peru.

When there is no mass taking place, one can enter the **Cathedral**
(3) via El Triunfo, the church adjoining it. Both churches were built on
the foundations of the Palace of Huiracocha, the eighth Inca.

El Triunfo (3) was built between 1729 and 1732 to commemorate
the Spanish victory over the fierce Indian rebellion of 1536, which
very nearly toppled the Spanish rule. The main altar is covered with
thin gold leaf, and like the rest of the church is made of grey andesite,
a hard volcanic stone rather like granite. The two paintings either side
of the altar are particularly striking; the *Descent from the Cross* is a
copy of a Rubens, while the *Carrying of the Cross* is a copy of a work
by Raphael.

The Cathedral was begun in 1560 using stones from the old Inca
palace and great blocks from the Sacsayhuamán (Saqsaywaman in
Quechua) Fortress. But the giant structure measuring 86m (282ft) by
46m (150ft) imposed a great financial burden on the few Spanish
inhabitants of Cuzco, so that it was 1645 before the Cathedral was
finally consecrated. The facade completely dominates the main
square, and shows the mixture of Renaissance and baroque styles

that is typical of Cuzco as a whole. The two towers are both 33m (108ft) high, and the left one contains the famous Maria Angola, a bell cast out of gold and bronze and weighing six tons that is supposed to be audible up to a distance of 40km (25 miles).

The Cathedral contains a wealth of art treasures, including 372 paintings, most of which were based on Spanish models but some of which show native Indian features. There is an example in the painting of the *Last Supper* hanging on the right-hand side behind the main altar, in which a guinea pig and *chicha morada* (a drink made from maize) are being served.

The vestry (to the right at the back) contains carved cedarwood furniture and portraits of former bishops of Cuzco. The Cathedral jewels are kept in a large safe. They include a 1.2m (4ft) high monstrance made of 21.66kg (47lb) of gold and 5kg (11lb) of silver and inlaid with 331 pearls, 263 diamonds, 221 emeralds, 89 amethysts, 62 rubies, 43 topazes and 23 other precious stones. The main altar is covered with solid silver; it is a much later addition, and hides the original altar, which is of greater artistic value. The latter is made of carved cedarwood inlaid with gold, and is a better match for the fine baroque choirstalls, which include life-size carvings of forty saints.

Two of the side altars are particularly popular with the people. The fourth on the right next to the entrance to El Triunfo is the altar to the Lord of the Earthquakes (*Señor de los Temblores*). The statue of the Crucifixion was made after the great earthquake of 1650, and is supposed to guard the city against earthquakes. It is processed through the city on special occasions. The altar facing it is to the Virgin of the Immaculate Conception (*Virgen de la Immaculata Concepción*). Popularly known as *La Linda* or 'the beautiful one', it is where young married women come to pray in order to have children.

The **Archbishop's Palace** (4) is one of the finest colonial palaces in Cuzco. It was built by the Marquises of Buenavista and Rocafuerte on the massive stone foundations of the Palace of Inca Roca, the sixth Inca. Formerly the Archbishop of Cuzco's residence, it is now open to the public and houses the **Museum of Colonial Art**. Apart from some fine antique furniture, there is a large collection of paintings by artists from the Cuzco school.

The walls of the great **Palace of Inca Roca** along the Calle Hatunrumiyoc (which is Quechua for 'great stone') are the finest in the whole of Cuzco. The heavy polygonal blocks have been shaped and fitted together with such perfect precision that after many severe earthquakes not even a knife blade can be inserted between them. The Stone of Twelve Angles is particularly famous, fitting into the blocks around it with the same accuracy as all the rest.

San Blas (5). This church built of sun-dried mud bricks looks very scruffy from the outside, but the interior is surprisingly rich in

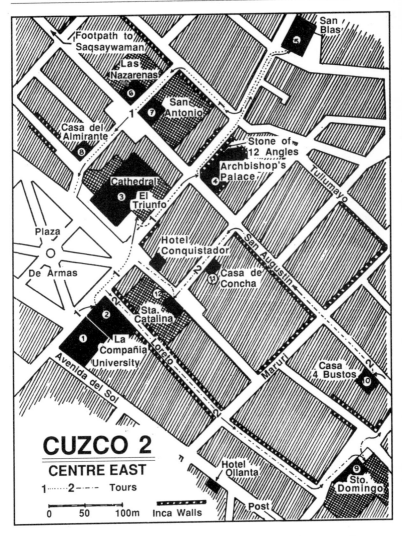

Footpath to
Saqsaywaman

Las
Nazarenas

San
Blas

San
Antonio

Casa del
Almirante

Stone of
12 Angles

Archbishop's
Palace

Tullumayo

Cathedral

El
Triunfo

Plaza

Hotel
Conquistador

San Augustín

De Armas

Casa de
Concha

Sta.
Catalina

Loreto

La
Compañia
University

Maruri

Casa
4 Bustos

Avenida del Sol

CUZCO 2

CENTRE EAST

1 ·········· 2 –·–·– Tours

0   50   100m   Inca Walls

Hotel
Ollanta

Sto.
Domingo

Post

treasures such as the beautifully carved churrigueresque altar and
the large paintings, eight of which show scenes from the life of St
Blasius. But the church's chief claim to fame is the baroque pulpit,
which is considered by experts to be the finest in the Western
Hemisphere. According to legend it was the work of the Indian
sculptor Juan Tomás Tuirutupa, who had been miraculously cured of

Preparing a meal in the streets of Cuzco

leprosy by the Virgin Mary and carved this pulpit as a thanks offering over a period of four years. Mary herself is given pride of place in the middle of the balustrade. Near her are the Four Evangelists surrounded by elaborate but tasteful ornamentation. These four Gospel writers are depicted along the bottom edge with bare breasts and long beards and surrounded by seven chimeras. The back of the pulpit shows St Blasius with his bishop's insignia, while the roof over the pulpit depicts nine more saints and is crowned with the figure of St Thomas carrying a cross in his hand.

The route returns from San Blas down the Callejón San Blas, and then goes right along the Calle Choquechaca, where there are some more Inca walls. The narrow passage to the left is the Callejón de Siete Culebras or 'Seven Snakes' Passage'. There was a school here under the Incas, where the sons of noblemen were educated in the practicalities of warfare and administration, and in the worship of the sun. Many of the stones are decorated with a small snake symbol as a sign of wisdom.

The Nazarene Convent or **Convento de las Nazarenas** (6) was founded in the sixteenth century by Spanish nuns of the Nazarene order to recruit young Indian women for their order. The only items of particular interest are the carved choirstalls.

The church of **San Antonio Abad** (7) contains some fine carv-

Chinchero market near Cuzco

ings. The adjoining building was previously a university, but is now a seminary for priests. The west door is typical of the mixed Indian and colonial style that developed in Cuzco. There is a statue of St Anthony and a Spanish coat of arms.

Casa del Almirante (8) belonged to an admiral in the seventeenth century, and was formerly one of the finest colonial mansions in Cuzco. Unfortunately it was so badly damaged in the great earthquake of 1950 that most of it had to be pulled down. However, the original façade built out of Inca stones has remained intact.

CITY TOUR 2
Length: 1km (half a mile)
Map: page 165

This tour again begins in the Plaza de Armas. The route runs along a narrow street to the left of La Compañía called Calle Loreto, which is lined on both sides by Inca walls. On the right-hand side is a simpler wall made up of smaller blocks that belonged to the Palace of Huayna Cápac, the eleventh Inca. The more elaborate stonework of the left-hand wall betrays a religious purpose in that the building was clearly designed to last for ever. Indeed, the wall once belonged to the House of the Sun Virgins, of which there were several hundred. All Inca families were obliged to choose the best-looking of their eight- to ten-year-old girls for this purpose. These girls then had to grow up as virgins living in complete seclusion. Their job was to maintain the sacred fire and make beautiful robes for the nobility out of vicuña wool. They usually became the Inca's concubines, although some were presented to noblemen as a reward for special achievements.

The stonework is typically Inca, being very slightly inclined inwards. The square blocks are slightly rounded like cushions, and have been worked and fitted with extreme precision. They are all very slightly narrower at the top, giving the impression that the building is taller than it actually is.

The route continues along the Calle Pampa del Castillo, passing a collection of souvenir stalls on the right, and arrives in the Plaza Santo Domingo, which once fronted onto the main Inca temple. The people used to assemble in this square when the Inca and the priests were performing religious ceremonies in the Sun Temple.

The monastery of **Santo Domingo** (9) is of even greater interest than the church, because the severe earthquake of 1950 exposed the foundations of the Qorikancha, the great Sun Temple of the Incas, which was previously thought to have been pulled down. Nowhere else are the peculiarities of Inca stonework more vividly shown. The carefully polished stones have been placed on top of each other without any mortar, and are precisely matched and keyed to prevent them moving in an earthquake. The walls are slightly inclined, with trapezoid windows, double-framed doors and niches for idols. The monastery entrance is to the left of the church. It leads directly into the cloister, which is surrounded by columns depicting scenes from the life of St Dominic.

In the near right-hand corner is the Moon Temple (*Templo de la Luna*), half of which was pulled down to make way for the church. The walls are thought to have been covered with silver, while the moon was represented by a large silver disc engraved with a woman's face. In front of it sat the mummies of the Incas' chief wives.

The Inca gateway next to the Moon Temple includes a particularly remarkable stone. It is the third stone from the bottom on the right-hand side, and belongs to both parts of the double frame. It has as many as twenty angles altogether, which is a remarkable technical feat considering that there are no surfaces at right angles and no fully vertical walls.

A corridor leads through to a thick rounded wall that runs along behind the chancel of the church. Some experts think this acted as a symbolic protection around the whole of the temple complex, while

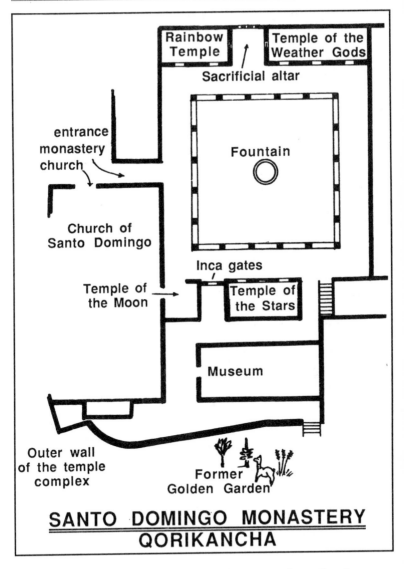

Rainbow Temple

Temple of the Weather Gods

Sacrificial altar

entrance
monastery
church

Fountain

Church of
Santo Domingo

Inca gates

Temple of
the Moon

Temple of
the Stars

Museum

Outer wall
of the temple
complex

Former
Golden Garden

SANTO DOMINGO MONASTERY
QORIKANCHA

others see it as part of the Sun Temple proper. According to historians, the Sun Temple was completely covered with gold. The sun was represented by a large gold disc inlaid with jewels, and the

The Cordillera Blanca

perfectly preserved mummies of the Inca rulers are supposed to have sat in front of it.

The wall looks out onto a series of terraces. These may have been the site of the famous Golden Garden which the conquistadors spoke of with such wonderment. It represented the agriculture of the Inca empire, and is supposed to have contained life-size gold and silver replicas of animals and plants, agricultural implements and even clods of earth. There are specific reports of twenty golden llamas guarded by herdsmen and a complete field of maize with gold stems, gold leaves and gold cobs.

If one returns along the corridor and through the Inca gateway, one comes to yet another temple. The Star Temple or Venus Temple (*Templo de las Estrellas*) was once similarly covered with silver, while the ceiling shone with the gold disc of the sun and numerous gold stars. The twenty-five trapezoid niches presumably contained idols.

On the other side of the cloister is the Temple of the Weather Gods (*Templo del Relámpago, Trueno y Rayo*), which is thought to have been completely covered with gold. The walls are noticeably inclined, and would have harmonised well with the steep roof, which is supposed to have been made out of wood and thatch.

The place of sacrifice (*sala de sacrificio*) is linked via a window to the Temple of the Weather Gods. The theory that the three channels through the back wall were where the blood flowed has yet to be proved. They could just as easily have been part of some kind of water cult.

The Rainbow Temple (*Templo del Arco Iris*) on the other side of the place of sacrifice was partly dismantled, but it appears to have formed a mirror image of the Temple of the Weather Gods.

The House of the Four Busts or **Casa de los Cuatro Bustos** (10), Calle San Agustín 400, is named after the four conquistadors whose busts are to be found at the entrance. This sixteenth-century colonial mansion now houses a luxury hotel. The route continues along the Calle San Agustín, which crosses the Calle Maruri and then runs alongside the walls of the **Palace of Túpac Inca Yupanqui**, the tenth Inca. The route goes left into the Calle Santa Catalina Ancha, where the lower storeys of many of the buildings consist of remnants of this same palace.

The **Casa de Concha** (11), Calle Santa Catalina Ancha, is typical of Cuzco's colonial mansions in that the ground floor consists of the original Inca structure, while the upper storey is a mud-brick addition. The carved balcony is one of the finest in Cuzco.

Santa Catalina (12) church may look very plain from the outside, but the interior is quite magnificent, especially the main altar, the choir, the mudejar balconies and several of the paintings. The 1950 earthquake exposed the Inca foundations of the adjoining convent to reveal the former House of the Sun Virgins. Part of the convent has now been turned into a museum.

CITY TOUR 3
Length: 1km (half a mile)
Map: page 175

Once again the tour begins in the Plaza de Armas, going from the corner by La Compañía along the tree-lined Calle Mantas and across the broad Avenida del Sol into the small square at the side of the Hotel Cuzco (the tourist hotel).

The church of the Mercedarian order, **La Merced** (13), has been heavily restored following the great earthquake of 1950, but the interior is among the finest in the whole of Peru. The main altar is covered with gilded stucco, while the side altars are of carved cedarwood and similarly gilded. But most remarkable of all are the beautifully carved baroque choirstalls, which resemble the pulpit in San Blas with their showy ornamentation.

The entrance to the monastery is to the left of the church. It leads into the cloister, which is decorated with paintings showing the life of San Pedro Nolasco, the founder of the Mercedarian order. The treasure chamber is famous for a particularly remarkable and valuable monstrance. This masterpiece of local goldsmith's work is 1.3m (4ft) high, weighs 22kg (48lb) and is encrusted with 1,518 diamonds, 615 pearls and countless other precious stones.

Casa Valle Umbroso (14), Calle Marquez 273. The colonial mansion that once stood here was burned to the ground in 1974, and it is not yet known when it will be restored. Visitors with the time and the inclination may carry on past the Plaza San Francisco along the Calle Santa Clara to visit the market (beware thieves!) and Santa Ana Station, where the trains go to Machu Picchu. But those who prefer to avoid the crowds in this poor sector of the city should turn right along the square towards **San Francisco** (15). The Franciscan monastery is well worth visiting for two reasons: the beautifully carved choirstalls in the church, and the considerable collection of large paintings that are on show around the monastery premises.

While walking along the Calle Garcilaso it is worth taking a glance into the fine courtyard of the old colonial mansion, **Casa de la Jara** (16), which is now used as a guesthouse. **Casa de Garcilaso** (17); this house is supposed to have been the birthplace of Garcilaso de la Vega, the press correspondent who revealed much of what we now know about the Incas. The house now contains a small museum.

The square in front of the **Old City Hall** (18) was used during the Inca period for religious festivals. It is therefore probable that the Inca walls that form the lower part of the structure once belonged to a religious building of some kind. The route now passes to the left of the City Hall along the Calle Santa Teresa.

The church of **Santa Teresa** (19) is best known for its large paintings showing the life of St Teresa. Many of the walls in both the church and the convent are clearly of Inca origin, but it is not known what the original structure was used for.

Archaeological Museum (20), Museo Arqueológico, Calle Tigre 165. The last building on the tour is full of materials, pottery, ornaments, mummies and metal implements from the Inca period.

SACSAYHUAMÁN FORTRESS
Map: page 161

The fortress of Sacsayhuamán (or in Quechua Saqsaywaman) is only half an hour's walk or a short taxi ride (3km, 2 miles) from the city centre. The cyclopean walls of the fortress are one of the most impressive sights in Cuzco, perched on the hillside 200m (656ft) above the city.

Half-way up the hill is the church of San Cristóbal (large paintings inside) and next to it the imposing remains of the former Palace of Manco Cápac, the first Inca. The building is known as Ccolcampata, and was later used by the Incas for storing grain. Strong-smelling mint-like herbs were mixed in with the grain to stop insect infestation.

Only the lower part of the Sacsayhuamán Fortress is left since the conquistadors took away all the lighter stones for building their city. But so gigantic are the stones that remain that some people have even suggested that it was built by some kind of supernatural being. It is not known when the structure was built, and some experts believe that it existed long before the Incas. However, its purpose is even more of a puzzle. It could have been a military installation — and yet Cuzco was never sufficiently threatened by enemies to justify such a cumbersome structure. On the other hand, there is very little to support the idea that it was some kind of religious temple. Maybe it was built just to keep the people busy, as often happened under the Incas. Or was it simply an enormous temple complex that never got finished?

There are yet more conundrums to be solved. The biggest stone measures 9m (29ft) by 5m (16ft) by 4m (13ft), and probably weighs about 360 tons. How on earth could such monstrously heavy blocks have been transported to the site? How could they possibly have been moulded and laid so accurately? The only credible theory is that they were pulled up the mountainside by a whole army of workers using wooden rollers and extremely strong cables, and that they were laid on top of each other by means of artificial ramps.

The gigantic walls are formed into three zigzag-shaped bulwarks, each of them 360m (1,180ft) long. The area behind them contains

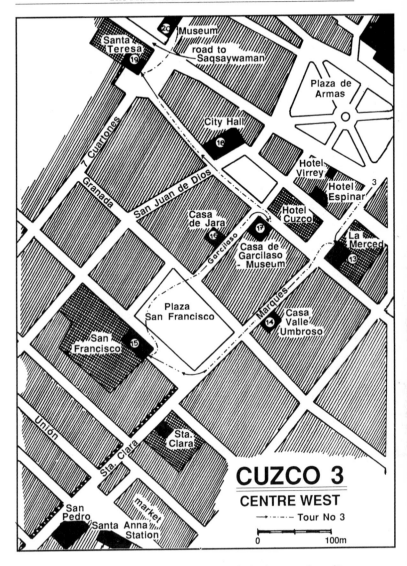

Santa
Teresa

20 Museum
road to
Saqsaywaman

19

7 Cuartones

Granada

San Juan de Dios

City Hall

16

Plaza de
Armas

Hotel
Virrey

Hotel
Espinar

3

Casa
de Jara

Garcilaso

16

17

Hotel
Cuzco

Casa de
Garcilaso
- Museum

La
Merced

13

Plaza
San Francisco

Marques

San
Francisco

15

14

Casa
Valle
Umbroso

Unión

Sta. Clara

Sta.
Clara

CUZCO 3

CENTRE WEST

⟶ ·–·–· Tour No 3

0   100m

San
Pedro

market

Santa Anna
Station

nothing but few foundation walls. These include the remains of two
square towers that were probably used for storing food, and the
foundations of a round tower that was previously thought to be a sun
clock. According to Garcilaso de la Vega, this round tower contained

a well that was supplied with clean water via a long underground channel. The precious water would no doubt have been distributed from here to the rest of the fortress.

The broad square in front of the fortress is used every year on 24 June for the great pageant of Inti Raymi, which re-enacts the great Inca festival of the sun god. This is part of a whole week of festivities, during which Cuzco is filled with the colour and spectacle of Indian folklore. Inti Raymi forms a fitting climax to the week. It is based partly on historical sources and partly on people's colourful imagination. The whole of the Inca establishment is represented, from the army, the nobility and the priesthood to the Sun Virgins and the divine ruler himself, and they celebrate the event with the ceremonial sacrifice of a llama. The soothsayer examines the still-pounding heart and makes predictions about war and peace, good and bad harvests and other important events in the coming year.

There are yet more Inca remains on the strangely shaped hill facing the fortress. Part of it has been cut out and smoothed off to form a rock slide known as the Rodadero, which was presumably used for recreation by the Inca nobility. Nearby are a series of steps hewn out of the rock and known as the Inca Throne (*Trono del Inca*). It is thought that the Inca and his nobles sat there to watch the building of the fortress. Further down on the other side of the hill are the Inca Baths (*Baños del Inca*), so-called because they include fragments of ancient water channels.

Excursions from Cuzco

1 DAY EXCURSION TO MACHU PICCHU
The ruined city of Machu Picchu is without doubt one of the most fascinating and beautiful sites in the whole of South America. Until a road link is built, however, it is only accessible by rail. A train departs at 7am every day from Santa Ana Station (**not** the main station) in Cuzco. Both the journey and Machu Picchu itself are described in full on page 200ff.

2 DAY EXCURSION TO CHINCHERO AND OLLAN-TAITAMBO
It is best to visit Chinchero on a Sunday, when the Indians hold a very traditional market that has not so far been spoiled by crowds of tourists. Ollantaitambo is the site of a fascinating Inca fortress. One option from here is to go up the Urubamba Valley and return via Pisac (see page 181). Another possibility is to continue over the Málaga Pass.

The route leaves Cuzco along the Abancay road, which is also

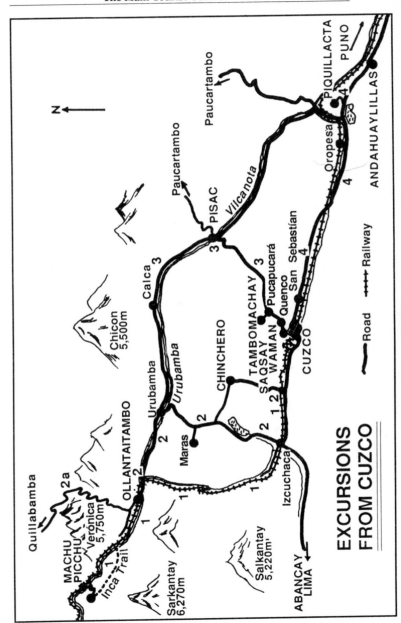

EXCURSIONS
FROM CUZCO

Road ———   Railway ＋＋＋＋

signposted for Lima (see map page 161). The road climbs through several hairpins over a steep pass into the Anta Valley. The turning for Chinchero (16km, 10 miles) is next to a fertiliser factory.

Chinchero (31km [19 miles], 3,760m [12,332ft]) is famous for its Indian market. This is held in the main square, which is a few steps up to the right of where the road comes to an end. Every Sunday the Indians assemble in their traditional costumes in order to exchange their wares. Almost noiselessly they set up their stalls in front of an Inca wall with ten niches. Items exchanged include maize, potatoes, coca, chicha and clothing.

Apart from the market, the mud-brick church is also very interesting, and is beautifully decorated inside. The slope below the market place is practically littered with Inca walls. These were probably part of the Palace of Túpac Yupanqui, the tenth Inca, for whom this was a favourite haunt.

The road from Chinchero to Urubamba runs through an undulating *puna* landscape scattered with small lakes and numerous tiny Indian dwellings. Every Sunday the Indians drive their llamas and donkeys towards Chinchero, laden with goods for market—although this traditional mode of transport is increasingly giving way to motor vehicles now that the road has been built.

There is a turning to the left (43km, 27 miles) for the village of **Maras** (3km, 2 miles). Seven kilometres (4 miles) beyond the village is the archaeological site of **Moray**. It is made up of crater-shaped depressions up to 150m (492ft) deep, each lined with shelf-like terraces created by the Incas for agricultural purposes. One can still see the original irrigation channels and drainage ditches. The site is thought to have been a nursery complex for the development and adaptation of new crop plants.

As the road drops down steeply into the Urubamba Valley, there is a fantastic view of the snow-covered mountains of the Cordillera de Urubamba, which has yet to be properly surveyed and mapped. **Urubamba** (56km [35 miles], 2,860m [9,380ft]) is the main town in the bottom of the valley. The tourist hotel offers both refreshment and overnight accommodation.

The road continues downstream towards **Ollantaitambo** (74km [46 miles], 2,750m [9,020ft]), where a rocky spur juts out into the valley. This is the site where the Incas built one of their border defences. It is described in more detail on page 211.

Mountain lovers who are used to high altitudes are recommended to carry on up the Málaga Pass, and maybe even to continue towards the tropical region of **Quillabamba**. This route goes through some of the most beautiful scenery in the whole of Peru. Six kilometres (4 miles) beyond Ollantaitambo the road leaves the Urubamba Valley and climbs up in an endless series of hairpins between two enormous

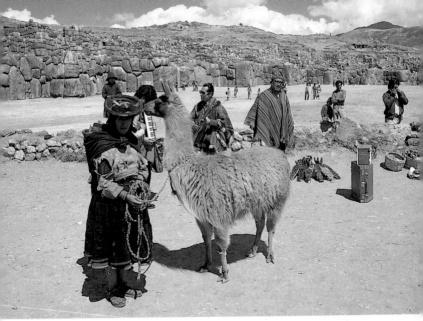

Sacsayhuamán Fortress

mountains called Huacratanca (5,500m, 18,040ft) and Verónica (5,750m, 18,860ft). Forty-five kilometres (28 miles) from Ollantaitambo, the road reaches the top of the **Málaga Pass** (4,320m, 14,212ft). It then begins the long descent through tropical gorges filled with dense cloud forests.

3 HALF- OR WHOLE-DAY EXCURSION TO PISAC VIA QUENCO AND TAMBOMACHAY

Pisac is very popular on Sundays because of its Indian market, whereas on other days of the week it is a rather lonely, depressing little place. But there are a number of fascinating ruins both on the way to Pisac and in the area around it. The route leaves Cuzco along the road past the Sacsayhuamán Fortress (see map page 161), and continues to climb up the hillside.

The **Quenco** (Kencco) site is 4km (2¹/₂ miles) further on. The amphitheatre is to the right just below the road. It consists of a semi-circular stage surrounded by seats hewn out of the bare rock. The rock standing in the centre of the amphitheatre resembles a puma when viewed from a certain angle. The purpose of the site is still the subject of debate. Some researchers think the rock had something to do with the cat-god cult of the Chavín period and was later demolished, while others think there was some kind of ancient cult

Ruins at Pisac

here based on the worship of certain natural phenomena. The area behind the rock has been hewn out into a labyrinth of passages and caves with stone altars. As for the many zigzag-shaped channels decorated with snake motifs, there are arguments as to whether they were for water or for the blood from sacrifices.

Further along the same road is the ancient site of **Pucapucará** (9km, 5$\frac{1}{2}$ miles), where the remains of an Inca fortress are clearly visible to the right of the road. It was presumably built to guard the entrance to the Urubamba Valley. There are usually Indians waiting here for tourists to take photos of them standing in front of these ancient walls, which are built of small unpolished stones.

Next to Pucapucará there is a left turn for **Tambomachay** (Tampumachchay), which is only about 100m away. This Inca site consists of a series of four stone terraces. The presence of a spring has led to the popular designation 'Inca baths', but most historians are agreed that the water served some kind of religious purpose. At religious ceremonies the Inca and his top noblemen are supposed to have stood and watched from the niches along the uppermost terrace. A short distance beyond Pucapucará the road reaches its

The mayors or alcaldes *at Pisac*

highest point before dropping down into the Urubamba Valley, the 'Sacred Valley of the Incas'.

A visit to the Sunday market at **Pisac** (30km [18¹/₂ miles], 2,970m [9,740ft]) seems almost to have become statutory for all tourists visiting Cuzco. Though originally a traditional Indian market in which goods were exchanged, it has now been totally transformed in response to the tourist market and the trade which this has inevitably brought with it. It is no longer a proper Indian market, and is only worth coming to for the sake of the large range of local textiles and handicrafts that are available.

One particular spectacle is the entrance of the mayors (*alcaldes*) from the surrounding villages. This colourful procession is announced by a few blasts on the *pututu*, a wind instrument made from large sea snails. The mayors enter the great Sunday fair dressed in beautifully made robes, and each carrying a silver-mounted staff as a sign of office.

On the mountainside about 300m (984ft) above the village are the fascinating Inca ruins of Pisac. They can be reached either via a new metalled road (9km, 5¹/₂ miles) or by an exhausting but very interest-

Pisac market

ing climb on foot taking about one and a half hours. The path goes up from the main square (keep bearing right). The road forks close to the site, and the left (ie lower) fork leads to a car park, which is an easy ten minutes' walk from the site.

The first section along the path down from the car park is thought to have been the residential quarter because the stonework is much simpler. The rock face behind it contains about 2,000 Inca burial caves. A tunnel leads through to what was once a watch tower, and from here a path leads down to the main temple complex.

The temple complex is one of the best-preserved and most carefully constructed of all Inca sites. The central structure was probably some kind of observatory (*intihuatana* or the 'sun's moorings'), where the time of year was determined from the shadow of a vertical stone hewn out of the rock. The buildings around it were presumably dedicated to the weather gods (rainbow and thunder), the moon and the stars.

There is a new road from Pisac going downstream along the Urubamba Valley. The hillsides are covered with old Inca terraces, which made it possible to cultivate even the steepest slopes and also prevented erosion. This suggests that the Urubamba Valley was very much the 'breadbasket' of the Inca empire.

Urubamba (60km [37 miles], 2,860m [9,380ft]) is the main town

Andahuaylillas church

in the valley. The tourist hotel offers both refreshment and overnight accommodation. There is a scenic road leading back to Cuzco via Chinchero. But before returning it is worth continuing another 18km (11 miles) downstream to the Inca fortress of Ollantaitambo, which is described later.

4 HALF-DAY EXCURSION TO PIQUILLACTA AND ANDAHUAYLILLAS

This excursion does not provide very much scenery, and the ruined sites along the way are not among the best, but the village church of Andahuaylillas is one of the finest in the Peruvian mountain region.

The route leaves Cuzco along the Puno road (see map page 161). Lovers of old churches should take a short turn through **San Sebastián** (5km, 3 miles), which has a fine baroque church built in 1650 by native architects.

Oropesa (25km, 15¹/₂ miles) is only a short distance from the main road on the opposite side of the valley. The mud-brick church is rather shabby on the outside, but contains some fine paintings and a skilfully carved pulpit.

Soon after the turning for Pisac and Paucartambo (30km, 18¹/₂ miles), there is another turning for **Piquillacta** (32km, 20 miles), which lies about 1km (half a mile) to the left of the main road. The ruins cover an area of 50 hectares (123 acres), and are surrounded by a 10m (33ft) high wall that is still partly intact. The purpose of the site is the subject of considerable scholarly controversy. Some consider Piquillacta (Piki Llacta) to be the remains of a pre-Inca city that was inhabited by Aymará Indians during the time of the Tiahuanaco culture. Others think it was the site of a vast Inca storage complex, where food, clothing and weapons were stored.

The **Rumicalca** (Rumiccolca) site (33km, 20 miles) is to the right of the road at the top of the pass. There are the remains of a large gateway built of enormous stone blocks that apparently guarded the entrance to the Cuzco Valley. It would also have served a dual purpose as an aqueduct for the water supply to Piquillacta.

Andahuaylillas (40km [131 miles], 3,090m [10,135ft]) is a village in the Urubamba Valley. The village church stands next to the main square about 1km (half a mile) to the right of the main road. It is built of mud bricks and looks rather plain from the outside. It is usually locked, so someone with a key must be found by asking at the presbytery next door. But the interior of the church is well worth the effort of getting a key. It is chock-full of baroque decorations, with an elaborately carved gilt altar, brightly coloured mudejar ceilings, large paintings mounted in extravagant frames and an organ adorned with angels playing seventeenth-century musical instruments.

5 DOWN INTO THE AMAZONIAN JUNGLE

There are several ways of visiting the tropical jungle from Cuzco. The simplest way is to fly to **Puerto Maldonado** (see page 215), which provides accommodation (including a jungle lodge) and boat trips of various lengths. The land routes are far more difficult, but offer some much more exciting scenery, especially the spectacular tropical gorges along the eastern flank of the Andes, of which Machu Picchu provides a small taster.

The most suitable destination is the area around the upper reaches of the Río Madre de Dios, where the inaccessible Manú National Park is also situated. From Cuzco one need only go as far as Pilcopata in order to get a good impression. The road via Paucartambo is so precipitous that a one-way system operates, alternating with each day. This means that at least two days must be allowed for the trip. There are several ways of undertaking the journey, depending on taste and on financial resources: By lorry. Most lorries take paying passengers. The journey is cheap and there are no problems apart from accommodation; By hire car. Deep ruts, large boulders and deep fords make the driving extremely slow and difficult (lorries are much faster). What is more, there is no fuel to be obtained on the way; On an organised expedition. Everything is provided by the travel company in Cuzco, though for a corresponding price! This also means that one can get out into the virgin forest of the Manú National Park.

The Journey to the Río Madre de Dios

The route goes from Cuzco via Pisac (30km [18 miles], see excursion 3 above) to **Paucartambo** (88km, 54$^1/_2$ miles). The traditional nature of this isolated little town is reflected in the bright colours even of everyday clothing, though the costumes worn on special festivals such as 16 July are more colourful still. Further on (113km, 70 miles) there is a turning for **Tres Cruzes** (14km, 8$^1/_2$ miles), which is famed throughout the country for its fantastic sunrises.

The road crosses a pass (3,800m, 12,464ft) and begins a spectacular descent through the cloud forests. It runs along gorges so full of mist and green vegetation that their depth can only be guessed at. The sides of the gorge are overgrown with tree ferns and orchids.

Pilcopata (194km, 120 miles) lies just above the point where several rivers join to form the Río Madre de Dios, which becomes a mighty river hundreds of kilometres downstream in Bolivia.

At **Salvación** (215km, 133 miles) there is some simple accommodation available. This is also where the Manú National Park has its offices. A permit must be obtained here for a visit to the park, which involves travelling by boat from Shintuya (247km, 153 miles) further downstream. The boat journey takes at least two days.

Huaraz and the Cordillera Blanca

Altitude: 3,090m (10,135ft)
Population: 52,000
Air links: Anta Airport 32km (20 miles) north of Huaraz
Road links: Pativica-Lima 402km [250 miles] (Route 2a), Casma-Lima 517km [320 miles] (Route 2b)

The Santa Valley, also known as the Callejón de Huaylas is without doubt one of the most beautiful valleys in the whole of Peru. The valley runs from south to north, and is dominated on the left-hand side by the mostly snow-free Cordillera Negra or 'Black Mountains'. To the right it is hemmed in by the heavily glaciated Cordillera Blanca or 'White Mountains'. The icy peaks of the Cordillera Blanca are among the most impressive in the whole of Peru. They also include Peru's highest peak, Huascarán, which at 6,770m (22,205ft) towers more than 4,000m (13,120ft) above the green fields at the bottom of the Santa Valley.

Huaraz is the main town in the valley. In 1970 it was almost totally destroyed in a disastrous earthquake. But a modern city has grown out of the rubble, which with its metalled roads and improved accommodation has made Huaraz even more popular as a tourist resort. However, apart from a few mountaineering enthusiasts, most visitors so far have been native Peruvians.

The market is especially interesting, with Indian women dressed in colourful costumes selling their modest wares. The museum is housed in a new building next to the main square. It chiefly contains carved monoliths from the Chavín period.

EXCURSIONS FROM HUARAZ

Huaraz is an ideal base for a whole range of marvellous excursions. However, with the exception of the metalled road along the valley and the roads to Casma and Chavín, the roads generally are so appalling that the average European would consider them impassable. But locals think otherwise, and one not infrequently sees a luxury car battling its way through terrain for which it appears totally unsuited. There are numerous travel agents offering a wide range of organised minibus tours to the most interesting places in the area. There are also large numbers of taxis available for excursions.

Lake Llanganuco and Chavín should on no account be missed out of the itinerary. The Puya Raimondii National Park is also highly recommended. Not everywhere is accessible by road, but there are countless paths for hikers and mountaineers going through the most unforgettable scenery. Full details of these are available at the Swiss-run Hostal Andino in Huaraz.

1 To Punta Callán (12km, 7¹/₂ miles)

Visitors who have not come via Casma should go at least some way up this road to see the view. As the road climbs the Cordillera Negra, a fantastic panorama opens up across the Santa Valley to reveal the whole mighty range of the Cordillera Blanca. It is not necessary to climb all the way up the pass (4,200m, 13,776ft), as the best view can be obtained only 12km (7¹/₂ miles) out of Huaraz.

2 Down Along the Santa Valley

(Huallanca 116km, 72 miles)

A whole day is needed for this trip, which offers a wide variety of scenery. The first part includes some fantastic views of the Cordillera Blanca. Then as the vegetation becomes continually sparser, the road begins a breathtaking journey through the Cañon del Pato (Duck Canyon), passing through a series of tunnels. Much of the route is shown on the map on page 191.

0 **Huaraz** (3,090m, 10,135ft). The road passes the last tourist hotel and heads through the eucalyptus forest directly towards the double peak of Huascarán.

6 **Monterrey**. There is a right turn for the Hotel Monterrey, which is

Puya raimondii *plants near Huaraz*

about 500m from the road. Next to the hotel is a hot spring that feeds water into thermal baths at a temperature of 30°C (86°F).

Anta Airport. Some of the icy peaks are particularly impressive from here, including Huascarán (6,770m, 22,205ft), Hualcán (6,130m, 20,106ft) and Copa (6,280m, 20,598ft).

32

Macará (2,750m, 9,020ft).

35

2a To the Quebrada Honda

A side road leads from Macará to the thermal springs of **Chanos** (3km, 2 miles) and on to **Vicos** (7km [4 miles], 3,050m [10,004ft]), where there is a marvellous view of Ranrapalca (6,168m, 20,231ft) and Tocllaraju (6,034m, 19,790ft). The road climbs in a series of hairpins up to the **Quebrada Honda** (*quebrada* means a deep valley with steep sides). A rough track frequented by locals runs up the valley and over a high pass called the **Portachuelo de Honda** (4,750m, 15,580ft) to **Chacas** (54km, 33 miles). The top of the pass provides one of the best views in the whole of the Cordillera Blanca.

35   **Macará** (2,750m, 9,020ft).

41   **Carhuaz** (2,650m, 8,692ft) is the second-largest town in the valley, lying below the mighty bastions of Hualcán (6,125m, 20,090ft) and Copa (6,200m, 20,598ft).

2b To the Quebrada Ulta

A new road from Carhuaz goes over the Ulta Pass (4,880m, 16,006ft) via a 280m tunnel and down to **Chacas**, from where it is possible to travel to Chavín — provided that the road is not cut off by rock falls, erosion or other damage).

After the village of **Chilla** (16km [10 miles], 3,050m [10,004ft]) the road climbs and twists until it finally enters the **Quebrada Ulta.** Just before that there is a steep path on the right leading up to Lake Auquiscocha (4,300m, 14,104ft) at the foot of Hualcán (6,125m, 20,090ft). The path takes two or three hours to climb, and goes through queñoa woods and past numerous waterfalls.

The top end of the Quebrada Ulta is dominated by the jagged peak of Contrahierbas (6,036m, 19,798ft) and the giant pyramid of the Nevada Ulta (5,875m, 19,270ft). As the road climbs the pass, the southern peak of Huascarán (6,770m, 22,205ft) and the glaciers of Chopicalqui (6,354m, 20,841ft) come more impressively into view behind.

---

41   **Carhuaz** (2,650m, 8,692ft). Further down the valley the icy flanks of Huascarán (6,770m, 22,205ft) come fully into view.

58   **Ranrahirca.** Little remains of this small village at the entrance to the Llanganuco Valley. Once a small town of some 5,000 inhabitants, it was mostly swept away after the great earthquake of 1970, when a massive avalanche of mud, stones and enormous boulders came sweeping down the valley from Huascarán. This was the most recent of many such catastrophes caused by the shifting of great ice masses on the precipitous north-western flank of the mountain. This, combined with glacial outflow and areas of loose scree, produced a mighty avalanche that fell some 4,000m (13,120ft) into the valley below.

61   **Old Yungay**. The road goes round a hill crowned by a statue of Christ. This was once the cemetery belonging to the town of Yungay. The top of the hill provides a depressing view of the swathe of mud and boulders covering the area where the town once lay. Yungay was normally spared the ravages of the landslides that came down into the valley, because a 200m (656ft) high ridge provided a barrier against them. But the 1970 earthquake loosed such a gigantic mass of mud and stones that it overshot the ridge and poured down over the town, burying 19,000 people. Only three minutes earlier, the earthquake had unleashed panic throughout the town. Only a small

number of people had managed to scramble up to the safety of the cemetery in the short time that remained as the avalanche came thundering across the valley. The former main square and church are marked by the tops of three palm trees and a rather larger pile of boulders.

Yungay (2,450m, 8,036ft). With the help of donations from all over the world, the survivors built a new settlement to the north of the disaster area, but it is only gradually beginning to gain an air of permanence. There is a turning here for the **Lake Llanganuco** (see excursion 3 below). 63

Caraz (2,290m, 7,511ft). There is a right turn here for **Lake Parón** (see excursion 4 below), and yet another right turn for Cashapampa and the Quebrada de los Cedros. 77

2c Quebrada de los Cedros

The second turning to the right in Caraz leads up to the small village of **Cashapampa** (16km [10 miles], 2,900m [9,512ft]), from which there are two possible paths for walkers (see map page 193).

The first climbs up along the **Quebrada Santa Cruz**, over the Punta de la Unión Pass to Colcabamba and eventually to Lake Llanganuco. This is one of the most popular mountain walks in the whole of the Cordillera Blanca. But it is much better to tackle it from the opposite end at Lake Llanganuco (see excursion 3b below), because the climbs are less punishing that way.

The second walk is extremely difficult and tiring on account of the large differences in altitude, so it can only be recommended to walkers who have become accustomed to the altitude (there is no way down for those suffering from mountain sickness).

The path climbs more than 2,000m (6,560ft) from the bottom of the valley via Lake Cullicocha (26km [16 miles] from Cashapampa, 4,600m [15,088ft]) to top of the Los Cedros Pass (4,800m, 15,744ft). It then drops down into the **Quebrada de los Cedros** (39km [24 miles], 4,000m [13,120ft]), where there are some Inca ruins to be found. The view from the top end of the valley (49km [30 miles], 4,500m [14,760ft] repays all the effort of getting there. For **Alpamayo** (5,947m, 15,506ft) has been declared the most beautiful mountain in the world on account of its almost perfect pyramidal form.

Caraz (2,290m, 7,511ft). The Santa Valley now becomes increasingly hot and dry, and the valley bottom is covered with a wilderness of cactuses and thorn bushes. 77

Sucre (2,180m, 7,150ft). This village marks the beginning of the famous **Cañon del Pato** or 'Duck Canyon'. This narrow gorge is continually threatened by landslides and floods, as the Río Santa runs its meandering course along the bottom. The road is no longer 91 metalled here, and it bypasses the most difficult sections by means of no less than thirty-five tunnels.

116 **Huallanca** (1,450m, 4,756ft). At the last hairpin along the road, the gorge suddenly opens out, and a tropical garden appears like a mirage in the valley below. In the vicinity is the famous Santa Hydroelectric Station, which has been tunnelled deep into the mountainside and provides electricity for the iron foundries in Chimbote on the coast. Permission to visit the station may be obtained at a restaurant situated among the workers' villas in the bottom of the valley.

3 To Lake Llanganuco (89km, 55 miles)

A day excursion is sufficient for visiting Lake Llanganuco, which is situated at the foot of Huascarán amid the wildest, most romantic scenery. The road is the same as for excursion 2 as far as **Yungay** (63km, 39 miles). There is a right turn in the new village just past the ruins of the old town.

The road climbs up through the Llanganuco Valley, which has been swept bare by numerous landslides. There are some fantastic views of the jagged peak of Huandoy (6,360m, 20,860ft) and the two more rounded peaks of Huascarán (6,770m, 22,205ft). The Indian huts around here are traditionally round, but are gradually giving way to the usually right-angled construction.

Later on the road enters a typical glacial U-shaped valley (*quebrada*), its 1,000m (3,280ft) high vertical walls sandwiched between Huascarán and Huandoy. The queñoa woods in the valley bottom are covered with epiphytes, whose rosetta-like water storage chambers are filled with millions of developing midges. Inspite of the altitude, these insects can be a real plague, especially in the rainy season, so that insect repellent is essential. (The route from now on is shown on the map on page 193.)

Lake Llanganuco (3,820m, 12,520ft) is 26km (16 miles) up from Yungay. It is surrounded by pretty queñoa woods and hosts of flowering herbs. All nature-lovers are recommended to follow the signposted walk (*Sendro María Josefa*) leading from the warden's hut. It takes about half an hour, and goes downhill and back onto the road, making it ideal for visitors who are less used to the altitude.

More energetic visitors are strongly urged to go on further up the valley. The route to the second lake admittedly brings no change in scenery. But as soon as the road crosses the river, it begins a twisty and precipitous climb up to a pass called the **Portachuelo de Llanganuco** (40km [25 miles], 4,750m [15,580ft]). The view becomes more spectacular with every hairpin. The mighty south face of Huandoy (6,360m, 20,860ft) towers up above the two blue-green lakes in the valley bottom. But Huandoy is only the first of a massive

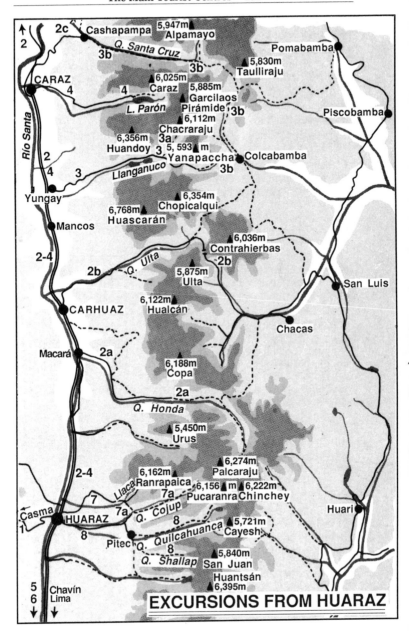

EXCURSIONS FROM HUARAZ

series of icy cliffs and pinnacles extending all the way to Chacraraju (6,112m, 20,047ft). On the other side of the valley are the eastern flank of Huascarán (6,770m, 22,205ft) and Chopicalqui (6,354m).

The meadow below the first hairpin after the second lake (see above) is frequently occupied by tents. This is the first bivouac point for mountain walkers wishing to tackle the two most popular routes through the Cordillera Blanca.

3a Quebrada Yanapaccha

There is a relatively easy path leading up to the end of the Llanganuco Valley (7km), where Lake 69 (4,500m, 14,760ft) lies at the very foot of Chacraraju (6,112m, 20,047ft).

3b Quebradas Huaripampa and Santa Cruz

This walking tour takes between four and six days to complete, and is one of the most impressive walks in the whole of the Peruvian Andes (see map page 193). Walkers along this much-frequented route will see as many as a dozen peaks above 6,000m (19,680ft) and many more that are nearly as high.

Equipment and mule parties can be hired from tourist agencies in Huaraz and Yungay. Early every morning a truck carries passengers from Yungay to the top of the Portachuelo de Llanganuco, thus saving the exhausting climb up to the top of the pass. It is 59km (36 miles) from the Portachuelo de Llanganuco to the final destination at Cashapampa (see excursion 2c above).

The path makes a long descent from the pass (4,750m, 15,580ft) down to Vaqueria (9km [5½ miles], 3,700m [12,136ft]) and eventually to **Colcabamba** (12km [7 miles], 3,300m [10,824ft]), where simple board and accommodation are available.

There follows a climb through damp meadows and mountain woodlands to the **Quebrada Huaripampa,** with views of the eastern side of the gigantic rock pinnacle of Chacraraju (6,112m, 20,047ft). There is a path up to the left (22km [13½ miles], 3,800m [12,464ft]) leading into the **Quebrada Paria** (4km, 2¼ miles), which is worth a short detour. This valley is overlooked by the mighty northern flank of Chacraraju and the Pirámide de Garcilaso (5,885m, 19,302ft).

The main route continues almost directly towards Taulliraju (5,830m, 19,122ft). It climbs up past the lower and upper Morococha Lakes (30km [18½ miles], 4,600m [15,580ft]) to the top of a pass called the **Punta de la Unión** (31km [19 miles], 4,750m [15,580ft]). There follows the long descent into the **Quebrada Santa Cruz**. Partway down the valley is Lake Jaruncocha (43km [26½ miles], 3,900m [12,792ft]). The final section is very steep but finally arrives in **Cashapampa** (59km [36½] miles 2,900m [9,512ft]), from which there is a road link to Caraz.

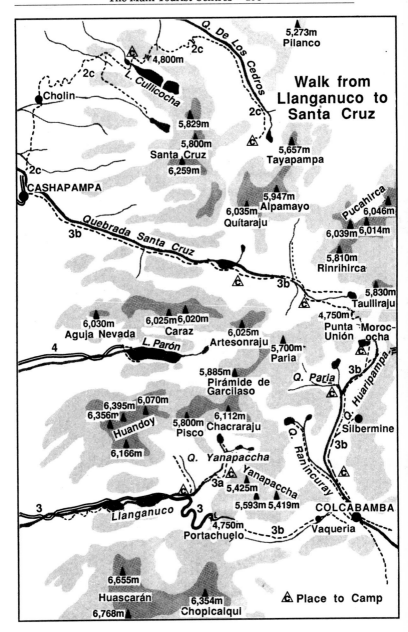

Walk from Llanganuco to Santa Cruz

Yungay cemetery — a reminder of the earthquake catastrophe

4 To Lake Parón (110km, 68 miles)

Lake Parón (4,150m, 13,612ft) is surrounded by even more dramatic scenery, though the steep banks mean that only short walks are possible from the end of the road. The route follows the same road as excursion 2 as far as **Caraz** (77km [48 miles], 2,290m [7,511ft]), from which there is a steep climb of some 1,900m (6,232ft).

Lake Parón lies at the top end of a 1,200m (3,936ft) deep gorge running between Huandoy (6,360m, 20,860ft) and the jagged ice pinnacles of Aguja Nevada (6,030m, 19,778ft). The massive glaciers that come down from these peaks lie directly above the lake and are reflected in its waters. The level of the lake has been reduced by 40m (131ft) by means of an underground channel. This is to prevent a disaster in the event of an earthquake, which could easily dislodge the glaciers, causing the lake to burst through the moraine and devastate the whole valley below.

5 To the Puya Raimondii National Park

(54km, 33 miles)

The landscape around the upper reaches of the Santa Valley is quite different from that further downstream, with large expanses of open plateau covered in *puna*. These highlands support some unusual vegetation, of which the most remarkable is a plant related to the pineapple called *Puya raimondii*, after which the national park has been named. It grows to about 4m (13ft) in height and looks rather like a dwarf palm covered in spines. But it produces a spectacular display of giant candle-shaped flowers up to 10m (33ft) high, which stand out against the snow on the mountains.

The route follows the Santa Valley along the metalled road for Pativilca and Lima (see Route 2a, Chapter 3). Six kilometres (19$^{1}/_{2}$ miles) beyond **Catac** (41km, 25 miles from Huaraz) the road makes a sharp bend through a gorge, and immediately afterwards there is a left turn for the national park. The warden's hut is just 13km (8 miles) up this road. The *Puya* plants are already visible on the mountainside above, and if one climbs up far enough (4,200m [13,776ft], 4,600m [15,088ft]), one can eventually see them next to the road.

One can carry on even further up the road until the beautiful peaks of Raria (5,576m, 18,289ft) and Huarapasca (5,430m, 17,810ft) come into view. Immediately before the top of the 4,800m (15,744ft) high Huarapasca Pass (30km (18$^{1}/_{2}$ miles) from the turning), the road crosses a river coming down from a valley to the right. A short walk up the valley leads to the foot of the glacier below Pasto Ruri (5,240m, 17,187ft). The blue ice of the glacier can be dangerous to walk on.

6 To the Ruins of Chavín de Huántar

(109km, 357 miles)

One of the most rewarding trips from Huaraz is across the Cordillera

Blanca to the fascinating pre-Inca remains of Chavín. The journey and the site are described in full on page 154.

7 To Huillcahuain and Lake Llaca (29km, 18 miles)
Just past the tourist hotel along the metalled road from Huaraz to Carhuaz (see map page 191), there is a right turn (2km, 1¼ miles) for Lake Llaca. The road is very steep and stony as it climbs up through the eucalyptus woods to a village. **Huillcahuain** (Willcawain) is just beyond the village and 8km (5 miles) from Huaraz. It consists of two ruined sites surrounded by stone walls that are probably pre-Inca.

The road continues to twist and climb up to **Lake Llaca**, from which there is a marvellous view of the mountains. To the extreme left are the horn-like peaks of Vallunaraju (5,686m, 18,650ft), which are linked by a razor-sharp ridge to the mighty south face of Ocshapalca (5,888m, 19,312ft). From the end of the road (4,400m, 14,432ft) there is a fairly easy 2-hour walk up to the Ocshapalca Glacier. Ice is hacked off the glacier here and carried down on muleback to Huaraz, where it is used in the production of icecream.

7a Quebrada Cojup
Just 15km (9 miles) up the Lake Llaca road (17km, 10½ miles from Huaraz), there is a steep path going up into the **Quebrada Cojup** (3,800m, 12,464ft) only 1km (half a mile) away. A broad path runs up along the valley to an old camp (14km [8 miles], 4,400m [14,432ft]). The last kilometre up to **Lake Polcacocha** (15km [9 miles], 4,500m [14,760ft]) is extremely tiring, but the view makes it well worth the effort. The mighty south face of Ranrapalca (6,162m, 20,211ft) glowers across the valley at Pucaranra, while the giant rock face of Palcaraju (6,274m, 20,578ft) straddles the end of the valley.

8 To Pitec (20km, 12 miles)
The village of **Pitec** (3,800m, 12,464ft) to the east of Huaraz forms the starting point for a number of fine walks. It can be reached from Huaraz via the Avenida Raimondi, which runs east-west through the town. The road deteriorates considerably on leaving Huaraz, and climbs 800m (2,624ft) within the space of 20km, 12 miles.

There is a fairly easy path up to **Lake Tallparaju** (15km [9 miles], 4,300m [14,104ft]), which is enclosed by a massive circle of mountains. Another path leads up through the **Quebrada Shallup**, which is famous for its waterfalls, ending at Lake Shallup.

Iquitos
Altitude: 95m (311ft)
Population: 125,000
Air links: Lima, Pucallpa, Leticia (Colombia), Manaus (Brazil)

Queñoa trees by the shore of Lake Llanganuco

Boat: irregular services downstream to Leticia and Manaus; primitive, unreliable services upstream to Pucallpa (about 8 days)

Iquitos, the chief town of the Peruvian jungle region, is a city full of superlatives; situated in the biggest jungle in the world, next to the river with the largest volume of water, it is the furthest from the sea of any deep-water port (3,700km, 2,294 miles). It has also been described by poets as 'a rainbow-winged butterfly next to a large silver snake'.

For those who remain unmoved by poetry or superlatives, Iquitos is still a unique and unforgettable experience. The jungle tours and the boat trips on the Amazon are by no means cheap, but they are an exhilarating adventure that can be experienced without too much effort or danger. They also provide a unique opportunity to see the strangely clad Indians of the jungle in their natural environment.

THINGS TO SEE IN THE TOWN
The great rubber boom around the turn of the century turned Iquitos into a great centre of prosperity, and most of the fine Portuguese-tiled buildings date from this period. The same is true of the **riverside promenade** along the banks of the Amazon, which is just 2km

198

Huascarán National Park: forest near Llanganuco

(1¼ miles) wide at this point. The rubber barons were also responsible for buying the **iron house** next to the Plaza de Armas, which was originally built by Eiffel as part of the Great Exhibition in Paris.

Five blocks from the Plaza along the Jirón Raymondi is the **Municipal Museum**, which contains a colourful display of the rich fauna from the jungle around Iquitos. The animals were once doomed to eventual extinction, but there is new hope for them now that the hunting and export of live animals has been banned. The museum also shows the costumes of local Indian tribes, and some of their artefacts such as the great wooden drums, whose message can be heard as far as 20km (12 miles) away.

The street going in the opposite direction from the Plaza is the Jirón Lima, which is the town's main shopping street. A good kilometre along here is the town's busy market quarter, from which the streets to the left go down to Belén.

Belén could easily be described as the Venice of the Amazon. The houses are built on floating rafts or long stilts. The canals are full of boats laden with bananas, sugar cane, timber, rubber and other local products that are unloaded and sold at Iquitos. The water level is highest from April to June. But during the dry season in September and October, the level drops by an average of 12m (39ft), so that the houses are left high and dry. The canals turn into streets, where the rubbish piles up until the next flood fortunately clears it all away.

SHORT EXCURSIONS FROM IQUITOS

1 To Lake Quistococha (16km, 10 miles)

To get here one must turn left off the wide metalled road to the new airport just before it reaches the customs buildings. Lake Quistococha has been turned into a beautiful safe bathing area amid a glorious tropical landscape. The large basins nearby are fish hatcheries containing genuine arapaima, the greatest delicacy of this region. However, the hotels often substitute zúngaro, a similarly large but much inferior fish, which they pass off as arapaima.

2 To Lake Moronacocha

This lake on the northern edge of the town is famous for the beautiful sunsets that can be seen from here. Next to the waterfront is a fish-breeding station (*criadero de peces*), from which tropical fish are exported to aquaria all over the world.

RIVER AND JUNGLE TOURS

The great Amazon experience is available from a number of different tourist agencies. The programme usually begins with a trip in a speed boat to a jungle lodge next to a quiet tributary. An excellent lunch is laid on, including various local specialities. After the usual midday downpour there is an opportunity to fish for piranha or even to bathe, though the latter is not recommended.

The next item on the agenda is a walk along slippery paths to visit a local Indian tribe (usually Jívaros or Yaguas). At the sight of strangers they quickly put on their warpaint and stage a shooting display with their metre-long blowpipes. Those who wish can have their faces daubed with red juice from the fruit of the achiote tree, which is supposed to repel mosquitos — though insect repellent (*repelente para insectos*) is probably a better precaution.

Visitors who do not have to get back to Iquitos may stay on to experience yet more unforgettable adventures, such as an evening boat trip or even a night in the jungle.

Other tourist agents offer similar well-organised excursions to the luxurious Amazon Lodge and to the Explorama Lodge at Yanamono, which is further downstream along the Amazon. Some of the smaller agencies provide a somewhat different programme, which makes a good complement to the main trip.

Machu Picchu

Altitude: 2,360m (7,740ft)
Railway: From Cuzco 112km [69 miles] — daily tourist service with bookable

seats, leaving at 7am, arriving about 11am and returning for Cuzco at 3.30pm.

The ruined city of Machu Picchu was discovered by an American called Hiram Bingham in 1911, perched inaccessibly above a steep-sided valley swathed in dense tropical jungle. The jungle has since been cleared, new paths have been created, a hotel built and much of the site reconstructed. But the great mysteries of Machu Picchu remain as ever unsolved. Speculation and theories abound, while hard evidence remains tantalisingly elusive.

The architectural evidence, backed up by the evidence of pottery finds, suggests that Machu Picchu was built in the mid-fifteenth century at the time of Pachacutec, but there is no clear evidence as to its purpose. Was it originally a large temple that required a large number of people for its upkeep? Or was it only one of a whole series of border defences along the Urubamba Valley? It was thought by some to have been the last undiscovered refuge of the Incas, so often referred to by Spanish historians. But this theory has now been discredited since the discovery of yet more remains.

THE JOURNEY TO MACHU PICCHU (see map page 177)

Until the new road is completed, together with a cable car to the new hotel, the only way to Machu Picchu is via a narrow-gauge railway. Not far out of Santa Ana Station, the railway has a steep slope to negotiate, which it does by means of several zigzags. Soon the roofs and towers of Cuzco are left far below, until they finally disappear behind the ridge that divides Cuzco from the Anta Valley.

At first the valley is fairly broad and level, but it soon turns into a steep, narrow gorge leading down into the Urubamba Valley. The Inca fortress of Ollantaitambo and the massive rounded peak of Verónica (5,750m, 18,860ft) are soon visible to the right.

Kilometre 88 is where the Inca Trail goes off (only local trains stop here). Trained hikers can walk from here to Machu Picchu in about four days. Tents, food and drinking water must be carried for the whole journey. The hike is extremely tiring, with several steep climbs and a pass over 4,000m (13,120ft). But hikers' efforts are rewarded with dramatic scenery and many fascinating Inca fortresses along the way. Some agencies lay on special organised hikes, in which tourists are relieved of backpacking and cooking responsibilities.

After Kilometre 88 the Urubamba Valley becomes gradually steeper and more covered in vegetation. When the train passes a hydroelectric power station, this is the sign for day-trippers to move towards the doors of the train, so that they can make a run for the buses (with small change at the ready) before they are full up with passengers. The bus carries visitors along a narrow zigzag road up to the Inca ruins 400m (1,312ft) up the mountainside. When the first

The landscape of the Puya Raimondii National Park

Cacti

party has gone, it takes at least half an hour before the buses return. Another way to save valuable time is to take a packed lunch from the hotel in Cuzco, as the hotel in Machu Picchu is too small to cope with the flood of midday guests.

THE TOUR OF THE SITE

There are many different routes around this mysterious city, whose treasures are not always immediately apparent. But the route suggested below is ideal for day-trippers with limited time. The most important places are included in the first half of the tour, so that visitors who are quickly exhausted or who run out of time have at least gained a good impression of the site. The numbers below correspond to those given on the maps on pages 205 and 209.

1 Farmers' Huts

The tiny restored huts immediately past the ticket office were probably inhabited by farmers who tilled the terraces beyond. They have occasionally been thought to have belonged to the watchmen who guarded the city. But if that was the case, they were very badly sited, as the only entrance to the city was much further up the mountainside.

2 The Terraces

These are typical of Inca cultivation terraces. They made irrigation easier and prevented the valuable soil from being washed down the mountainside during the rainy season. Maize was probably the main crop. Just past the first row of terraces, there is a steep stairway to the left leading up to the old Inca Trail. This formed the original boundary of the city, but the walls are only partly preserved. There was only one gate in the walls through which people could enter (see number 16 below).

3 The Fountain Steps

The next flight of steps is so named because of a row of water basins linked by pipes and channels running downwards. If one turns left up a short series of steps, one comes to a group of buildings dominated by a skilfully constructed round tower.

4 The 'Mausoleum'

This is the name given to the cave underneath the round tower, although no human remains or other such clues have been found here. Next to the entrance there are six steps hewn out of the rock, which are thought to have represented Mamapacha, the earth mother. The niches inside the cave are supposed to have contained the mummies of important Incas, though there is no tangible proof of this. But there is a kind of altar inside, suggesting that this might have been some kind of underground sanctuary.

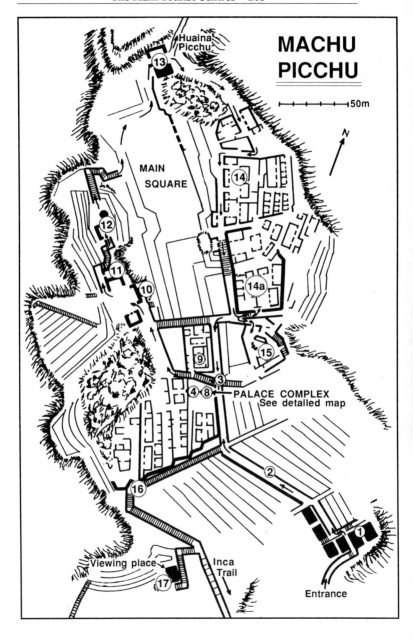

MACHU PICCHU

The road from the station to the ruins of Machu Picchu

5 The Round Tower

Hiram Bingham called this a 'military tower', but there is considerable confusion surrounding the actual purpose of the tower. There are channels along the window that looks out towards Huayna Picchu, the rocky mountain overlooking the site. Hiram Bingham thought they represented snakes and that these formed part of some religious rite. The window is therefore known as the *Ventana de los Amarus* or 'Window of the Holy Snakes'. Other experts think the channels were used as part of some water cult.

Yet another theory is that the building was never finished, and was never actually used for its intended purpose. This theory is based on the fact that the rock in the middle of the tower is of an irregular shape. However, the horseshoe-shaped plan of the tower and the trapezoid niches in the adjoining courtyard show marked parallels with features in buildings associated with sun worship.

Finally, there are those who believe that the building was the home of the Sun Virgins, who were to be found at every Inca religious centre. One point in favour of this is that of the 135 bodies found at Machu Picchu, 109 were those of young women.

There are many more theories as to the purpose of the tower. But all of them are agreed on one point: the building must have served a religious purpose, this being the only reason that could possibly

Machu Picchu

have justified such a complex structure.

6 The 'Grain Stores'
Such is the designation given to several buildings with much simpler stonework, which can be reached from the 'mausoleum' via a series of steps hewn out of the bare rock.

7 The 'Princess's Palace'
The *Palacio de la Ñustra* is the name given to the two-storey building standing between the round tower and the grain stores. A stairway goes up past them into the courtyard with the trapezoid niches, leading back inside the round tower. The window facing Huayna Picchu also looks out onto the ceremonial fountain.

8 The Ceremonial Fountain
Some experts believe this was used for some kind of baptism for the remission of sins.

9 The 'Inca's Palace'
This can be reached along a passage behind the round tower and across the Fountain Steps. The entrance to this complex of buildings is via a trapezoid door that is topped by a three-ton lintel hewn out of a single stone. The quality of the stonework and of the massive lintel

led Bingham to conclude that the building must have belonged to some high official, or even to the Inca himself.

The Fountain Steps divide into two flights next to the entrance to the Inca's Palace. The steeper of the two flights leads up to a terrace, to the right of which is the main temple area. This section includes the main temple (11), the Three Windows Temple (10) and the priests' dwellings, little of which now remains.

10 The Three Windows Temple
This is built out of massive stone blocks, of which the one that forms the lower part of the middle window is particularly remarkable. There is no wall on one side, but there is a tall stone column which presumably supported the roof.

11 The Main Temple
Behind the fine monolithic altar is one of the finest walls in the whole of Machu Picchu. The regular, almost rectangular stone blocks are slightly tapered towards the top, giving the impression that the building is much taller than it is. A staircase leads up from behind the temple to a hill top that is covered with the remains of various religious buildings.

12 Intihuatana
This is a Quechua word meaning 'the sun's moorings'. It refers to a skilfully carved stone 1.8m (6ft) high that stands on the summit, and which is thought by some experts to have been used as a sundial. Others see this strange stone as symbolising a universe that revolved around an axis running between the sun and the earth.

The most important part of the tour is now finished. There are two possible options from here. One alternative is to return to the temple area and go on up through the city gate (16) and along part of the Inca Trail to enjoy the view (17). The other option is to continue the tour by going down the other side of the hill to the main square, which was once used for big festivals.

13 The Temple of the Sacred Rock
Next to a rather nondescript hut with a reconstructed roof is a 3m (10ft) high rock surrounded by a low wall. There is a path leading up from here to the summit of Huayna Picchu, which takes about forty minutes to climb from this point (see the Huayna Picchu walk below).

14 The Eastern Quarter
The part of the site along the route back to the hotel is characterised by a much simpler style of building, suggesting that the common people lived in this quarter. There is a stairway leading down to the south-eastern corner of the main square.

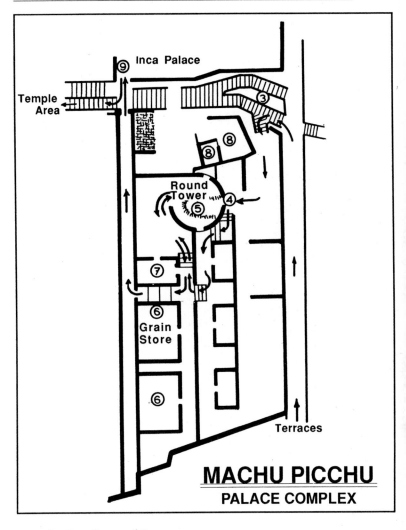

MACHU PICCHU
PALACE COMPLEX

14a The Intellectual Quarter

If one turns left at the bottom of the stairway, one comes into an area surrounded by a high wall, which is claimed by some to have been inhabited by the great thinkers of the empire. One of the houses contains two flat receptacles hewn out of the bedrock. These are thought to have been used for the production of dyes for robes

Among the ruins,
Machu Picchu

belonging to the nobility. This, however, would mean that the Sun Virgins lived here, since this was one of their tasks.

15 The Prison

This section lies immediately below the Intellectual Quarter towards the hotel. The complex is made up of several chambers, in which prisoners are supposed to have suffered a variety of tortures. There are a few niches in the walls with holes bored in the stone either side of them. It has been suggested that prisoners were held here with their arms through the holes and their hands tied together in front. Having been thus immobilised, they are supposed to have been slowly strangled by means of a heavy wooden collar placed around their necks.

The route leads back to the entrance across the Fountain Steps (3). But if there is time and energy left, it is worth making a short detour up the line of the old wall and along the first part of the Inca Trail.

16 The City Gate

This forms the beginning of the great Inca Trail from Machu Picchu to Ollantaitambo (see the Inca Trail walk below).

17 The Cemetery

There is a small stairway off the Inca Trail leading up to where a small hut has been restored next to the cemetery terraces. There is a marvellous view from here of the whole city with the Urubamba Valley and the steep summit of Huayna Picchu in the background.

WALKS FROM MACHU PICCHU

1 Up Huayna Picchu

Looking up at the steep granite pinnacle of Huayna Picchu, it is difficult to imagine that there is a path leading up to the top. But experienced mountain walkers will have no great difficulty climbing it in about an hour from the hotel. It is essential to have a good head for heights, as the narrow path runs along precipitous drops of nearly 1,000m (3,280ft), and is often slippery to boot. But there are ropes to hang on to along the most difficult sections. The early morning is recommended for the climb, as the path is then still in shadow.

The summit (2,720m, 8,921ft) is 360m (1,180ft) above the main square, and is littered with artificial caves, remains of houses and even cultivation terraces. Bingham thought that beacons were often lit on this mountain top, which had special, magical and religious significance. He also thought the watchmen lived up here and tilled their own fields.

2 Along the Inca Trail

The walk along the old access route to the city is much easier than climbing up Huayna Picchu. The road is built out of granite slabs, and can even be mastered by less experienced walkers. Indeed, the most difficult section is the long stairway leading up to the city gate (16). Given the landscape around, it almost goes without saying that there are some amazing views along the way.

Two hour's walk from the hotel are the ruins of **Huiñay Huayna**, which are situated next to the trail at a height of 2,650m (8,692ft). Apart from thirty ruined houses and a plethora of cultivation terraces, there is a remarkable tower with seven large windows.

Ollantaitambo

Altitude: 2,750m (9,020ft)
Railway links: Cuzco (Santa Ana Station)
Road links: Cuzco via Chinchero 74km [242 miles], via Pisac 80km [50 miles] (see excursions 2 and 3 from Cuzco)

The plan of the modern village of Ollantaitambo still reflects that of the original Inca settlement. Above the village on a massive rocky spur jutting out into the valley are the remains of an Inca fortress that was built to guard the fertile valley from the attacks of fierce jungle tribes. The site also had a religious significance, and according to legend the hearts of the Inca rulers were buried here. The many half-prepared stones and unfinished structures lead one to suppose that building was still in progress when the Spaniards swept in.

TOUR OF THE SITE

The path from the car park leads up through a series of cultivation terraces to a wall with several trapezoid niches, where idols are presumed to have been displayed. It passes through a trapezoid archway that was probably the entrance to the temple. A narrow path continues up the hillside to a rock shaped like a chair that is known as the **Inca's Throne**.

The route continues past a stone shaped like an altar to a structure known as the **Unfinished Temple** or **Central Palace**. The two names reflect the present uncertainty as to the purpose of the building. But the remains are nonetheless very impressive. They consist of giant blocks of reddish-coloured porphyry that have somehow been brought across from a quarry on the opposite side of the valley. On the right-hand side where the stairs go up, one can see the system of slots and keys that held the stones together.

The buildings above the temple are of a much simpler construction. The narrow path running up behind them leads to the Sun Temple or **Intihuatana**, which is reached in about fifteen minutes.

In a private field on the other side of the car park is the so-called **Princess's Bath**, which consists of a stone decorated with geometrical designs with a fountain running onto it. The owner of the field will fill the water channel that supplies the fountain in return for a tip.

Paracas

Altitude: sea level
Road links: Lima 285km [176 miles], Pisco 22km [13 miles] (see Route 4)

The Paracas Peninsula is famous for its mysterious pre-Inca cemeteries. In recent years it has also become increasingly popular as a seaside resort on account of its sunny climate. The village of Paracas consists of no more than a few villas and hotels (including a luxury hotel), but it is within easy reach of the towns of Pisco and Ica.

There are a large number of excellent bathing beaches along the south side of the peninsula. But bathing is not recommended from the muddy beach near the Hotel Paracas, as it is much frequented by stingrays. The **Archaeological Museum** 2km ($1^1/_4$ miles) beyond the village is small but very interesting.

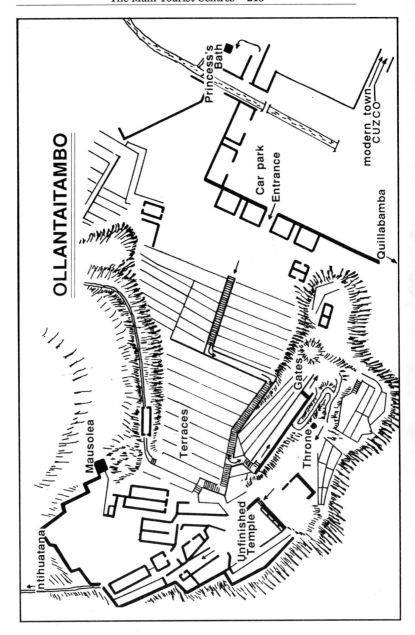

OLLANTAITAMBO

Princess's Bath

modern town CUZCO

Car park Entrance

Quillabamba

Gates

Throne

Terraces

Mausolea

Intihuatana

Unfinished Temple

Ollantaitambo

Visitors to Paracas are strongly recommended to take a boat trip to the **Islas Ballestras**. There is a boat every morning from in front of the Hotel Paracas, provided there are enough passengers to fill it. The waves have eroded these islands into gigantic rock platforms perched on columns of rock which emerge from the boiling sea. The caves below are inhabited by hundreds of seals and sea-lions, while the steep cliffs above are covered with the guano from the thousands of birds which nest here.

The boat also runs along the rocky shore of the peninsula to where a giant Nazca carving is visible from out at sea. This 150m (492ft) high picture has been scratched out of the loose surface rock, and was thought by Dänneken to indicate a landing place for creatures from outer space. Experts are in no way agreed as to what it is supposed to have represented — a gigantic candelabra according to some (hence the name El Candelabro), a columnar cactus according to others, while others again have suggested a 'tree of life' or some kind of marine navigation signal. The position and dimensions of the carving suggest that it might even have represented the constellation known to Europeans as the Southern Cross. But its purpose remains as obscure as ever, especially that of the flower-like decorations along the 'branches' and the square 'foot'.

Pucallpa

Altitude: 200m (656ft)
Population: 119,000
Air links: Lima, Iquitos, Tarapota
Road links: Lima 790km [490 miles] (see Route 3a)
Boat: primitive and unreliable connections to Iquitos (4-8 days)

Pucallpa has grown enormously in recent years, thanks to the new road link to Lima and the frenetic search for oil fields in the Peruvian Amazon. But as a town it still retains the somewhat provisional appearance of a gold-mining settlement.

The town itself may be uninspiring, but the jungle around offers much to interest the visitor. However, given a choice between Pucallpa and Iquitos as the base for a visit to the jungle, then Iquitos is much the better alternative, offering a greater variety of activities.

The most interesting part of the town is the port of La Hoyada, with its many floating dwellings. From here it is possible to hire a kind of dug-out with an outboard motor for a ride on the Ucayali, the 1,900km (1,178 mile) long tributary of the Amazon.

The main local tourist attraction is **Lake Yarinacocha**, which is an oxbow lake formed from a bend in the Ucayali that has become separated from the main river. It can only be reached by boat when the river level is high. It can be reached overland via a track that goes to the right off the Lima road at the edge of the town. About 5km (3 miles) further on (there is a regular bus service) is the small port of **Puerto Callao**, where boats are available for trips across the lake.

Only an hour away by boat is the famous village of the Shipibo Indians, whose pottery and textiles are available in Pucallpa. Another popular trip is across the river to the German-owned Hotel La Cabaña on the opposite shore, from which further trips into the jungle are possible (bookings can be made in Lima from the office behind the Hotel Bolívar).

Puerto Maldonado

Altitude: 250m (820ft)
Air links: Cuzco
Road links: Cuzco 531km [329 miles] (only by lorry; 3 days in good weather conditions)
Accommodation: tourist hotel.

This small frontier town in south-eastern Peru has grown amazingly quickly in recent years, thanks to the recently built road link, the prosperity of the timber industry and the luck of a few gold diggers. It is favourably situated at the confluence of the Río Tambopata with the great Río Madre de Dios. Although still largely made up of wooden huts reminiscent of the American Wild West, it is now showing considerable signs of progress.

The tourist trade has benefitted from the relative proximity of Cuzco. An hour's boat trip away along the Río Madre de Dios is a jungle lodge called the Albergue Cuzco Amazónico. Four hours away up the Río Tambopata is the Explorer's Inn, which is in the middle of a nature reserve. Three-day packages are arranged so as to include the boat trip from Puerto Maldonado, board and lodgings (almost luxurious by jungle standards) and various trips into the jungle. Travellers who book from Cuzco or Lima are met at the airport and need make no further arrangements.

The jungle regions around Puerto Maldonado belong to the southern part of the tropical rain-forest zone, and are different in many respects from the central Amazonian regions. The relatively long dry season means that the flora and fauna are less rich than further north. However, there are plants here that are much rarer to the north, such as the gigantic Brazil nut tree. A large proportion of the resident population live from collecting and preparing the Brazil nuts (*castañas*).

Most trips from Puerto Maldonado require a boat, but there are plenty of these available for hire around the harbour. Should a guide be needed, there are plenty of them offering their services. **Lake Sanoval** is well worth a visit, requiring a one-hour ride followed by a 2km (1$^1/_4$ mile) march through the jungle. It is also possible to hire a motorbike in order to visit the gold diggers of Laberinto.

Puno and Lake Titicaca

Altitude: 3,830m (12,562ft)
Population: 53,000
Transport links:
Air links: Arequipa
Railway links: Juliaca-Arequipa 350km [217 miles] (9 hours); Juliaca-Cuzco 381km [236 miles] (10 hours)
Road links: Arequipa 288km [178 miles] (Route 6); Cuzco 386km [239 miles] (Route 8); Juli-La Paz (Bolivia) 263km [163 miles] (Route 7)
Boat: daily service from Juli to Huatajata/Bolivia (10 hours including lunch stop at Copacabana), connecting with a bus to La Paz.

Puno is much feared by tourists on account of its high altitude and the severe cold at night, which can cause problems in unheated hotel rooms. In the winter period (May to September) night frosts below temperatures of -10˚C (14˚F) are the norm. But the warm daytime sunshine means that the cold nights are swiftly forgotten. Indeed, visitors can return from boat trips on the lake with severe sunburn or even sunstroke if they are not careful.

Puno's greatest attraction is Lake Titicaca but there are also some marvellous overland trips (see below), of which the most rewarding are those to the burial towers of Sillustani and the colonial churches of Juli. The Cathedral is the chief attraction in Puno itself. The carved stone decorations on the façade show strong Indian influences. The cross near the entrance is carved with a sun and a moon and other symbols of Inca gods.

EXCURSIONS FROM PUNO

1 To the Uro Indians on Lake Titicaca

There is a boat every morning from Puno harbour to the floating islands of the Uro Indians. This is not only cheaper than the trips organised from the hotel office, but the boat is less crowded, making photography very much easier.

An effective sun-tan lotion and a head covering are both absolutely essential when travelling on Lake Titicaca. Those wishing to photograph the Indians should take plenty of small change for tips. It is also advisable to arrange two of the islands to be visited before setting off. The Uro Indians living closest to Puno have long since adapted to the endless stream of tourists, and no longer follow their original lifestyle.

The Uro Indians have lived on floating islands of reeds since before the Incas. They live in reed huts and make strange boats out of reeds. These remain seaworthy for about two years, after which time they are so saturated with water that they are virtually impossible to manoeuvre, and they are left to rot on the edge of the floating villages. The floating islands themselves are similarly perishable, and must be continually covered with fresh reeds. Visitors are advised to avoid the dark patches on these shifting islands, or else risk sinking up to their waists in freezing cold water!

At one time the Uro Indians lived exclusively from fishing and from the edible parts of the reeds — and these are still basic to their way of life. Those living nearer to Puno now supplement their income by making brightly patterned coverlets and model reed boats for tourists, not to mention the tips from photographers. But their basic lifestyle has changed surprisingly little. Greater material prosperity is reflected in a floating school made of corrugated iron, a floating football pitch and a rise in the consumption of alcohol.

2 To the Burial Towers of Sillustani (35km, 22 miles)

About 19km (12 miles) north of Puno along the metalled road to Juliaca, there is a turning along a metalled road leading to the shores of the beautiful Lake Umayo.

Among the ruins on a rocky peninsula jutting out into the lake are a number of strange towers known to the Indians as *chullpas*. Their

Puerto Maldonado — house on the Río Tambopata

construction varies enormously, suggesting that they were built at different periods. Some *chullpas* are round and some square. Some are built of rough stones with the gaps filled with earth, while others are carefully shaped and constructed in true Inca fashion. Some contain only one room, while others consist of a series of rooms one on top of another. However, all of them have a very low entrance.

The finest and best-preserved of these towers are for some strange reason wider at the top than the bottom. They are thought to go back to the Tiahuanaco period in the ninth and tenth centuries AD. Experts are surprisingly unanimous as to the purpose of the *chullpas*. They were graves in which the mummified remains of important people or noble families were laid to rest.

3 To the Colonial Churches of Juli (85km, 53 miles)
There are many very interesting churches on the Altiplano around Puno, all of which bear the stamp of Amerindian influence. Among the finest of these churches are those in the town of Juli. The journey from Puno and the town itself are described in Route 7, Chapter 3.

4 To the Folk Festivals of the Altiplano
Few tourists will be able to visit Puno during the first week in November, when it is the location for one of the most impressive folk festivals in the whole of South America. But there are plenty of

Market at Desaguadero by Lake Titicaca

opportunities at other times of the year for witnessing a similar if more modest festival somewhere in the region. It is best to enquire locally about festivals in the area and to hire a taxi to go and see them. But beware of any Indians who are drunk! Friendly bonhomie can quickly turn into aggression at the slightest provocation.

Sechín

Altitude: 90m (295ft)
Road links: Lima 372km [230 miles], Trujillo 193km [119 miles] (Route 1); buses to Casma and then by taxi (5km, 3 miles)

At the point where the Panamericana Norte crosses the Casma Valley, there is one of the most important archaeological sites on the whole of the Peruvian coast. Unfortunately the site was built mainly of mud bricks, so that most of the temples, forts and pyramids have been destroyed. More is left of the giant temple pyramid of Alto Sechín (Peru's largest pre-Inca structure), because it was partly built of granite. Its resemblance to the sanctuary at Chavín leads one to believe that the buildings at Sechín were subject to Chavín influence.

The most interesting place for tourists to visit is the structure on Cerro Sechín, which though smaller has been partially reconstructed. It is situated to the right of the road from Casma to Huaraz.

The mud-brick sanctuary is surrounded by a wall made of tall stone columns with smaller blocks in between. The pattern of the stonework is similar to that of a building at Tiahuanaco near Lake Titicaca in Bolivia, which has led some experts to suggest that a culture based in the southern Altiplano spread its influence as far as Sechín. On the other hand, the designs on the stones have frequently been compared to the Dancers of Monte Albán in Mexico, leading to the theory that the coastal cultures of Peru owed much to developments in Central America.

The drawings on the stones are highly realistic, showing tall, scantily dressed figures that could be either soldiers or priests. They each wear a belt and a flowerpot-like helmet, and hold a weapon or some kind of object for use in religious ceremonies. The faces and the feather-like hair decorations show a certain resemblance to the cat-god figures of Chavín.

The smaller stones reveal the artists' considerable anatomical knowledge. They show disgestive tracts, vertebrae, gouged-out eyes, torn-off extremities and disembodied heads with horrific facial expressions. Such pictures suggest war trophies or conquered enemies, but they could also represent the victims of some gruesome religious cult. The stairway is flanked by two particularly high columns, which are so carved as to be reminiscent of flagpoles.

The mud-brick building inside the outer walls was once a temple, and was apparently extended several times. In the centre was a symmetrically planned structure made up of a central chamber (*cámara sagrada*), two side chambers and an anteroom. The paintings and coloured bas-reliefs are quite remarkable, but their meaning has proved very elusive.

The drawings on the walls of the central chamber show two strange cat-like creatures 2.6m ($8^{1}/_{2}$ft) tall by 1.5m (5ft) high which are leaping towards the doorway; their heads are unfortunately missing. One of the bas-reliefs in the side chambers is particularly puzzling, showing a scantily clad figure drawn upside down. He could either be standing on his head and wearing a turban with a snake-like projection, or else he could be hanging from a hook with his skull split open. As for the meaning of the two fishes measuring 3.7m (12ft) by 1.5m (5ft) on the front of the building, this is simply yet another of the many unanswered questions of Sechín.

Trujillo

Altitude: 40m (131ft)
Population: 350,000
Air links: Lima, Cajamarca, Talara, Yurimaguas, Tarapoto, Iquitos

Road links: Lima 561km [348 miles] (Route 1, bus 8 hours); Chiclayo 208km [129 miles] (Route 1, bus 3 hours)
Cajamarca 299km [185 miles] (Route 1b, bus 7 hours)

Trujillo is the fourth-largest city in Peru, after Lima, Callao and Arequipa. The Peruvian government plans to turn it into the second major industrial and commercial centre, forming the northern counterpart to the Lima conurbation. The introduction of new industries has led to massive expansion in recent years, and the atmosphere of the old colonial city has been increasingly swamped by modern developments.

The city's chief interest for tourists lies in the many remains of ancient Indian cultures that flourished here in the valley of the Río Moche. The Mochicas left behind an incredible number of pottery vessels, though few of these have been found in Trujillo. However, there are many of their *huacas* to be seen (ie archaeological sites, from *huaco* meaning 'antique vessel'), which are still most impressive despite the ravages of natural disasters and the vandalism perpetrated by countless treasure hunters in search of building materials.

Also situated in the Moche Valley are the ruins of **Chan Chan**, the great capital of the Chimús, who were the successors to the Mochicas and the great rivals of the Incas. These ruins form the most important site in the whole valley. The reconstructed **Rainbow Temple** (*Huaca del Arco Iris*) is also particularly fine. Other items worth seeing are the **Emerald Temple** (*Huaca Esmeralda*) and the **Sun Temple** (*Huaca del Sol*), not to mention the colonial buildings in the city centre.

One day is just sufficient to see the most important sites. If more time is available, one can continue outwards from Chan Chan to the fishing port of **Huanchaco** (10km, 6 miles), where the fishermen use a special kind of fishing craft made of reeds.

THE CITY CENTRE

The city contains a number of beautiful colonial buildings from the prosperous seventeenth and eighteenth centuries, when several Spanish noble families settled in Trujillo. They are easy to recognise with their wooden balconies and wrought-iron window grills. The short walk described below gives a good impression of what there is to be seen.

The **Plaza de Armas** is the broad central square, in the centre of which is a massive statue of liberty. This is a reminder of the fact that Trujillo was the first Peruvian city to declare independence, and that Simón Bolívar set up his headquarters here.

The tourist hotel at the northern end of the square is graced with a colonial balcony. Next to it is the rather nondescript **Cathedral**, which contains some very fine choirstalls. The Bishop's Palace next

Selling souvenirs by Lake Titicaca

to the Cathedral possesses a fine colonial courtyard that is worth a quick glance. But the building opposite the tourist hotel is very much finer, with its carved wooden columns.

If one goes up the street out of the square on this side, one comes to a fine building on the right called the **Casa El Mayorazgo**, which is well worth a visit on account of its beautiful colonial interior.

Two blocks from the Plaza de Armas along the right-hand side of the Calle Pizarro is the **Club Central**, which is housed in one of the most elegant colonial mansions in the whole of Peru. If one turns right past the third block into the Calle Colón, one can see a fine church on the left beyond the next crossroads. This is known as the **Templo del Carmen**, and contains the finest churrigueresque altar in the city.

RAINBOW TEMPLE (*Huaca del Arco Iris*)

This site is also variously known as the *Huaca del Dragón* (Dragon Temple) and the *Huaca del Ciempies* (Centipede Temple). It is located about 2.5km (1$^{1}/_{2}$ miles) from the city centre in the suburb of La Esperanza, to the left of the main road to Chiclayo.

All the indications are that this building was once a temple. It is surrounded by a high wall, and the ground plan and pyramid-shaped structure suggest a religious purpose. The meaning of the ornamental carvings on the mud bricks is still very unclear. Depending on the

Sechín

eye of the beholder, they can be variously interpreted as dragons, centipedes or weather symbols such as rainbows — hence the variety of names given to the site.

EMERALD TEMPLE (*Huaca Esmeralda*)
This pyramid-shaped structure is hidden behind a church to the left of the Huanchaco road about 2km (1¹/₄ miles) from the city centre. The mud-brick stairways leading up to the sanctuary platform are covered with carpet-like decorations that are among the finest ever to have been found.

CHAN CHAN
In the fifteenth century, shortly before the Inca conquest, the capital of the Chimú empire numbered some 100,000 inhabitants and covered an area of about 18sq km (7sq miles). It is the largest city ever to have been built of sun-dried mud bricks (*adobes*). Many cities in the desert regions of the Middle East were built of a similar material, but none of them were as large as this one. To feed and water a city of this size in the desert must have required the kind of tight organisation that is only possible under a very strict regime.

The Incas eventually overcame the Chimús by cutting off the vital irrigation channels that brought water from far up in the mountains.

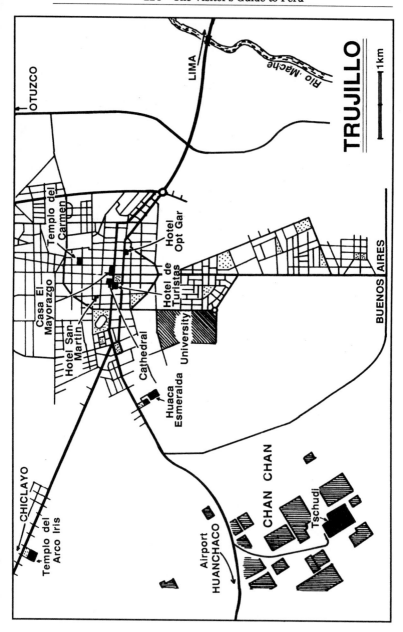

The Chimú craftsmen, who were in many respects more advanced than those of the Incas, were carried off to Cuzco. It is not known for certain what happened to the rest of the population, who would have been unable to survive here now that the fields were unirrigated. However, when the Spaniards arrived, the city was already abandoned and deserted.

The extensive site includes a number of large enclosures surrounded by high walls and known as *ciudadelas* or 'citadels'. They were all built according to the same plan, and comprised broad squares, gardens, cemeteries, large water cisterns and various buildings, all of which were linked together by a confusing maze of streets. The areas between the citadels contained a number of simpler structures. These were often built on the same plan as the citadels, but on a much smaller scale.

Countless theories have been produced to explain the purpose of these citadels. However, the five most important ones are as follows:

• That the citadels were enormous palace complexes, each covering an area of up to 29 hectares (2.47 acres), and which housed a vast retinue of officers and attendants. According to this theory each ruler built a new palace for himself, while the old palace was abandoned following the death of his predecessor, or else gradually became depopulated. Against this theory is the fact that some of the rooms were much too small to live in.

• That the citadels were palace complexes which were all inhabited at the same time. Each was ruled over by a separate ruler, who was in turn subject to the supreme ruler.

• That the citadels formed the barracks for the Chimú army.

• That the citadels were 'manufacturing communities' in which craftsmen belonging to the same guild lived and worked together, mass-producing goods as on a conveyor-belt. It has certainly been proved that the Chimú pottery was mass-produced by means of a system similar to that used on a conveyor belt. But this does not explain why the citadels were all built alike.

• That the citadels were enormous storage compounds. According to this theory the high walls and the maze-like street plan were to ward off thieves. The small chambers were for storage, while the larger rooms were occupied by officers in charge of supplies. However, this theory does not explain the presence of cemeteries, gardens and water tanks.

The Tschudi Citadel

This citadel was named after the Swiss archaeologist Jacob von Tschudi. It has been partially restored, and is therefore by far the most interesting of all the citadels. It can be reached from Trujillo via the road to Huanchaco. A track goes off to the left about 5km (3 miles) out of the city centre (there are bus services to here), which ends at

Indian rush house

the citadel carpark about 1.5km (a mile) from the road. (The numbers given in brackets below refer to the circled numbers on the map.)

The citadel is entered via a gateway that is not quite square. This leads into a large **ceremonial square** (1). As will be obvious from the variety of theories, the names of the various sections are based on no more than the inspiration of the person who discovered them. According to the storage compound theory, this area could have been a large market place or square where the supplies were distributed among the people.

The animal drawings along the bottom of walls probably represented coypus. The coypu is an aquatic animal similar to a beaver that was once common in this area (in Britain it has been accidentally introduced to East Anglia). The right-hand wall has a zigzag band running along the top of the outside (2). This is decorated with fishes, and there is a row of pelicans along the bottom of the wall.

Beyond the ceremonial square are the so-called *adoratorios* or **'prayer chambers'** (3). These were so named because of the rather complicated honeycomb pattern of the stonework, which is decorated with large numbers of pelicans and cormorants. According to the storage compound theory this area would have been occupied by the chief administrators. The tiny niches in the walls would have contained marked beans which could have been used to record the

Fishermen's 'reed ponies'

amount of stock available.

The path leads via a second, smaller **ceremonial square** (4) to a **basin** (5) that still contains a number of water plants. This may have been one of the many water cisterns that were fed by groundwater. The destruction of the irrigation channels caused the water table to drop, so that most of the cisterns dried up. The basin could also have been one of the gardens, which were created by removing the soil nearly down to the water table. One such garden is still to be found around the back of the citadel. Advocates of the storage compound theory see this area as a source of material for making mud bricks.

The **cemetery** (6) occupies the back portion of the citadel. The grave vaults are built out of a concrete-like mixture of dried mud and shellfish remains. They would no doubt have contained some valuable items, but would have been stripped of their contents as soon as they had been discovered.

The path now runs back through a structure made up of numerous tiny chambers that is commonly known as the '**barracks**' (7). It returns along a retaining wall that is up to 9m (29ft) high in places, and goes past the prayer chambers (3) to a set of reconstructed buildings adjoining the larger ceremonial square. Among them is the so-called **Hall of the 24 Niches** (8), which according to some historians contained various idols. Those who think the citadel was a vast

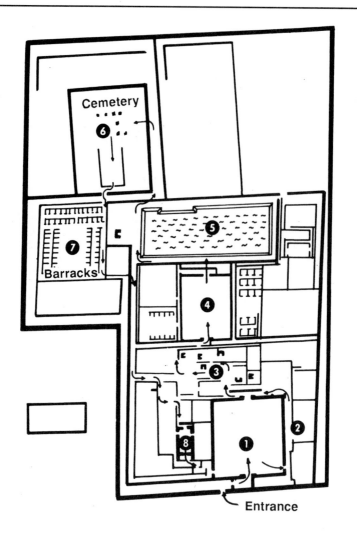

CIUDADELA TSCHUDI

palace complex are of the opinion that the ruler's private quarters were here.

EXCURSION TO HUANCHACO (10km, 6 miles)

The main attraction of Huanchaco is the fishing area, with the famous *caballitos de totora* or 'reed ponies'. These consist of bundles of reeds which the fishermen 'ride' on the sea as if on horseback. The fish caught are kept in a small depression on the top of the craft until the fisherman arrives inshore. Then the 'horse' is propped up to dry. If there are no fishermen to be seen offshore, then one of them can no doubt be persuaded to demonstrate one of these strange craft in return for a tip.

EXCURSION TO THE SUN TEMPLE (8km, 5 miles)

This site can be reached via the road to Lima. Two kilometres ($1^1/_4$ miles) beyond the turning for Huamachuco there is a track going off at a sharp angle to the left. It leads right up to the Sun Pyramid (*Huaca del Sol*), which is visible from a wide area around. A rocky outcrop forms the natural foundation for a temple built of millions of mud bricks that are layered to create a vast platform towering 40m (131 miles) above the Moche Valley. It was presumably built during the Mochica period between the fourth and tenth centuries AD.

From the top one can see a second pyramid at the foot of a mountain. This in turn is thought to have been the **Moon Temple** (*Huaca de la Luna*).

USEFUL INFORMATION FOR VISITORS

TRAVEL PREPARATIONS

Documents Required

UK, Irish and American visitors to Peru do not require visas to enter the country, only a passport. Australians, and New Zealanders as well as several other nationalities *do* require a visa and may obtain this from the Peruvian embassy in their country. On arrival in Peru, Europeans will be issued with an entry permit for 90 days (renewable). US and Australian citizens are given only 60 days but may renew. To prolong your stay, show your return ticket at the Dirección General de Migraciones, Paseo de la República 585 in Lima.

Visitors to Peru must complete a tourist card (issued by the airline or at a border checkpoint) and this should be attached to your passport and carried at all times. A new tourist card must be obtained for each re-entry or when an extension is given. An exit or onward ticket is required when entering Peru. Upon departure from any of Peru's international airports, an airport tax will be charged.

Students should carry student cards at all times as they may be eligible for discounts.

Health Precautions

Most serious diseases have now been eradicated in South America. There are one or two exceptions however and travellers to Peru should take preventative measures. Those wishing to explore the jungles, for instance, should take along anti-malaria pills and take precautions against yellow fever. There are sometimes outbreaks of typhoid in Lima and elsewhere and hepatitis should be protected against. Consult your doctor about possible vaccinations and/or medicines.

Avoid drinking tap water or boil it first, and purify it with chlorine tablets, *or* drink bottled water only. Always ask for drinks *sin hielo*, without ice, as this is likely to be made with tap water. Be wary of salads and fruits washed in tap water especially in markets. Vegetables and fruit prepared in *good* restaurants are usually acceptable. Be cautious about eating at the cheaper cafés and market vendors — always check that conditions are hygienic first. Avoid drinking unpasteurised milk.

If you should have the misfortune to be bitten by a rabid dog in or near Lima, make your way to the Centro de Antirabia in Lima, where they will give you an anti-rabies injection.

On the whole, in Lima and other large cities, medical services and sanitary conditions are good but do set out well-prepared for all eventualities.

Altitude Sickness

Altitude sickness (*soroche*) occurs when you ascend the high altitude quickly, so the best way to prevent this is to spend a day or two travelling slowly to the higher altitudes, rather than fly in suddenly from sea level to places like Cuzco. Even at Cuzco you probably won't suffer severe symptoms, possibly just shortness of breath or a headache, but higher still and you could experience vomiting, tiredness, loss of appetite, loss of sleep, rapid pulse and breathing problems. Tablets such as Coramina Glucosa can provide immediate relief especially from nausea and are available all over Peru. The best way to combat altitude sickness is to take it easy until you get used to it and avoid smoking and alcohol. If symptoms are severe, obtain more oxygen by descending to a lower altitude. People with high blood pressure or with heart or circulatory disorders should not visit high altitude locations such as Cuzco or Puno without first consulting their doctor.

Items for the First Aid Kit

• all medicines that are regularly needed at home
• remedies for mountain sickness (eg Coramina Glucosa) for use when travelling at high altitudes (these are readily available in Peru).
• remedies for diarrhoea and intestinal infections, which often result from unfamiliar diet (Pentofuryl and Imodium have proved particularly effective).
• cold and flu remedies.
• painkillers, elastoplast and disinfectant for minor injuries.
• suntan lotion for use at high altitudes.
• insect repellent for use in the jungle.

Bathing

• Bathing in still waters is always dangerous, even if local people are happy to do so. Tropical dwellers are immune to many bacteria that Europeans have no resistance to.
• Muddy shores can be dangerous, whether on the coast or along rivers in the jungle. Soft mud is the habitat of stingrays, which can inflict painful and dangerous injuries.
• There are dangerous tidal currents at many points along the Pacific coast, which can prove too much even for strong swimmers.

Mountain Sun

The sun can be very dangerous at high altitudes, and especially on Lake Titicaca. This is because the air, being relatively thin, absorbs less of the high-energy ultraviolet radiation from the sun. It is even possible to be cold and to get sunburn or even sunstroke at the same time.

The head should always be kept covered and sunbathing should be avoided at high altitudes. Where there is snow cover or on Lake Titicaca, a highly absorbent suntan lotion should be used to filter out the extra light reflected by the snow or the water.

ARRIVAL IN PERU

The Best Time to Travel

Coastal Regions
The period from December to May is best suited for the Lima area, but other seasons are not too bad either. Only the narrow coastal strip is subject to sea fogs.

Mountain Regions
The rainy season from December to May should be avoided, as many of the traffic routes are cut off by bad weather. The rest of the year is fine.

Jungle Regions
This region is damp all the year round, but the period from August to October offers the best chance of some respite from the rain.

Arrival by Air

Many airlines fly from London to Lima with connections in Paris, Milan, Bogota, Madrid, Amsterdam, Frankfurt or Caracas. From the US, airlines such as Aerolineas Argentinas, LAN-Chile etc provide direct flights from Miami, New York or Los Angeles to Lima. Aeroperú and Faucett also provide flights. The most direct route from Australia is to fly to Tahiti and connect to Santiago and from Chile to Peru. From Canada, there are flights from Vancouver or

Toronto to Lima.
NB Air tickets bought in Peru are liable to a surtax so you should therefore purchase a return ticket at home.

Arrival by Land

The Panamerican Highway provides a metalled road link from Peru to Santiago (Chile) or to Guayaquil and Quito (Ecuador), either by car or by bus (with various travel companies). You cannot drive all the way into Peru from North or Central America because of the jungle of the Darien Gap (see 'Driving in Peru').

The roads to La Paz (Bolivia) are much less good by comparison. The section from Puno to La Paz is now fully metalled, but the road to Puno from the coast will remain difficult for some time to come. However, the rail connection to Puno is very comfortable, and one can continue by ferry across Lake Titicaca and pick up a connecting bus to La Paz.

Arrival by River Boat

It is possible to travel by river boat from the mouth of the Amazon at Belém in Brazil to Iquitos in Peru, an exciting way to travel. For details consult the main tourist office.

Arrival by Sea

The sea route is very time-consuming and expensive, and the lack of demand means that there are very few bookings available. Passenger services have virtually ceased, while freight carriers are increasingly reluctant to carry passengers. Cruise specialists may, however, be able to help.

The Time Difference

Peru is in the same time zone as the eastern USA. Peruvian time runs 5 hours behind Greenwich Mean Time and 6 hours behind British Summer Time.

Customs Controls

Tourists are normally treated fairly leniently by customs officials although people have reported frequent identification checks and searches at provincial borders when touring by bus. Often illiterate soldiers interrogate foreign passport holders while the bus leaves with the tourist's luggage! Mechanical apparatus and drugs are the chief items which are searched for at airports and backpacking foreigners may be searched for cocaine, including a body search. Personal essentials may be freely imported (camera and photo equipment should have been used), together with 400 cigarettes or 50 cigars or 500g tobacco, and 2 litres of alcoholic drinks, new items for personal use or gifts up to US $200. NB. No object of archaeological interest may be exported from Peru.

Currency and Exchange

The monetary unit of Peru is the Inti (I/.) which is comprised of 100 céntimos. Coins are in denominations of 1, 5, 10 and 25 céntimos, notes in denominations of 10, 50, 100 and 500 intis. The money unit used to be the sol (inti = 1,000 soles) and although there are very few notes in circulation, Peruvian people still think in terms of soles or of 'libras' (10 soles).

Visitors to Peru are advised to take US dollars or travellers' cheques as it is difficult to change currencies other than US dollars or Deutsche marks. All major credit cards, though are accepted by most businesses. Be careful of dealing with black market money changers — verify their reliability if possible and count your money carefully. For cash dollars, money changers will give you local currency at higher rates than the banks offer and usually, with less red tape. Local currencies are notably unstable, however, and exchange rates can vary enormously from week to week.

Banking hours: Monday to Friday 9.15am-12.45pm in winter and from 8.45-11.30am in summer. Some are open in the afternoon and on Saturdays. Most airports have facilities for changing foreign currency because if you arrive at a weekend or on a holiday you probably won't find a bank open.

NB. Left-over currency from other South American countries can usually only be exchanged at the border, and then only with great difficulty.

TRAVEL WITHIN PERU

Air Travel

All major cities and tourist attractions are linked by air, railroad and bus services. However, as distances are long and road conditions are poor, the best way to travel is by internal flight. Peru's two international airlines, Aeroperú and Faucett, serve the country with frequent flights. Flights are generally inexpensive and as one-way tickets are usually half the price of a return, you could make your journey more interesting by flying one way and return by land. You can buy a 30 or 60 day 'Visit Peru' pass for unlimited travel within the country. Students are sometimes eligible for a small discount.

The following cities are served with internal flights: Arequipa, Ayacucho, Cajamarca, Cuzco, Chachapoyas, Chiclayo, Húanuco, Juanjui, Juliaca, Iquitos, Lima, Piura, Pucallpa, Puerto Maldonado, Rioja, Tacna, Talara, Tarapoto, Tingo María, Trujillo, Tumbes and Yurimaguas. NB. Flights are often fully booked so make reservations well in advance.

Rail Travel
There are only three railways in Peru offering passenger services:
Lima – La Oroya (Cerro de Pasco) – Huancayo – Huancavelica
There is one train a day along this route. The section from Lima to Oroya follows a breathtaking route through some magnificent scenery, but takes twice as long as a bus or *colectivo*.

Arequipa – Juliaca – Puno – Juliaca – Cuzco
The route from Arequipa via Juliaca to Puno is much more scenic than that from Puno to Cuzco. The railway is also the most comfortable means of transport between Arequipa and Puno. However, *colectivos* are preferable for the less scenic journey between Puno and Cuzco. They cost more than the train, but are marginally quicker.

Cuzco – Machu Picchu
For this journey the railway is the only alternative to walking. The daily tourist train is much more expensive than the local train, but is also much more comfortable. First-class travel is advisable on all trains. Second-class passengers may even have difficulty finding standing room! Seats can usually only be reserved one day in advance. However, travel agents will take earlier bookings and buy the tickets at the station on the day before. **Warm clothing** is essential on all railway journeys. The trains from Arequipa to Puno and Cuzco provide a buffet car and a sleeper for night journeys. But an emergency supply of food is always advisable.

Buses
Bus services are provided even along routes which cars cannot manage because of the appalling road conditions and fares are usually cheap. They vary in quality and comfort from the luxury bus to a rusting heap of metal. It is therefore worth checking out the vehicle before travelling. Unfortunately, the worse the road conditions, the less roadworthy the vehicle.

However, there is usually a choice of several bus companies for each route. The addresses are given in the yellow pages of the telephone directory under *Transportes terrestres*. Seats may be reserved on services belonging to the better companies (Tepsa, Ormeño, Roggero). But travellers wishing to board in small towns or villages may often have to wait for hours at the bus stop. In such cases it is advisable to buy a ticket on the bus, to be able to travel on the bus which comes first.

Colectivos

These large taxis or minibuses are available all over the country, and especially on overland routes. The prices are so cheap that many tourists will buy up all the seats and travel alone in them as if in a taxi. There are several *colectivos* a day along the main routes. Along some routes such as between Puno and Juliaca there are always vehicles waiting, and they will set off as soon as they are full. Seats on other routes must be booked one day in advance. The local offices are usually easy to find, and are labelled *Comite* followed by a number. They can also be found in the yellow pages of the telephone directory under *Transportes terrestres*.

Taxis

Taxis can be hailed simply by shouting and waving. The taximeter always manages to break down with a foreign passenger on board! It is no use trying to argue against this, and the most one can do is to agree on the fare beforehand. Considerable reductions can often be negotiated for longer journeys. The best policy is to find out the normal rate for the journey at the hotel beforehand. However, taxis are very cheap by European standards. After midnight and on holidays there is a surcharge. Beware of black 'pirate' taxis — they usually charge 50 per cent more!

Hire Cars

Cars may be hired in Lima, Arequipa, Cuzco and Iquitos from Hertz, Avis, Budget and other car-hire firms. The current rates can be obtained from your local offices of international hire firms, where it is also possible to make an advanced booking; this is strongly recommended for Cuzco and Arequipa. To drive a hire car you have to be over 25 and leave a deposit by credit card.

Many visitors to Peru will hire a minibus and kit it out as a dormobile, using a board and airbed for sleeping on. This serves the dual purpose of providing overnight accommodation and carrying essential supplies.

Driving in Peru

Driving is on the right-hand side. Foreign vehicles must bear the entry permit Customs Duty Payment Voucher issued by Customs on entry. You may also obtain this from your Touring and Automobile club. Foreign drivers of their own car must obtain an international driver's licence, valid for 30 days and a *carnet de passage* obtainable from an automobile club.

If you do bring your own car, stock up on spare parts and ensure your documents are in good order. Ensure, also, that your car is in good condition and always have enough fuel for the return trip as service stations are few and far between. It must be said that driving in Peru is not easy as the roads are poor and theft is common. It is also very expensive to import your car by ship. You cannot drive all the way to Peru from North America because of the 200km section of jungle called the Darien Gap which begins at Panama and ends in Colombia. The Darien Gap has to be crossed on foot, by canoe or flown over.

Accidents

These are relatively uncommon in towns or on mountain roads, but the Panamericana and the Carretera Central can be extremely dangerous. There are frequent pile-ups on these roads, mostly as a result of irresponsible behaviour when overtaking.

When an accident occurs, costs are usually settled on the spot. A foreigner is normally assumed to be 'stinking rich', and being unused to the situation is likely to have to pay over the odds. But bringing the police in can waste several days and is usually of no help. Full comprehensive insurance is therefore advisable. Most Peruvian drivers do not even have third-party insurance, and whatever their personal circumstances they are usually hard-up when an accident is involved.

Accidents involving personal injury must always be reported to the police.

Fuel

There are two sorts of fuel in Peru: 85 octane and 95 octane. The Panamericana is adequately served by filling stations, but they are extremely infrequent on mountain routes. Sometimes the only filling station has just sold out or the attendant has gone for a walk. A 20 litre reserve can is therefore very useful.

Road Conditions

These are in no way comparable to Europe or North America. Even the Panamericana, which is one of the few metalled roads, can often be in an appalling state. Deep sand along the roadside can cause vehicles to overturn if they go too near the edge.

Earth roads tend to form deep ruts which can only be negotiated at very high or very low speeds. The surface has very little grip, so that the braking distances are much greater and vehicles skid very easily on corners. The rainy season creates further problems with mud, causing even deeper ruts, and fords that may often be impassable.

When negotiating river fords, it is always advisable to let another vehicle go first to give an indication of depth and show the best route across. As there are often large boulders under the surface, it is important to go very slowly with high revs (in first gear, with the clutch slipping if necessary). A broken axle or a ruptured fuel tank is much more serious than getting stuck in the middle of the river.

Food and Drink

Lima has some of the best cuisine of South America and has many gourmet restaurants which often specialise in seafood. In the smaller towns and villages native cooking is mainly prepared. Popular dishes include: Ceviche, raw fish marinated in lemon juice and spices and served with raw onions and hot peppers (aji) and anticuchos which are grilled beef hearts pickled in vinegar and spices and served on a skewer. Pisco sour is a strong cocktail made with lime juice, egg white, sugar and Pisco, a kind of brandy.

Many Peruvian restaurants called Chicherias or Picanterias specialise in good inexpensive national dishes and hundreds of

Creole restaurants specialise in mixed Spanish and Indian dishes. Peru also abounds in Cantonese restaurants called *Chifas*.
NB. Standards of hygiene and quality vary enormously. Beware especially of eating fresh fruit and vegetables — always peel and cook first.

Some of the best places to eat are as follows:

Trece Monedas, Jirón Ancash 536. International cuisine and a colonial atmosphere.

El Cortijo, Avenida Panamá 675, Barranco. Meat from the spit.

Tambo de Oro, Avenida Belén 1066. International and Creole cuisine.

Granja Azul, 2km (1 1/4 miles) off the Carretera central, signposted to the right 11km (7 miles) out of the city. Chicken from the spit in the pleasant atmosphere of an old hacienda.

Pavillón de Caza, Monterrico, near the Gold Museum. Good but expensive, serving French and international cuisine.

Chifa Kuo Wa, Paseo de la República 5046, Miraflores. High-class Chinese restaurant with a nice garden.

Chifa Lung Fung, Avenida Limatambo 3165, San Isidro. High-class Chinese restaurant with a Japanese garden.
    Many other restaurants and peñas (restaurants offering local colour) can be found in the yellow pages of the telephone directory under the heading *Restaurantes*.

PLACES TO VISIT

CHURCHES IN LIMA

The Cathedral
Plaza de Armas
Open: 10am-12noon and 3-5pm daily.
Museum of religious art in the cathedral.

Church of Jesus and Mary
Eighteenth-century church open only in the afternoons.

Church of San Marcelo
Avenida de la Emancipación
Originates in the mid-sixteenth century.

Convent of Los Descalzos
Alameda de Los Descalzos
Rímac
Open: Monday-Saturday 9.30am-1pm, 2-5.30pm.
Contains over 300 paintings. Museum.

La Merced and Monastery
Plazuela de la Merced
Jirón de la Unión
Open: 8am-12.30pm, 4-7.30pm daily. Monastery open: 8am-12noon and 3-5.30pm.
Colonial façade and attractive cloister. Built on the site of the first mass in Lima in 1534.

Las Nazarenas
Av. Tacna
Open: 7am-11.30pm and 4.30-8pm daily.
Built in the eighteenth century.

San Agustin
Jirón Ica 251
Open: 7am-12noon, 3.30-7pm daily.
Interesting Churrigueresque façade.

Santo Domingo
Jirón Camaná
Open: 7am-1pm, 4-8pm daily.
Monastery open: 9.30am-12.30pm,
3.30-5.30pm, Sunday 9am-1pm.
Remains of Santa Rosa de Lima in
an urn on the altar.

San Francisco
Jirón Lampa
Open: 9.30am-12noon and 3-6pm.
Baroque church, completed 1674.
Catacombs and monastery.

San Pedro
Jirón Ucayali
Open: 8am-1pm, 5-8pm daily.
Completed 1638. Rich wood
carving and beautiful altars. One of
the finest examples of colonial
architecture in Lima.

Santuario de Santa Rosa
Av. Tacna
Open: 8am-12noon, 3-7pm daily.
Preserved here is the hermitage
built by Santa Rosa and the house
where she was born.

MUSEUMS IN LIMA

Amano Museum
Calle Retiro 160
Miraflores
☎ 412909
Open: Monday-Friday afternoons
after telephoning, with guided tours
at 2, 3, 4, and 5pm. Fine private
collection of artifacts from the
Chancay, Chimú and Nazca
periods. Telephone at least one
day in advance for an appoint-
ment.

Bullfight Museum
Hualgayoc 332
Plaza de Acho
Rímac
Open: daily 9am-1pm and 3-6pm.
Closed Saturday, Sunday and
holidays in the afternoon. Paintings
and engravings, matadors' relics.

Contemporary Folk Art Museum
Saco Olivero 163
Open: Tuesday-Friday 2.30-7pm
and on Saturdays from 8.30am-
12noon.

Gold Museum
Prolongación Av.
☎ 352919
Open: daily 3-7pm, Saturday 9am-
1pm.
Underground museum with pre-
Inca metals, weavings, mummies
and arms collection.

Museum of Anthropology and Archaeology
Plaza Bolívar
Pueblo Libre
☎ 611312
Open: Tuesday-Saturday 10am-
6.30pm, Sunday 10am-6pm.
Closed Mondays.
The art and history of the aborigi-
nal races of Peru.

Museo Banco Central de Reserva
Av. Ucayali and Lampa
Open: Tuesday-Friday 10am-5pm.
Pottery and gold items. Nine-
teenth- and twentieth-century
paintings.

Museo Etnográfico de la Selva
Av. Tacna 120
Open: daily except Mondays until
7pm.
Household and cultural objects
from Madre de Dios.

Museum of Italian Art
Paseo de la Rebública
Open: Tuesday-Sunday 9am-7pm
and 9am-8pm on Fridays.
Italian works of art, lithographs and
etchings. Houses the Institute of
Contemporary Art.

Museum of the Inquisition

Plaza Bolívar
Calle Junín 548
Open: Monday-Friday, 9am-7pm
and 9am-5pm on Saturdays and
9am-1pm Sundays.
Accurate depiction of the tortures
of the Inquisition.

Museo Histórico Militar

Real Felipe Fortress
Callao
Open: 9am-12noon, Tuesday,
Wednesday and Thursday and 3-
5pm and from 2-5.30pm at
weekends.
Military relics.

Museum of Mineral Specimens

Krystal S.A.
León Uelarde 537
Lince
Lima 14
☎ 710713/711379

Museo Miniatura de la Plaza de Armas del Siglo XIX

House of Dr César Revoredo
Salaverry 3052
Private small-scale reproduction of
the Plaza de Armas in the
nineteenth century. Prints by water
colour artist Rancho Fierro.

Museum of National History

Plaza Bolívar
Pueblo Libre
Open: 9am-5.30pm except
Saturdays.
Paintings, Manuscripts, uniforms
etc.

Museum of Natural History

Av. Arenales 1250
Open: Monday-Friday 8.30am-
3.30pm and on Saturdays from
8.30am-12noon, Sundays 9am-
1pm.
Flora, fauna, butterflies, insects,
minerals and shell collection.

Museum of Peruvian Culture

Av. Alfonso Ugarte 650
Open: Monday-Friday 10am-5pm
and 9am-5pm on Saturdays.
Pottery, art and costume of
Peruvian Indians.

Museo Peruano de Ciencias de la Salud

Jr. Junín 270
Open: Monday-Saturday 9am-
5pm.
Ceramics and mummies.

National Museum of Art

Paseo Colón 125
Palacio de la Exposición
Open: Tuesday-Sunday 9am-7pm.
Over 7,000 exhibits showing the
history of Peruvian art and culture
— paintings, silver, furniture etc.

Pinacoteca Municipal

Plaza de Armas
Open: Monday-Friday 9am-1pm.
Paintings by national artists.

Philatelic Museum

Central Post Office
Plaza de Armas
Open: Monday-Friday, 8am-
1.30pm, 2-4pm and on Saturdays
8am-1.30pm and Sundays 9am-
12noon.
Complete collection of Peruvian
stamps. Shop.

Rafael Larco Herrera Museum

Av. Bolívar 1515
Open: Monday-Saturday 9am-
1pm, 3-6pm, Sunday 9am-1pm.
Exhibits from the Mochica,
Cupisnique, Nazca, Chimú and
Inca periods.

MISCELLANEOUS

Safety in Peru

There are thieves to be found
everywhere, and they have always

thought of tourists as easy prey. Peru is a hotbed of thieves, especially in Lima and Cuzco and in the market at Huancayo, where professional thieves will skilfully relieve tourists of money, watches or jewellery without their even being aware of it. Accomplices make the task easier by distracting the victims, pushing them or even running into them with a motorbike. Women walking alone may suddenly have their handbags or cameras ripped off them, sometimes by other pedestrians or sometimes from a passing car.

Fortunately, however, most tourists still manage to keep their possessions intact. Just a few precautions are needed to make sure they are properly protected:

1 Larger sums of money should be kept in a pouch hung around the neck or sewn into the lining of your trousers. Carry most of your money in the form of travellers' cheques.

2 Important documents should always carry the hotel address, as thieves in Peru normally return these within a few hours.

3 No jewellery should be worn openly in the street.

4 Handbags and items of value should always be held tightly, preferably under your arm. Backpacks may be razor-slashed and the contents taken so move quickly.

5 Valuables should never be left in the hotel room, but should be handed in at reception in return for a receipt.

6 Valuables should never be left in cars, while cars should always be parked in supervised car parks.

7 Luggage should always be kept in sight when travelling by public transport.

8 Avoid standing still for too long in crowded places.

Avoid any places where there has been guerrilla activity and be careful of what you photograph. The provinces of Junín, Huancavelica, Ayacucho, Loreto, Apurímac, Huánuco, San Martín and Pasco are currently under martial law and since 1986, Lima and Callao have been under curfew (*toque de queda*) between 1am and 5am.

If your belongings are stolen and the value exceeds US$20 make your way to the PIP International Police. If the value is under US$20 go to the Guardia Civil. Visitors to Lima can go to the Tourist Police (see Useful Addresses) where you will have to obtain a statement of theft or *denuncia* signed by the police if you wish to claim insurance.

Hitch-Hiking

This is difficult in Peru and not advisable. Hitch-hikers are usually picked up by lorries or vans; private cars are rare. Drivers usually ask for money so ask first how much they are going to charge.

Taking Photographs

Indians frequently make marvellous subjects, but are often very reluctant to be photographed. A short explanation, even in sign language, can often work wonders — maybe a little joke or just saying *Permitame un recuerdo* (Let me have a souvenir). However, Indians who are drunk should always be given a wide berth. Some Indians in the areas around

Cuzco and Puno (including the Uros) are keen to make money out of tourists, and will only pose for the cameras if they are paid first.

Photographic materials are very expensive in Peru, so it is important to take enough films for the whole holiday, together with spare batteries if necessary.

Souvenirs

Alpaca wool (from a kind of llama) is soft and silky and makes lovely warm pullovers, jackets and ponchos, which may come in useful in the cold climate of the mountains. Hand-woven cloths, knitted caps, lacework, ponchos and other items of Indian clothing all make marvellous souvenirs. But modern mass-produced goods with old Indian designs are also in plentiful supply.

Apart from the rich variety of textile products, there are also alpaca skins, gold and silverware and a variety of pottery goods. The choice is vast. Cheap earthenware comes in every shape and size imaginable, from a simple flowerpot to a life-size model of a pig! Beautiful but rather heavy to carry are the strange windblown 'Ayacucho Churches', which come in a variety of sizes. Ayacucho is also the home of the little collapsible wooden altars with their brightly coloured carvings.

Other items for sale include *huacos*, ancient vessels from precolonial sites. These are not only very expensive, but will be confiscated by customs as their export is banned. They are frequently forgeries anyway, so it is best to buy cheap imitations.

FESTIVAL CALENDAR

Jan 1 New Year (official holiday).

Jan 1-12 Sullana: Popular annual fair with cockfights.

Jan 6 Ollantaitambo: (near Cuzco): Epiphany processions and dances. **Huancavelica:** The main city square is turned into a representation of Jerusalem, in which Herod holds court and the Three Kings look for the Christ Child. There is a procession on the following day. **Huánuco:** Great festivities including dances, the main theme being the black slaves awaiting their freedom (*Baile de los Negritos*).

Jan 18 Huánuco: Repeat of the dance performances of 6 January.

Feb 2 Puno: The Candlemas Festival, or Purification of the Blessed Virgin Mary (*Fiesta de la Virgen de la Candelaria*). The innumerable costumed dance groups and the devil's dancers make this one of the most memorable experiences of a Peruvian holiday. The festivities build up to a climax on the following Sunday.

Shrovetide carnivals
Abancay: A wonderful day-long pageant, showing the province's rich folklore. Costumed dancers and musicians perform in the streets. **Huaraz:** A lovely carnival full of colourful costumes.

2nd week March
Ica: Peru's wine capital holds its great wine festival (*Festival de la Vendimia*), including the election of a wine queen and dancing competitions.

Holy Week (March)
  Ayacucho: On Palm Sunday a great folk drama begins and is enacted on the streets throughout the week. Representations of Christ's passion are interspersed with glorious mass-processions, while streetside markets do a roaring trade. **Arequipa**: Daily processions through the city from Palm Sunday onwards, with countless worshippers dressed in mourning. **Cuzco**: On Monday there is great procession in which the *Señor de los Temblores* (Lord of the Earthquakes) is carried through the streets of the city. **Catacaos** (near Piura): Another famous Monday procession attracting vast numbers of people. **Tarma**: The streets are beautifully decorated with flowers for the Easter processions.

May 1 May Day (official holiday).

Corpus Christi
  Cuzco: A vast procession made up of Indians from the surrounding countryside, wearing festival garb and playing traditional musical instruments — one of Peru's greatest tourist events. **Cajamarca**: Corpus Christi here is combined with a kind of harvest festival inherited from the Incas. The main attraction is a procession to which Indians come from miles around.

June 24 Cuzco: The climax of the so-called Cuzco Week is a replay of the great Inca sun festival *Inti Raymi* in front of the battlements of the Sacsayhuamán Fortress.

June 29 Zepita (Lake Titicaca): The Festival of St Peter and St Paul is celebrated with the kind of colourful pageant for which the Lake Titicaca region is famous.

July 16 Quillabamba, Paucartambo (near Cuzco); **Pucará** (near Puno): In all three villages the Festival of Our Lady of Mount Carmel (*Fiesta de la Virgen del Carmen*) provides the occasion for colourful dancing, especially at Paucartambo.

July 25 Pomata (Lake Titicaca): The Festival of St James (Santiago) coincides with the ancient Inca festival of lightning. Various costumed dances in the streets, including those of the famous devil's dancers.

July 28-29 Independence Days (official holiday). **Andahuaylas**: The festival programme includes a gruesome bullfight, in which a condor is tied to the back of the bull. If the condor succeeds in killing the bull, this is considered a favorable omen for the coming year. **Huánuco**: Colourful dance presentations to mark the national holiday.

Aug 5-8 Copacabana: Lake Titicaca's biggest and most exciting festival takes place just across the Bolivian border. Hundreds of costumed dance troops come from Bolivia, Peru and Chile to dance and play in the streets.

Aug 15 Arequipa: The city celebrates the anniversary of its foundation. The programme includes processions, fireworks and several fairs.

Aug 20 Azángaro (near Puno): St Bernard's Day provides a reason for people to dance in the streets dressed in some striking disguises.

Aug 22 Rosaspata (near Lake

Titicaca): This small village celebrates the so-called Octave of the Assumption of the Blessed Virgin Mary with a pageant of local folklore.

Aug 30   Lima: The procession in honour of Santa Rosa of Lima takes hours to move through the city centre, with much singing and praying.

Sept 8   Ayaviri (near Puno): The Nativity of the Blessed Virgin Mary is the occasion of a week-long festival, with costume dancing and a fair during which local products are sold.

Sept 14   Moho (Lake Titicaca): The famous devil's dancers and other local costumed dancers can be seen here on the occasion of the Festival of the Holy Cross.

Sept 5   Acora (Lake Titicaca): The Seven Sorrows of the Blessed Virgin Mary is celebrated with processions, dances and bullfights.

Sept 24   Vilque (near Puno): Another Marian festival (*Nuestra Señora de las Mercedes* or Our Lady of Mercies) provides an opportunity to see a procession and some costumes from Lake Titicaca. There is a similar procession in nearby Juliaca.

Carhuaz (near Huaraz): This Marian festival is marked by processions, folklore presentations, bullfights and fireworks.

1st Sunday October
   Chucuito (near Puno): A colourful folk scene with music and dance groups, including the devil's dancers, for the Festival of Our Lady of the Rosary, with similar celebrations in the nearby villages of **Acora** and **Tiquillaca.**

Oct 9   Day of National Honour (official holiday).

Oct 10   Yunguyo (Lake Titicaca): The Festival of St Francis of Borgia marks the beginning of the main annual festival in this border village. There are thousands of costumed dancers from Peru and Bolivia, including of course the devil's dancers from Oruro.

Oct 18, 19, 28   Lima: On each of hese three days there is a procession through the city headed by a painting called *El Señor de los Milagros* (The Lord of Miracles), which shows Christ on the cross.

Oct 28   Callao: The anniversary of the great earthquake of 1746, which almost completely destroyed the town. A statue of Christ was found intact among the ruins near the harbour, and has been greatly venerated ever since. This statue, known as *El Señor del Mar* (The Lord of the Sea), is carried through the city at the head of a long procession.

Nov 1   All Saints' Day (official holiday).

1st week Nov
   Puno: The Puno Week is the occasion for a unique spectacle of folklore, with the whole gamut of costumes and music from the Lake Titicaca region. The week includes a pageant of the legend of Mama Ocllo and Manco Cápac, the founders of the Inca empire, who are supposed to have risen from the waters of Lake Titicaca.

Dev 8   Juli (Lake Titicaca): The Conception of the Blessed Virgin Mary is celebrated throughout the Lake Titicaca region with the usual rich display of native dancing. This festival is most impressive in Juli, though the celebrations at *Parcarcolla* just outside Puno are also quite splendid.

Dec 25 Christmas Day (official holiday).

ACCOMMODATION

Hotels

In Lima and in towns along the coast there is normally an ample supply of hotel beds available. Hotels in holiday areas (Huaraz, Tarma, San Ramón, Ica, Paracas) are fully booked at long weekends and for national holidays such as 28 and 29 July. In Cuzco there will normally only be problems during the high season (June to August). Machu Picchu is almost always fully booked for months in advance, but one can still try to book a room on arrival in Cuzco at the state tourist hotel. Puno is often similarly booked up, but in emergency one can resort to nearby Juliaca.

Reservations at all state tourist hotels can be obtained from the following sources:
• Entur Perú Avenida Javier Prado Oeste 1358, Lima-San Isidro, P.O. Box 4475, ☎ 287815/282742/274077.
• the main Peruvian tourist offices in Britain and the USA etc.
• all tourist offices and tourist hotels in Peru.

Hotels are divided into four categories — Hotel, Hostel, *Residencial* and Pension. Hotels and hostels give a better service and charge higher prices plus tax and a service charge. Prices in *residenciales* and pensions include tax, are cheaper but the service is less good. Youth hostels are not common in Peru.

Key
1 first-class hotel
2 good hotel by local standards
3 basic hotel
T state tourist hotel (*hotel de turistas*) — rooms bookable from Lima ☎ 52 86 26

Abancay
Hotel de Turistas (T 2) Av Diaz Barcena 500
Gran Hotel (3) Av Arenas 196
Abancay (3) Av Nuñes 202

Ancón
Playa Hermosa (1-2)

Andahuaylas
Hotel de Turistas (T) Av Lázaro Carrillo

Arequipa
Hotel de Turistas (T) Selva Alegre 218
El Portal (1) Portal de Flores 116
El Conquistador (1-2) *Mercaderes* 409
Jerusalén (1-2) Jerusalén 601
Crismar (2) Moral 107
Presidente (2) Pierola 201
Viza (2-) Perú 202
Las Mercedes (2+) Consuelo
La Casa de mi Abuela (2-3) Jerusalén 606
Fernández (2-3) Quesada 106, Yanahuara
El Virrey (3) San Juan de Díos 605
Arequipa Inn (3) Rivero 412
Extra (3) Av Olímpica 300

Ayacucho
Hotel de Turistas (T 2) Jr 9 de Diciembre 108
Marqués de Valdelorios (2) Alameda Bolognesi 706
Hostería Santa Rosa (2-3) Lima 166

Samary (3) Callao 335

Barranca
Hotel Chavín (2) in the main street

Cabo Blanco see **Talara**

Cajamarca
Hotel de Turistas (2) Lima 773
Hostal Cajamarca (2-3) 2 de Mayo 311
Casablanca (2-3) 2 de Mayo 446
Sucre (3) Jr Amalia Puga 815
Atahualpa (3) Pasaje Atahualpa 686

Camaná
Hotel de Turistas (T 2-3)

Cerro de Pasco
Cerro de Pasco (2) San Juan Pampa

Chaclacayo
Los Cóndores Tambo Inn (1) Av Garcilaso de la Vega 900
Centro Vacacional Huampani (2) Carretera Central km 26

Chala
Hotel de Turistas (T 2-3)

Chavín
Hotel de Turistas (2)

Chiclayo
Hotel de Turistas (T 2) Av Federico Villareal 115
Inca (2) Luis Gonzales 622
Obby (2) Miguel Grau
Costa de Oro (2) Av Balta 399
El Sol (3) Elias Aguirre 115
Europa (3) Elias Aguirre 466
Splendor (3) M Pardo 315
Royal (3) Plaza de Armas

Chincha
El Sausal (2+) Panamericana Sur 197$^1/_2$km (122 miles) Hacienda San José (2)
Panamericana Sur 205km (127 miles)

Colón (2-3) Plaza de Armas

Chimbote
Hotel de Turistas (T 2-) José Gález 109
Presidente (2) L Pardo 536
San Felipe (2-3) José Pardo 514
Riviera (2-3) Elias Aguirre 385
El Sol (3) Av Enrique Meiggs 1595

Chosica
Kalua Inn (2) Carretera Central 35km (22 miles)

Chucuito see **Puno**

Churín
Internacional (2-) Victor Larco Herrera
(prebooking necessary:
☎ Lima 61 189 32)
San Juan de Churín (3) Larco Herrera 315
Las Thermas (30 Larco Herrera 411

Coina see **Trujillo**

Concepción see **Huancayo**

Cuzco
Libertador (1) San Agustín 400
Savoy (1) El Sol 954
El Dorado inn (1) El Sol 395
Picoagua (1-2) Santa Teresa 344
Cuzco (2+) Heladeros 150
Alhambra 1 (2+) Tecsecocha 490
Alhambra 2 (2+) El Sol 594
San Agustín (2) Maruri 390
Royal Inca (2) Plaza Recocijo 299
Conquistador (2) Santa Catalina 149
Tambo (2) Ayacucho 235
Inti Raymi (2-) Matará 260
Wiracocha (2-3) Mantas 114
Del Inca (2-3) Calle Querra 251
El Solar (2-3) San Francisco 162
Espinar (2-3) Portal Espinar 142
Virrey (2-3) Portal Comercio 165
Garcilaso (2-3) Garcilaso 233
Ollanta (3+) El Sol 346

Málaga (3+) Av Infancia 535
Del Angel (3+) Afligidos 124
El Sol (3+) San Andrés 338
Corona Real (3+) Av Huáscar 226
Mantas (3+) Mantas 115
Los Marqueses (3) Garcilaso 226
Tambo Real (3+) Belén 588
Santa Catalina (3) Santa Catalina 366
Raymi (3) Av Pardo 954
Chavín (3) Calle Matará 215
Plateros (3) Plateros 340

Huacachina see **Ica**

Huacho
Hotel Milagritos (2) Av Centenario 28 de Julio 840

Huallanca
Cañon del Pato

Huancavelica
Hotel de Turistas (T 2) Plaza de Armas
Tahuantinsuyo (3) Jirón Cabaya

Huancayo
Hotel de Turistas (T 2) Jirón Ancash 729
Presidente (2) Calle Real 1138
Hostal Santa Felícita (2-) Giráldez 145
Kiya (2-) Giráldez 107
Mirador (2-3) Taylor 1438
Acolla (2-3) Antonio Lobato 505
Percy's (2-3) Calle Real 1399
Piura (3) Piura 132
Colón (3) Calle Real 455
Confort (3) Ancash 297

Concepción
Huaychulo (2) Carretera de Satipo 1¹/₂km (nearly a mile)

Huánuco
Hotel de Turistas (T 2-3) Jr Dámasco Beraun 775
Hotel Cuzco (2) Jr Huánuco 616
Hostal La Pileta (2-3) Jr 28 de Julio 988

Huaraz
Hotel de Turistas (T 2+) Av Centenario (near exit for Caraz)
Hotel Andino (2+) Pedro Cochachín 357
Colomba (2) Francisco de Zela 210
El Pacífico (2-3) Av Luzuriaga 630
El Tumi (2-3) San Martín 1121
Cataluña (2-3) Av Raymondi 622
Yanett (2-3) Av Centenario 102
Los Portales (2-3) Raymondi 903
Premier (3) Av Luzuriaga 651
Raymondi (3) Av Raymondi 820
Landauro (3) José de Sucre 109
Barcelona (3) Av Raymondi 612
Tabariz (3) Raymondi 827
La Suiza Peruana (3) San Martín 1133
Hotel Monterrey (T 2) 7km (4 miles) along Caraz road (thermal bath)

Huarmey
Hotel de Turistas (3+) Panamericana Norte

Huaychulo see **Huancayo**

Ica
Las Dunas (1) Panamericana Sur 300km (186 miles)
Hotel de Turistas (T 2) Av Los Maestros
La Posada del Sol (2) Abraham Valdelomar
Hostal El Carmelo (2) Panamericana Sur 301km (186 miles)
Las Brisas (2) Castrovirreyna 246
Silmar (2-) Castrovirreyna 110
Inti (2-3) Amazonas 235
Los Medanos (2-3) Panamericana Sur 303km (187 miles)
Hostal Piso (3) Plaza de Armas
Siesta (3) Independencia 196
Embassy (3) Mcal Castilla 216
Presidente (3) Amazonas 223
Confort (3) La Mar 257
Amazonas (3) Amazonas 235

Progreso (3) Progreso 254

Huacachina
Mossone (2-3)

Ilo
Hotel de Turistas (T 2+) Carretera Pampa Chica 1940
Hotel de Turistas (T 2-) Malecón Trapacá

Iquitos
Ambassador (2-) Pevas 260
Safari (2-) Napo 118
Europa (2-3) Brasil 216
María Antonia (2-3) Calle Próspero 616
Dos Mundos (3) Tacna 631
Perú (3) Próspero 318

Jungle Lodges:
Travellers are picked up in Iquitos at the lodge office or at their hotels.
Amazon Lodge (2) 2 hours down the Amazon (office: Putumayo 165)
Explorama Lodge (2) 2 hours 30min down the Amazon (office: Putumayo 150)
Amazon Safari Camp (3) 1hour along the Momón tributary (office: Putumayo 196)
Explornapo Camp (office: Putumayo 150)

Jauja
Albergue Turistas Lago Paca (T 2-3) 5km (3 miles) beyond Jauja

Juliaca
Hotel de Turistas (T 2) Jr Manuel Prado 335
Royal Inn (2-3) Jr San Román 158
Arce (3) Plaza 10 de Mayo

La Merced
Mercedes (2-3) Tarma 575
Cristina (2-3) Tarma 582

Lima: Centre
Sheraton (1) Paseo de la República 170
Crillón (1) Av Nicolás de Pierola 589
Gran Hotel Bolívar (1) Plaza San Martín 958
Hotel Carusso (1) Av Arenales 1800
Riviera (1-2) Av Garcilaso de la Vega 981
El Plaza (2) Av Nicolás de Pierola 850
Savoy (2) Jirón Cailloma 224
Hostal San Francisco (2-) Jirón Ancash 340
Maury (2-) Jirón Ucayali 201
San Martín (2-3) Av Nicolás de Pierola 882
Grand Castle (2-3) Carlos Zavala Loayza 218
Columbus (2-3) Av Arequipa 1421
Continental (2-3) Jirón Puno 196
Wilson (2-3) Jirón Chancay 633
La Casona (3) Moquegua 289
Oriental (3) Jirón Cuzco 696
Gran Hotel (4) Av Abancay 546
Europa (4) Jirón Ancash 376

Lima: San Isidro and Miraflores
César (1) Diez Canseco
El Pardo (1) José Pardo
El Condado Miraflores (1) Alcanfores 465
María Angela (1) Av La Paz 610
Los Galgos (1-) Alcanfores 329
Suites del Golf (2) Los Eucaliptos 550
Exclusive (2) San Martín 550
Garden (2) Rivera Navarrete 450
Country Club (2) Los Eucaliptos
El Marqués de San Isidro (2) Chinchón 461
Hostal Aristo (2-3) Av La Paz 769
José Antonio (2-3) Av 28 de Julio 398
Hostal El Dorado (2-3) José Pardo 486

Hostal Miramar (2-3) Malecón
Cisneros 1244
Hostal Polonia (2-3) Panamericana
6599
Hostal Palace (2-3) Av 28 de Julio
1088
Grand Hotel Miraflores (2-3) Av 28
de Julio 151
Hostal Residencial San Isidro Inn
(3+) Juan Pezet 1765
Hostal El Ovalo (3) Av Pardo 1110
Hostal Residencial Benavides (3)
Av de la Merced 119
Hostal Residencial La Castellana
(3) Grimaldo de Solar 222
Hostal El Ejecutivo (3) Av 28 de
Julio 245
Hostal Señorial Miraflores (3) José
Gonzales 567
Hostal Residencial Collacocha
Andrés Reyes 100
Hostal Residencial Santa Mónica
Juan Pezet 1419

Lima: Surroundings
Granja Azul Inn (1-2) Carretera
Central 11km (7 miles)
Santa María Beach Hotel Santa
María, 50km (31 miles) south of
Lima
(☎ 27 84 28)

Machu Picchu
Hotel de Turistas (T 3)
Albergue de Turistas (T 3) Aguas
Calientes

Mollendo
La Cabana (3) Comercio 240
Salerno (3) Arequipa 209
Mollendo (4) Arequipa 100

Monterrey see **Huaraz**

Moquegua
Hotel de Turistas (T 2+) on a hill
2km (1¼ miles) from centre
Los Limoneros (3) Lima 441

Nazca
Hotel de Turistas (T 2+) Bolognesi
Montecarlo (2) Callao 123
La Maison Suisse Panamericana
Sur 447km (277 miles)
Maria Reiche Panamericana Sur
447km (277 miles)

Ollantaitambo see **Urubamba**

Oxapampa
San Martín (3) Jr Mullembruck 540
Santa Isolina Jr Bolognesi

Paracas
Hotel Paracas (2)

Pisac see **Urubamba**

Pisco
Embassy (3+) Comercio 180
Progreso (3) Progreso 254
Portofino (4) Miranda 295

Piura
Hotel de Turistas (T 2) Plaza de
Armas
Vicus (2-3) Av Guardia Civil B-3
Santa María (2-3) Arequipa 247
Piura (2-3) Loreto 910
Las Palmeras (2-3) Loreto 945
San Jorge (3) Loreto 925
Bolognesi (3) Bolognesi 427
see also **Sullana**

Pucallpa
Hotel de Turistas (T 2) Jr San
Martín 552
Hotel Inamburu (2) Federico
Basadre 271
Mercedes (2-3) Raimondi 610
Tariri (2-3) Raimondi 745
Sisley (3) Coronel Portillo 658
Pinedo (4) 7 de Junio 583
Alex (4) Coronel Portillo 381

Laguna Yarinacocha
Ucayali Lodge (2) book from Lima
(☎ 27 15 02)
Bungalow La Cabaña (German-
owned)

Puerto Maldonado

Hotel de Turistas (T 2) León
  Velarde
Wilson (2-3) Gonzales Prada 355

Jungle Lodges

Travellers are picked up from the
airport. Prebooking necessary via
a travel agent in Cuzco or Lima.
Albergue Cuzco Amazónico (2+)
  15km (9 miles) downstream
  along the *Río Madre de Díos*
Explorers Inn (2) 4 hours
  upstream along the Río
  Tambopata

Puerto Pizarro

Motel Puerto Pizarro (2-3)

Puno

Hotel de Turistas (T1-2) Isla
  Esteves
Ferrocarril (2-) Av La Torre 185
Don Miguel (2-3) Av La Torre 545
Internacional (2-3) Jirón Libertad
  161
Palace (2-3) Jirón Tacna 786
Italia (2-3) Teodoro Valcárcel 122
Jerusalén (3) Arequipa 380
Monterrey (3) Pasaje Grau 148
Lima (3) Jirón Tacna 247
Los Uros (4) Teodoro Valcárcel
  135
Nesther (4) Jirón Deustua 268

Chucuito

Tambo Titikaka (2) 17km ($10^1/_2$
  miles) from Puno on La Paz
  road

San Ramón

Conquistador (2-3) Progreso 298
San Ramón Ex-Base Aerea
  (airport)
Chanchamayo Progreso 289

Satipo

Majestic (2-3) Colonos Fun-
  dadores 408

Sullana

Aypate (2-3) José de Lama
Wilson (3) Tarapacá 378

Tacna

Plaza (2+) San Martín 421
Hotel de Turistas (T 2) Bolognesi
  300
Gran Hotel Central (2) San Martín
  561
Camino Real (2) San Martín 855
Holiday Suites (3) Alto de Lima
  1476
Hostal Hogar (3+) 28 de Julio 146
Emperador (3) San Martín 558
Lima (3) San Martín 442

Talara

Gran Hotel Pacífico (2+) Av
  Aviación
Talara Motel (2) Parinas

Cabo Blanco

Fishing Club (2) 40km (25 miles)
  north of Talara

Tarapoto

Hotel de Turistas (T 2) Jr Pablo
  Cruz
Edinson (2-3) Jiménez Pimentel
  177
Brasilia (3) Martínez de Com-
  pagnón

Tarma

Hotel de Turistas (T 2) Mcal
  Ramón Castilla
Galaxia (3) Lima 262
Colmena (3) Jauja 618
El Dorado (3) Huánuco 488

Tingo María

Hotel de Turistas (T 2)
Marco Antonia (3) Jr Monzón 364
Royal (3-) Benavides 214
La Cabaña (4) General Prado 821

Trujillo

El Golf (1-2) Urbanización El Golf
Hotel de Turistas (2) Plaza de
  Armas

Residencial Continental (2-3)
  Gamarra 603
San Martín (3+) San Martín 749
Vogi (3+) Ayacucho 663
Turismo (3+) Gamarra 747
Opt Gar (3+) Grau 595
Los Jardines (3+) América del
  Norte 1245
Continental (3) Gamarra 663
Palermo (3) Palma 250
Los Angeles (3-) América Sur
  1313
Est-Mor (3-) César Vallejo 134
Royal (3-) Sinchi Roca 1138
San José (3-) Grau 515

Coina
Hostería El Sol in the mountains
  145km (90 miles) from Trujillo
  (for information
  ☎ Trujillo 23 19 33)

Tumbes
Hotel de Turistas (T 2) San Martín
  275
Punta Sal Club (2) Panamericana
  Norte 1,195km (740 miles)
César (2-3) Huáscar 353
Continental (2-3) Huáscar 135
Lourdes (3) Mayor Bodero 150
Toloa (3) Tnte Vásquez 444
Kikos (3-) Bolívar 464

Urubamba
Centro Vacacional Urubamba
  Carretera Urubamba 70km (43
  miles)
Hostal Naranjochayoc (2-3)
  Carretera Urubamba 69km (42
  miles)

Yura
Hotel de Turistas (T 2-3)

Zorritos
Hotel de Turistas (T 2-3)
  Panamericana 186
Albergue Zorritos (2-3) Panameri-
  cana

TOURIST INFORMATION OFFICES IN PERU

Almost every major city has a tourist information bureau but often the staff only speak Spanish so do go armed with a few phrases in that language. Here are a few of the main offices.

Arequipa
Portal Municipal 112
☎ 21-31-01

Cajamarca
Jirón Silva Santisteban 138
☎ 92-2228

Chiclayo
Elías Aguirre 830-832 ofc 202
☎ 22-7776

Cuzco
Portal Bélen 115
Plaza de Armas
☎ 23-7364

Huánuco
Gral Prado 714
Plaza de Armas
☎ 21-24

Huaraz
Edif. del Correo
Plaza de Armas

Ica
Av. Grau 148
Postal 82
☎ 23-5247

Iquitos
Prospero 163
Plaza de Armas
☎ 23-8523

Lima
Foptur
Fondo de Promocion Turistica
Av. Angamos 355
Miraflores

Lima
☎ 432524

Piura
Ayacucho 377
☎ 333720

Pucallpa
Saenz Peña 298

Puno
Jirón Dos de Mayo 775
☎ 29-45

Tacna
San Martin 405
☎ 71-5362

Tarapoto
Gregorio Delgado 240

Trujillo
Jirón Independencia 628
☎ 24-1936

USEFUL ADDRESSES

Peruvian Tourist Office (Foptur)
First Floor
10 Grosvenor Gardens
London SW1W OBD
England.
☎ 01-824-8693

Peruvian Tourist Office
50 Biscayne Boulevard
Suite 123
Miami
Florida
USA
☎ (305) 374-0023

Peruvian North American Cultural
Institute
Cuzco 446
Peru

Peruvian — British Cultural
Association
Av. Arequipa 3495
San Isidro
Lima
Peru

Peruvian Tourist Ministry
Jirón de la Union 1066
Lima
☎ 323559

Amazon Tours and Cruises
1013 S. Central Avenue
Glendale
California 91204
USA
☎ (818) 246-4816
☎ (800) 423-2791

Worldwide Student Travel Limited
37/38 Store Street
London WC1E 7BZ
England
☎ 01-580-7733

Embassies/Consulates

Peruvian Consulate
52 Sloane Street
London SW1 9SP
England
☎ 01-235-6867

Peruvian Consulate
Richmond House
1 Rumford Place
Liverpool L3 9RT
England
☎ 051-227-5161

Peruvian Consulate
20 Wellington Street
Dun Laoghaire
Co. Dublin
Republic of Ireland
☎ 0001-800-256

British Embassy
Edificio Washington
Plaza Washington
Avenida Arequipa
Lima
Peru
☎ 283830/283836/9

Canadian Embassy
Av. Libertad 130
Miraflores
Lima

Peru
☎ 463890

US Embassy and Consulate
Grimaldo del Solar 346
Miraflores
Lima
Peru
☎ 443621/443921

New Zealand Embassy
Av. Salaverry 3006
San Isidro
Lima
Peru
☎ 621890

Help
Pharmacy
Botica Inglés
Jirón Cailloma 336
Lima
Peru

Anglo/American Hospital
Av. Salazar
San Isidro
Lima
Peru
☎ 403570

Hospital de Niñas
Av. Brasil
Lima
Peru

Policía de Turismo (Tourist Police)
Salaverry 1156
Jesus María
Lima
Peru
☎ 237225/246571

Peruvian Touring and Automobile
Club
Av. César Vallejo 699
Lince
Lima
Peru
☎ 403270

Travel
Aero-Perú
Plaza San Martin
Av. Nicolas de Pierola
914 Lima
Peru
☎ 322 995

Faucett
Suite 163
4th Floor
London SW1 5BN
☎ 01-930-1136
    or
Av. Inca Garcilazo de la Vega
865 Lima
Peru
☎ 275-000

INDEX